TURNING POINTS

Also by Off Campus Writers' Workshop

A Reason to Be Here:
Tales from the Writers Convention

Overcoming:
An Anthology by the Writers of OCWW

TURNING POINTS

Short stories, memoirs, and creative non-fiction from members of
Off Campus Writers' Workshop

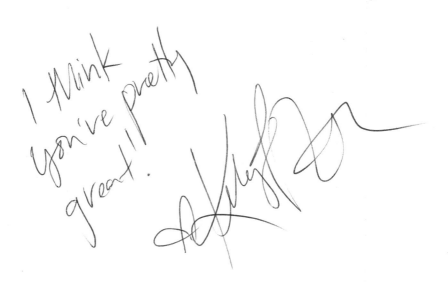

TURNING POINTS

Short stories, memoirs, and creative non-fiction from members of
Off Campus Writers' Workshop

Windy City Publishers
info@windycitypublishers.com

Published in the United States of America

ISBN:
978-1-953294-05-0

Library of Congress Control Number:
2020926006

Main Cover Image: Maciej Błędowski © 123RF.com
Additional Cover Graphic: stillfx © 123RF.com

WINDY CITY PUBLISHERS
CHICAGO

WWW.WINDYCITYPUBLISHERS.COM

DEDICATION

To the pioneering women who founded Off Campus Writers' Workshop in 1946,
and in tribute to other pivotal members who in the decades that followed
contributed materially to developing the organization we recognize today,
we dedicate this anthology.

Their efforts are directly responsible for energizing and supporting the development of
generations of writers, culminating in—but not limited to—
this amazing collection of short stories, memoirs, and creative non-fiction.
That the mix of work includes both well-published writers and neophytes
is a testament to their vision of an organization that supports the writing dreams
of all authors, no matter their previous experience, age, or writing education.

To all those who have come before us,
who've helped build this unique organization
into the thriving institution it has become—
we extend our gratitude.

CONTENTS

LIFE'S LESSONS *Short stories from long lives*

TRUE TURNING POINTS *Memoir and Creative Non-Fiction*

STORIES BY OUR STAFF *Fiction by the Anthology staff*

FROM THE EDITORS

TURNING POINTS celebrates the 75th anniversary of Off Campus Writers' Workshop, a member-managed non-profit organization that has helped thousands of aspiring writers learn the art and craft of creative writing.

Our anthology project started in the autumn of 2019, with a session on the elements of short story writing led by Patricia McNair, an accomplished short story writer and gifted university educator. Since that time, our authors have written first drafts, subjected them to the rigors of critique group analysis, then worked with OCWW editors to refine and revise their works. In addition to this exacting internal effort, the organization retained the copy editing and production services of Windy City Publishers.

Our combined works represent a full spectrum of OCWW members, from those engaged in creative writing for the first time in their lives to established authors with many publishing credits to their names. What we have in common is a passion for creative writing and an eagerness to work together to make each person's writing better.

We hope you enjoy this collection, and we hope it's worthy of the 12 women who founded Off Campus Writers' Workshop all those years ago.

ANTHOLOGY STAFF

RENEE JAMES	EDITOR
PETER HOPPOCK	EDITOR
TRACY FORGIE KOPPEL	MANUSCRIPT EDITOR
BARBARA BARNETT	MANUSCRIPT EDITOR
CHARLES DICKINSON	CONSULTING EDITOR
JASON LAVICKY	PRODUCTION & ART
WINDY CITY PUBLISHERS	COPY EDITING, PRODUCTION & ART

THE FIELD GLASS

Foreword by Fred Shafer

When Henry James wrote that "the house of fiction has in short not one window, but a million," he had in mind the seemingly endless possibilities raised by the attitudes, impressions, beliefs, and life experiences of all the writers on earth. In this remarkable anthology, *Turning Points*, there are forty-three windows—short stories, memoirs, and essays written by the members of Off Campus Writers' Workshop in honor of its seventy-fifth anniversary. Each piece of writing has achieved its own identity; together, they pay tribute to the unique purposes of an organization that has helped countless people realize their potential as writers.

In Henry James's formative years, there were no programs or classes in creative writing, and if there had been any, it seems unlikely that he would have joined. He had friends with whom he discussed literature and an active social life, from which he drew ideas for his fiction, but when it came to the writing itself, he valued his privacy. In his notebooks, he can be seen rejoicing in his freedom at the start of a day's work: "Ah, once more, to let myself go! The very thought of it soothes and sustains, lays a divine hand on my nerves, and lights, so beneficently, my uncertainties and obscurities. Begin it—and it will grow." Only in solitude, James believed, will a writer become capable of living "in the world of creation," close to the heart of a story, where the characters and situations are alive and real, and anything seems possible.

In 1884, a leading British novelist and literary critic, Walter Besant, called for a program of study in fiction writing similar to the plan followed in academies of the fine arts. In the belief that fiction, like the art of painting, is "governed and directed by general laws," he proposed a series of courses devoted to separate areas of technique, "taught with as much precision and exactness as the laws of harmony, perspective, and proportion." Henry James took issue with Besant's ideas in an essay called "The Art of Fiction." He rejected the idea that there are laws for fiction and dismissed the curriculum Besant proposed, because it would rank technique over content. Singling out one technique from the others would be another serious mistake, James said, because the techniques are all interrelated—"I cannot imagine…a passage of description that is not in its intention narrative, a passage of dialogue that is not in its intention descriptive." A writer needs to sort out these connections in the process of finding each story, James insisted, and he believed that the mentor or teacher who points out problems in technique or content would interfere with a writer's freedom.

If Henry James had lived long enough, he might have been surprised to see the emergence, several decades later, of workshops, classes, and entire programs in fiction writing; well into the 21st century, they have become fixtures on college campuses. Few if any programs have been organized around separate topics, but it has become a common practice for instructors to try to address what James felt should remain unexamined, the role technique assumes as a means of discovery. Technique is discussed now as a craft issue, not an element of high art. Teachers who haven't reflected closely on the process of writing and who insist on setting rules may, as James feared, impede or mislead their students. But the best instructors know there is a fine line between dominating and enabling and that their responsibility is to give students the equipment needed to pursue their own stories.

The plan for Off Campus Writers' Workshop, even before that was its name, was for it to become a home for the study of craft issues. In 1946, early in the rise of writing workshops, twelve women approached Dr. Frederic Litton, the dean of Northwestern University's Medill School of Journalism, and asked him to meet with them in their homes, share ideas from his classes on fiction writing, and comment on manuscripts. At first he referred the women to one of his graduate students, but two years later, he took over, and the group became known as the Off-Campus Fiction Writers. Nearly twenty years passed, with a significant rise in enrollment and changes in both the leadership and the venue. When the group adopted its present name in the late 1960s, it moved to the Winnetka Community House, where it still meets. The organizers installed a program similar to the one Henry James opposed, with workshops on distinct craft issues, not only in fiction writing, but also in poetry, non-fiction, stories for children, and other genres. When I was invited to speak in the late 1980s, the plan was firmly in place, and since then I've had the privilege of watching Off Campus Writers' Workshop progress and grow. The current president, Fred Fitzsimmons, vice-president Paco Aramburu, and the other leaders have brought in advanced methods of organization and advertising, and carried the instructional model to new heights.

The strength and beauty of the pieces of writing in *Turning Points,* along with the present enrollment figures (340 members and as many as 150 attending sessions on Zoom during the pandemic) testify to the continuing success of Off Campus Writers' Workshop. But how has this organization managed to last for so many years, and why has its craft-based model mattered, when the meetings are conducted in front of such large audiences, without the close contact between teacher and student found in smaller classes? An obvious reason is the effort the program directors put into planning the schedule. In addition to lining up workshops in other genres, the current program director, Susan Levi, has organized a series on fiction writing that covers a wide range of perspectives, delivered by writers and editors who are known to be excellent teachers and communicators, capable of inspiring an audience without demanding that their ideas be accepted as rules.

Another reason, the speakers will agree, is the quality of the audiences. It would have been impossible for Henry James to foresee a group made up of that many people who are committed to the study of technique without feeling vulnerable to a speaker's influence. These days, writers expect to hear craft issues discussed. They know there are issues they cannot learn by themselves, but that it is their job to find out if a technique applies to their stories. Nearly everyone comes to Off Campus Writers' Workshop hoping to publish. There are sessions led by agents and editors about the intricacies of submitting manuscripts, as well as weekly reports by members on recent sales. But the talk of publishing isn't allowed to dominate. Experienced and newer writers alike understand that their greatest need is to continue to learn, while staying focused on the writing. Because it isn't necessary to show one's work, a freedom not permitted in smaller workshops, they can go home after a session, weigh the ideas discussed that day, and re-enter the private worlds of their stories. They own their solitude.

When members would like to receive comments, they can submit manuscripts to the speakers for evaluations in writing. The saying "the manuscript belongs to the writer," is cited by Henry James to explain why a teacher or mentor should refrain from mentioning anything about a work in progress. James recommended that teachers tell their students, "Ah, well, you must do it as you can!" What he failed to grasp is that a teacher's comments, when offered constructively, can help a writer to identify possibilities and needs, and that even the act of rejecting a suggestion might lead the writer to her own way of solving a problem and a new sense of the story. At Off Campus Writers' Workshop, "the manuscript belongs to the writer" means that the writer's freedom to make these decisions is honored. This attitude has undoubtedly informed the sub-groups and mentorships set up for members to share their writing with peers, as well as the critique sessions through which the pieces in *Turning Points* passed. The state of finish attained by each story and essay shows that the editors, Renee James, Peter Hoppock, and their team treated the writers' purposes with respect and care.

Turning Points has been organized into six sections, like the floors in Henry James's house of fiction, with as many as nine pieces of writing, or rooms, on each floor. James imagined the writer to be sitting inside a room, gazing out the window with "a pair of eyes or at least a field glass...a unique instrument, insuring to the person making use of it an impression distinct from any other." The field glass stands for technique used as a means of discovery.

The effects of this process shine throughout the pages of *Turning Points*. There are vivid details that confirm a sense of reality—a room full of exotic flowers, a miniature seascape made of lint, two male and female cardinals singing to each other inside a bush, an expensive watch worn on the same arm as a cheap plastic wristlet, three neatly rolled joints that turn out to contain oregano; metaphors and similes that preserve strong impressions—the sun "tangled in a distant stand of trees," a group of women who resemble "a flock of flamingos" in their dark pink hospital gowns, a "sea" of premature babies "with the translucent skin and fragile bodies of jellyfish," and a family of Cambodian refugees "huddled together in a pile like puppies;" places in dialogue when a character's motives and needs come into the open, and the balance between the two people shifts; sequences of physical action, as subtle as one hand grazing another, or as conspicuous as a gun being fired into a ceiling, a woman pepper-spraying a friend's violent husband, two people fooling around with cutlasses, or a man hurling a locket into a coffin as it is lowered into the ground; and finally, scenes in which someone is lying in bed, sitting at a computer, riding in a car, or walking on a once-familiar college campus at night, when a secret or a memory surfaces, catching the character and perhaps also the writer by surprise. At these moments and many others like them, even the rhythms of the sentences convey truth.

Each story and essay deserves its own paragraph, to acknowledge what sets it apart from the others. But you, as the reader, have already made it inside this house. When you walk down the halls, you'll need only to step through each door, take a seat, and you will see, hear, enjoy, learn, and be moved by everything the writer found outside the window.

— FRED SHAFER

Fred Shafer was an editor with *TriQuarterly*, the international literary journal published by Northwestern University, where he taught fiction writing in the School of Professional Studies for many years. He now leads three private workshops on short story and novel writing. He began appearing at Off Campus Writers' Workshop in the 1987-88 series and has been the opening speaker for more than twenty years.

PREFACE

by Scott Turow

Sometime while I was in high school, more than 50 years ago, my mother became a member of a writer's group known as Off Campus Writers' Workshop. My mom, like so many other writers, was at loose ends about how to further her literary ambitions. She had written sporadically and in isolation for many years. Joining a group was a step in the right direction for her. It was a public declaration of her hopes, and a way to make her efforts more disciplined, to share the thoughts and company of other writers, and to think out loud with them about what worked and didn't in the pieces that were discussed during each session.

Over the years OCWW became uniquely important to my mother. She made some of her closest friends there. She contributed work that was workshopped, and also liked putting on the hat of critic when other members' pieces were discussed. The comments that often stayed with her the longest came from the established writers who visited or presided over the workshop, offering tips and their own assessment of the members' works.

My mom managed to publish one book and several articles during her years as an OCWW member. But she was also very proud of the success of a number her OCWW colleagues, who regularly published short stories in national magazines, or who were the authors of well-received books across a number of genres.

Because of my mother's experience with OCWW, I have regularly recommended to people who want to know how to develop as writers, that they try to find a local writers' workshop, although I'm not sure anyone will locate an organization that is quite the equal of OCWW. The nurturance, education and exposure OCWW has offered writers for seventy-five years now, has made it the premier writers' group in the Chicago area, and the oldest, continuously-running writer's organization of its kind in the United States. These days its in-person membership neighbors three-hundred and fifty, a far cry from the days when my mother met with a group that numbered in the teens.

One of the most unique aspects of OCWW, as my mom experienced it, was that writers who began publishing regularly did not turn their back on the group, but remained active members, continuing to treat as peers writers who were still seeking their voice. The works in this book reflect the variety of expression and experience that has always characterized OCWW. There are polished pieces by serious pros, and others from writers still in the aspirational phase. They vary in mood and genre; there are both short stories and memoirs. But all are worthwhile reading, both in themselves and as a testimonial to a uniquely successful organization that has advanced the careers of writers for 75 years now and created a community among them.

— SCOTT TUROW

Scott Turow is a lawyer and the best-selling author of more than a dozen novels, including *Presumed Innocent, The Burden of Proof*, and *Reversible Errors*. His books have been translated into more than 40 languages, and sold more than 30 million copies. He continues to practice law, specializing in criminal litigation, and has done extensive pro bono work, actively pursuing judicial reform. His most recent legal thriller is *The Last Trial* (2020).

FAST READS
Stories under 2,000 words

Slam

by Janet Souter

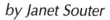

Sunlight catches Mr. Kranik's glasses, making them resemble distant spotlights as he squints around the room. Someone whispers, "Hey, it's Kranik the Martian," and the class giggles. Julie feels a rush of compassion, certain the man heard, yet because he's so eager to share his love of poetry—especially this poem—he's willing to suffer a few seconds of quiet humiliation. Such desperation.

"Okay, can anyone tell me what the author meant when he wrote this?" Kranik's voice emphasizes "anyone" as though he has little hope.

Julie could raise her hand to lessen his discomfort, but hesitates. No, she won't answer this time. It's better not to look too eager, or appear to suck up. Anyway, it's only five minutes 'til the end of fifth period.

Dead silence. Well, let it be silent. She'll save herself for reading the poem she wrote for extra credit and handed in last week—the one that he returned to her yesterday with his words penned at the top of the page in high-spirited red ink: "Excellent! I want you to read this in class tomorrow!" Imagining herself reading her work aloud makes heat rise in her cheeks. Maybe they won't care all that much, but if nothing else, they'll know that she's good. That's enough. "The Snow Ballet." It's even a good title for a poem talking about snowflakes and how they look like ballerinas against the soft, blue-black night.

The other kids often make fun of Kranik, who always wears a scarf, shuffles down the hall in loose-fitting loafers, and never seems to remember anyone's name. But Julie loves the way he reaches into the words on a page and draws out the author's deepest thoughts. Someday she'll meet someone like him and they'll go to New York and read plays and hang around in coffee shops. She can live with her breasts that refuse to grow, the freckles that should have disappeared by now, the owl-like glasses—what she is inside will see her through the next couple of years. Later, in New York, the laughter and friends will come.

Oh, what the heck. She'll give the answer to show the class how it's done, and save Kranik too. She starts to lift her arm off the desk.

Then Kranik points, past Julie to someone in the back of the room. "Yes—um, Anita…uh?"

"Platt. I'm *Alyssa* Platt."

Julie turns her head sharply. Oh, come on, not Alyssa Platt. Really? Alyssa Platt, always rattling on about guys, who she's going to the sophomore dance with, or what she's going to have pierced next. Not all that pretty either. Blue eyes and dimples, sure, but her teeth protrude and her nose is massive. The boys hang around her anyway, so she must be giving them something really special. In gym that morning, one of the girls said that Alyssa Platt and Jimmy Moran took a train into the city last Friday after the Valentine Dance. They tried to check into a hotel, but the desk clerk said they didn't look old enough and refused to give them a room. *Two 15-year-olds—what were they thinking?*

So Alyssa Platt will tell everyone what the poem means. Well, good luck, Alyssa. *Jesus!*

Alyssa stands up slowly and leans on her desk. Everyone looks at her, relieved that she broke the silence, relieved that they won't be singled out. Not caring what Alyssa says, hoping she'll jabber on until the bell rings.

"Okay," Alyssa begins. "Now I'm not sure about this, but it seems—well it seems that he's talking about himself as a person, like maybe what he hopes to become—that the poem is what he will become and what he will become will sing. Like to the world or like maybe, oh I don't know, like an instrument of God, or something."

Kranik nods all the while Alyssa's talking and Julie thinks that he resembles those little plastic dogs that people put in their car's back window. "Anita, that's—"

"*Alyssa.*"

"Alyssa, sorry. That is what he meant when he wrote this poem. You have a good insight into poetry. Keep it up. Don't ever lose it." Kranik gazes at her, his eyes soft, his tone quiet, almost tender.

Alyssa shrugs, looking like she's trying to appear modest, and sits down. There's a stillness in the room. Julie feels a sudden dryness in her mouth as she struggles to believe what she just heard. Alyssa's answer *was* better than the one she had. Alyssa *did* read more into it. How did she do it? Who and what is Alyssa Platt?

Don't ever lose it? Such admiration in his voice. Such caring.

A guy in the front row turns to Alyssa and gives her a thumbs up. In less than a minute Alyssa has invaded the only good part of Julie's world and with so little effort, managed to stay in her own as well. Alyssa has no right to get it all. Couldn't she keep her mouth shut?

"Anyone else?" Kranik asks.

A dense moment of silence sends the message. No one thinks they can top Alyssa's unexpected stroke of near-genius.

On the other hand, he did write *Excellent!* on her poem. But all of a sudden there's Alyssa and her "insight." If Alyssa has insight, *and* her endless gaggle of BFFs, then she has it all and what's left for Julie? Is it possible that Alyssa has become the favorite? If so, Julie herself may never have a moment of glory like the one Alyssa has today. Maybe New York and her Kranik-like person will slip away too, but that's the future. She has to be the best *now*, and implores a favor from the God she'd always pictured as a benevolent mechanic—The Fixer of All Things. *Let it be here, at least 'til I'm out of this place and I won't ask for it again. Please, let me have something here.*

"Okay," Kranik says. His voice is brusque, but the room stays silent. He takes a deep breath, looks down, and then glances up at the clock.

"Julie." Kranik sounds like he's certain of Julie and who Julie is and he's proud of being so sure of himself. "We have a few minutes left. I believe you have a poem for us?"

You have a poem for us? Is that all? It couldn't be that hard to say, "Class, Julie has written a poem with such vivid imagery, such an excellent use of personification, I want to share it with the rest of you. This is what poetry is all about."

Julie swallows as she opens her notebook. The poem is there in front of her, the words fall into step, march like perfect toy soldiers underneath Kranik's red, scratchy handwriting. *Excellent!*

She imagines herself reading, all the while sensing the kids yawning, grateful for another few minutes of easy boredom, or worse, secretly laughing at her too. And Kranik—look at him, relieved that someone has filled the agonizing silence. Maybe Kranik has been humoring her all along. Oh, shit. That's it. He actually pities her. He knows where she stands—or doesn't stand—among the others, so he's taken her on as his own little service project. Throwing a few little *Excellent* crumbs her way just to make her feel better.

She's been betrayed. Not just by Kranik, but—in reading it over—by the poem as well. The phrases that came onto the paper so easily two weeks ago, as she watched the snowflakes outside her father's apartment, suddenly appear silly and childish. They were snowflakes and they fell. Big deal. It's only a bit of word plaster to fill in Kranik's time holes.

She looks up at Kranik. His eyebrows are raised as if to say, "Well?" There's even a hint of a smile in his expression. Anyway, it's too late. The poem is trite. Anyone in the room could have written it. She must show him that she knows what he thinks of her work, but most of all, he must be punished for his pity. For his *Excellent!*

Her eyes don't leave his as she slides the poem deep among her other papers. She'll get the words out—words that once they are said, will show him that she doesn't need "Excellent" from him. With or without an exclamation point.

She revels in the feel of her shrug, the tilt of her head and especially her smile. "Nope. Sorry."

— JANET SOUTER

Janet's careers include: graphic artist, travel agent, and community news coordinator/columnist for the *Daily Herald* newspapers. She and her husband Gerry have written more than 50 traditionally published books on American history, biography, and fine arts. Janet is currently working on an historical fiction novel set in 1909 Chicago.

Nameless Child

by Elizabeth DeSchryver

The doorbell rang.

"Could you keep her steady?" Nina asked. "I have to get that. I'll just be a minute."

Deborah tentatively slid her hand around the small curve of the baby's back, slippery with soap. Nina was bathing the child after a messy lunch, a lunch Deborah had watched with discreet fascination.

Deborah hadn't meant to stay. She was just—well, it didn't matter. Nina had invited her to stay for coffee, after she fed the baby. The baby—Millie, she must start calling her by name—made a game of it, moving her mouth away at just the right moment and then waving her hands gleefully as squash puree formed a wound-like streak across her cheek. What little she got into her mouth she giggled back out.

Apparently she did manage to eat something, because her system made room for it out the other end with infernal speed and a waft of pungent odor. The child was one big squishy train wreck.

No, that wasn't fair. She wasn't fair. Deborah wanted to dislike this soft, gurgling, helpless creature—Millie—to reject the whole package of motherhood. Gently, she used her thumb to move a soapy curl off the baby's forehead. The baby made that sound again, a sort of wet giggle as it—she—splashed her arms in the water. Bubbles popped, releasing a sickly, powdery scent. Flecks of lather landed on Deborah's blouse. Never wear silk to a baby's house.

And it *was* the baby's house. Millie. *I must call her Millie*, Deborah reminded herself. Millie's toys and clothes and supplies were strewn around the townhouse, a playset occupying most of the living room, the fireplace blocked by random pieces of cardboard. Deborah tried to imagine her home turned into this, this jigsaw puzzle of baby-ness. What would it have been like?

Deborah shook her head. No point in thinking about it.

Nina had moved next door just a few months ago, husband and baby in tow, although Deborah had yet to meet the husband. She'd seen him through her window—well, the back of his head—as he got into the car. It seemed like a very nice head. Blond, like the baby.

Deborah had been away when they'd moved in. She'd been back over a week before it registered that someone *had* moved in. That first week, it was all she could do to get dressed. But then, she started hearing things.

"You're just imagining it," her sister said. "I bet if you asked your therapist, she'd say it was perfectly normal."

"I'm not imagining it. I hear a baby crying. Every night."

"Are you sure it wasn't just a cat? They can sound—"

"It was a baby. I know what a baby sounds like."

"Could you be dreaming it? Dreams can seem so—"

"I wasn't dreaming! Stay overnight if you don't believe me."

"Okay, okay, I believe you."

Deborah hoped her sister hadn't just been patronizing her. Jane had been so supportive when David left. And after, at the hospital. But Jane had such a normal life; new husband, good job, hopeful future. Her happiness leached through her studied sympathy like over-soaked ladyfingers.

If only she'd been able to cry. Denial, she'd been told. Denial, then shock. "You have to cry," David kept telling her. As if it were that easy. As if she could just throw a switch and release the pain. But she couldn't. She couldn't. She felt trapped in a sort of viscous goo, like that ballistic gel on crime shows, the test bullet ripping into the pseudo-flesh, death suspended by inches.

The water had soaked into the cuffs of her blouse. She should have rolled them up. Wet silk clung to her scars. Why was she wearing silk? Oh, well. The blouse was old, anyway.

The—Millie—was returning her stare now, in quiet, wide-eyed contemplation. Did it sense something through Deborah's hand, her expression? How old did babies need to be before they could focus on faces? Deborah tried to remember from her clutch of baby books. What was that tiny, half-formed brain thinking? Could it think yet?

Millie. Not it. Millie. What kind of name is Millie? Is it short for Millicent? Mildred? Who names their baby Mildred these days?

When was that damn woman going to get back here?

She'd finally met Nina when the weather started warming up. She saw the stroller first. *I am not insane*, she thought with a tangled surge of triumph and relief. *These townhouses just have thin walls.* Her sense of vindication carried her outside to introduce herself.

"We're going to the park," Nina said with a breathy laugh, tucking a Thermos into her elbow. "Millie's a bit young for the swings, but she loves to watch the other kids. Do you want to come with us?"

Deborah said yes, robot politeness kicking in before her brain could invent an excuse. She made the obligatory cooing noises over the stroller. Thankfully, the child was barely visible between the blankets and the knitted pink cap dotted with dropped stitches. Deborah was hopeless at knitting, but she knew mistakes when she saw them.

"What a lovely cap. Did you make it?"

"No, my sister did. It's a hand-me-down. Good thing we had a girl."

Deborah winced. "How lovely," she said mechanically. She wasn't sure if she meant the cap, the baby, or the sister.

"Is something wrong?"

"No, no. The sun is just brighter than I expected. I should have brought my sunglasses."

"We could go back if you want."

"No, no, I'll adjust."

She'd made more of an effort after that, waving hello when she saw them outside, clipping coupons for their brand of diapers and wipes and baby food, dropping them through the mail slot. She'd brought over cookies—chocolate crinkles, her standard go-to for hospitality—and so began a series of coffees and lunches and walks to the park, always in the company of the baby, but never this close before. Never touching.

This is good for me, Deborah told herself, looking down at the plump little creature. *This is what I need.* Desensitizing, they call it. Or was that just for allergies?

I'm allergic to babies, she thought with a smothered giggle. Millie responded with her own version of a giggle, squirming a bit. Deborah tested the water's temperature, considered adding a bit more heat. She imagined scalding water pouring out of the faucet, turning the translucent skin pink, then red…that story about how to boil a frog crept into her mind. She could spread the heat around, warm the water slowly, so the baby wouldn't even notice, until…

You are a horrible person. Horrible, horrible.

"No," she heard her therapist in her head. "Don't blame yourself. It's normal to have dark thoughts after this kind of trauma. As long as you don't act upon them. If you are tempted, call me."

I don't deserve a baby, Deborah thought. *I don't deserve to be a mother.*

The baby squirmed again, falling backward. Deborah caught her just before her head hit the edge of the sink. She put her whole arm behind the—behind Millie, letting the water wick up her sleeve. Why don't they have a baby bath? Maybe they can't afford it. Nina mentioned hand-me-downs. Maybe they'd spent more than they could afford, buying a townhouse in a good school district. She could give them her baby bath. She knew she should have returned all the baby things, all that lovely ruffled pinkness. Call it a gift. Come up with some excuse.

Deborah swirled the water around the baby's plump little tummy. Millie giggled again. So infectious. "You little squirmy-wormy thing." She wanted to pick up the baby's tiny foot and stick it into her mouth. "Squirmy-wormy-ermy."

"Sorry about that," Nina said, walking into the room. Deborah stepped back as Nina slid into place, an exchange of warm bodies, supporting hands. Did the baby even notice? Deborah reached for a towel to dry her arm.

"Why, aren't you just the happiest baby?" Nina cooed. "Yes you are! Yes you are!" She bent down and blew against Millie's tummy, making a buzzing sound. Millie giggled with her whole body.

"Here," Deborah said, holding out the towel. Nina drained the water from the sink, and then gently rinsed off the soap, cupping her hand under the faucet to pour it over Millie's head. "There. All soft and pink and clean." Nina took the towel and wrapped it around that sturdy little body. Millie twisted around and reached back toward Deborah, her head wobbling a bit.

"She really likes you," Nina said. "She doesn't respond like that to everyone. You have a real way with babies."

Deborah stared at the two of them, that image: a baby's head tucked under a mother's chin. Love and hope. Madonna and child.

With a shudder, Deborah began to cry.

ELIZABETH DESCHRYVER

Elizabeth is a published poet, playwright and short story author. She earned her PhD in English from Northwestern University, so logically she spent the next 24 years working for a technology consulting firm. Now retired, she divides her time between writing, thinking about writing, and volunteer work.

Unfortunate Certainty

by Paco Aramburu

Doris didn't know if she would make the last few steps to her room. Her shaking hands supported her weight on the comfort-fit handles of two canes. The hallway of the nursing home was, as usual during lunchtime, deserted. In the doorway, a flash of pain seized her muscles.

Doris tottered and fell on her chair, landing on her carefully arranged pillows. In between spasmodic sighs, she adjusted her body over the seat. The two discarded canes made an X on the carpet, reminding her that every step she took had brought her closer to the end.

Another seizure overtook her body. While the intense pain subsided, a liquid darkness drenched her consciousness, becoming intimate with her limbs. The absence of discomfort, the final rest of not being anymore, the abyss of not feeling overcame her. When a feeble, scratchy breath returned, Doris—who had been dreading this moment for weeks—readied herself to take the last one.

She had hoped for something less prosaic, more like the movies of old Queen Elizabeth surrounded by mourners, bells ringing, whispers in the hallways of power. Yet, as she approached the end, her only witnesses were the carpet, the canes, and the Posturite bed the girls had bought her.

A rude new pain seized her body. She searched for her daughters' photo on the night table. They had managed to be together and smile for one shot. In that instant, her breath faltered. The vacuum in her lungs surprised her. There were no sounds, no sights, no other sensation.

Just time stretching silently, blindly, deadly.

Within the darkness, in the deliberate way honey pours lazy and gold, memories of her life oozed from somewhere in her dying brain.

Her family's old house, with the crooked roof and battered wood siding, materialized in her mind. The vision became more defined, more painful, as she remembered the rich neighborhood surrounding their unkempt front yard, a neighborhood with judgmental trimmed hedges, better-than-thou gardens

11

manicured by illegal immigrants, and shiny new cars swallowed by attached garages. Her mind repeated the litany of lame excuses she used so she could leave the house through the alley to avoid being seen in her front yard.

Her family had the habit of failing at every business they endeavored. The contempt their neighbors had for the second-hand clothing that all members of her clan were forced to wear, their old car, their pockmarked garden gnomes, had been obvious to her ever since she was a child. Doris's outfits would be examined by the girls at school the way a general inspects the troops, and they talked about their parties in front of her so she would be humiliated by not being invited.

Clattering memories followed one another like train cars. John F. Logan—Jack—moderately wealthy suitor, husband, dad, daddy, good old reliable, the departed. From his awkward courting in college, Doris had known he would be the highest she could reach up the social ladder. She had come down from the ideal portrayed in romance novels to settle for a life of relative comfort. From the concessions to complacency on their wedding day to suffering the every-dayness of every day, to his serene way of consuming time, Jack waited for life to pass through his gray existence. When the opportunity came in the form of a heart attack, Doris absconded to the kitchen and listened for the moment his moaning and pleading calls to her stopped.

Then, like a caboose rattling behind that memory, the joy of holding her babies washed over her. She witnessed how, in time, her two daughters had become a worn photocopy of their father, spending all their energies making sure their lives and those of their husbands and children were absolutely pre-dictable, so not one of them was in danger of being really alive. Like rocks in a river, they just stood in the current waiting to be eroded.

Time didn't move backward or forward. She had ceased to be. A thin sliver of her self witnessed, from the empty colorlessness of the emerging memory, her brother-in-law Albert—Al, Uncle Al, the You to my Me, My Life Love, my very own sweetheart.

Al's mischievous smiles let her know that life was a play in which the two of them were both the actors and the audience. Their hearts had conversed in whispers ever since they met. He rode a motorcycle in a leather outfit, was not afraid to stay up late to discuss a poem, had a weakness for French bread and Doris's legs.

Silence, darkness and time stretched until a feeling ripped through the nothingness. Her twin sister Corine—Aunt Cori, Albert's wife, my lover's wife. Cori had spent a life pretending her ailments were her most interesting feature and, because unfortunately they were, her incessant prattling about them made her presence unbearable.

Doris re-experienced the contempt she held for her sibling who had a petty blindness to Albert's gifts. Killing her had been easy. Because of Cori's obsession with telling everyone—whether they wanted to hear it or not—those things that were bad for her health, it became a simple matter of switching the contents of her many capsules. When Corine finally died, Doris's joy was the most intense, the most satisfying feeling she had in her life. A victory over her sister allowed Doris to dispose of an intimate reflection of her own self. Her ugly mirror. Elated to have won over her less-talented reflection, she now had Albert all to herself.

A precious few years later, a dark cloud cut Al's light forever. Doris re-lived the devastating grief of his passing. He left her like a nutshell; useless, tasteless, disposable.

As a new, thicker darkness oozed over her known world, she understood that getting rid of her sister had been the moment that defined her. Her victory claimed two lives so she could live one. While memories drowned in the dark, time stretched silently, blindly, deadly.

PACO ARAMBURU

Paco is an adopted son of Chicago where, in the 1980s, he began writing in English. He learned to merge his South American experience with the wide river of ideas offered in the U.S. Paco is Vice President of OCWW, has two finished novels, and one in progress.

Birds of a Feather

by Caroline Winkler

Everyone in outer London raised hens as part of the war effort. Mum told Little Lenny and me that owning female chickens was the only way to get fresh eggs.

Our russet-red hens were gentle and friendly, and tending them was a pleasure for my little brother and me.

But our notions about chickens changed abruptly when our next-door neighbor added a strutting Banty cockerel to his clutch. We discovered the bird one dawn when we were awakened by loud crowing—and dad's rant.

"Bloody hell!" our old man screamed, banging the upstairs window. "Hear that dreadful racket, Jimmy lad?" Before I could answer, he said, "A female chicken is one thing, but a male cockerel? You'd think we lost enough sleep last night out in that air raid shelter! Now this blighter invades our peace!"

Us two boys gawked out the window. Dad rushed into the back garden in his tattered pajamas, enraged at the sight of a tiny orange and green cockerel with flowing black tail feathers. A different breed, smaller than a chicken, it strutted proudly atop our next-door neighbor's fence, shaking the huge red comb on its tiny head and crowing.

Dad came back fuming. "The neighbors got one of those damn bantam cockerels. Said it would keep stray cats away from their henhouse."

"Well," Mum began in her soft voice, "it's a pretty wee rascal. And having a male around s'posed to encourage hens to lay more egg—"

"But a bantam!" Dad's cheeks flamed and he shook his head. "Sure, he's a handsome fellow, but believe you me, those pointed little orange claws—"

"Blimey!" I turned back to the window, a shiver of excitement along my spine. "Let's see!"

"Not only do those damned bantam cockerels crow all day," Dad declared, "I've seen firsthand why they've such a fierce reputation in cockfights. Slash a rival bird's throat in one well-placed sweep of those needle-sharp talons!"

"Charlie!" Mum shook her head. "You know cockfights are illegal. You promised!"

"Ah…" Dad backtracked, an embarrassed flush on his cheeks.

Mum grabbed my arm and blessed herself. "I can't have that thing attack my boys!"

"I doubt this one's trained to fight, but better safe than sorry." Dad's eyes softened in a rare glance of affection at me. "You'll be fine if you just stay away from it when you go out there."

Back when we'd got our own chickens, Dad had assigned me—the elder at 12—to clean out their shitty coops, which were right by the neighbor's fence. When I'd protested, Dad pointed a finger in my face.

"Quit bellyaching and be a man! Maybe you'd like to switch jobs with me? Still driving that bloody bus, day in, day out, bomb sites, dust, smoke."

That look in Dad's eye had told me not to interrupt and I'd put my arm around Little Lenny.

"Grown men blubbering on the curb. Homes, loved ones, everything lost!" Dad shook his head, then glanced at my scared face as if he'd seen me for the first time. "No? I didn't think you'd switch. And don't try conning Little Lenny into swapping chores with you either."

I'd resisted cringing as Dad reached out to ruffle my hair. I'd felt the back of that hand before. Mum said Dad could barely help it. He was what she called "sort of shell-shocked" from all the tragedy he'd seen. So I'd determined to always be strong in front of Little Lenny. Though but 10 months younger, at age 11, Little Lenny was much smaller and a real fraidy-cat. I had my hands full keeping bullies off him at school.

So right then, I resolved to also protect Little Lenny from the bantam cockerel. And since that very day just happened to be Little Lenny's birthday, I volunteered for his job as well, cutting the grass. No need for him to even set foot outside.

I snuck another glance out the window. I couldn't help but admire the bantam's spunk, strutting atop the fence and squawking fiercely as he spied a cat. Dad took one look out and immediately agreed to my taking on Lenny's chore.

"Smashing!" I said. "Then I'll do it later, after the cake!"

Mum had scrimped, saved, and traded eggs to get ingredients to make a birthday cake. I could already hear rattling pots and pans. How I longed to be in the kitchen, smelling it bake. I barely remembered the last time we'd had anything sweet.

When I slipped into the kitchen under the pretense of looking for cereal, Dad wouldn't brook what he called my dawdling.

"Just get on with it!" he scowled.

"And shut that bloomin' door behind you," Mum added, "so's—"

"I know, I know," I said, "so I don't let those *bloomin'* flies in."

"So cheeky!" Mum tutted as I dodged a swipe of her dishtowel on my way out. Dad sneered at me. "And the flies is why your coops always need cleaning!"

Soon as I stepped into the muggy July warmth, beads of sweat rolled down the back of my neck. Dozy on the early heat, a bee buzzed by, perhaps in search of Mum's prize red roses. But they'd been ripped out when we got the hens. Dad only permitted tall, golden sunflowers because their seed made chickenfeed. I picked a handful for our hens before grabbing the push-mower.

As the blades flipped up the smell of mowed grass, I sensed a movement along the fence. Before I realized what was happening, the bantam had flown off the fence and landed right on my shoulder. I froze and he clucked at me. He even sounded kind of friendly. Perhaps he approved of how I took care of our chickens.

Then he became more daring. That pesky little bird reached over and pecked my earlobe. As I yelped and swatted him off, my fingertips connected with a flutter of soft down and I caught a flash of orange wings. He landed on my shoe. I wriggled my foot but he wouldn't get off. I tried to run, but he crowed and plucked at my shoelaces, worrying them back and forth like a dog with a bone. He seemed ready for a game!

I stretched my leg and lifted my foot, flipping the bantam up into the air. He took off but flew right back down, landing on my shoe. We had a smashing game of kick and fly until he alighted on my shoulder. The bantam leaned gently against my sweaty neck, exhausted. Crikey, he was actually snuggling against me. He panted a bit while his tiny heart throbbed. And this time when he clucked, I reached up. Carefully avoiding his sharp beak, I gingerly ruffled the yellow-speckled feathers under his chin. He clucked softly as if he enjoyed it.

My brother burst from the house. The startled bantam flew back onto the fence. Little Lenny raced over to show me his new boxing gloves. Just what I had always wanted. But Dear Old Dad had told Lenny *he* needed some toughening up.

Let me tell you, it worked too well. Before I even knew what happened, Little Lenny donned a glove and bopped me one in the eye! I grabbed the other glove, ready to defend my title as eldest and strongest. All I had to do was extend my arm onto Little Lenny's chest and hold him at arm's length. Then I had a good laugh! No matter how furiously he struggled, short Little Lenny couldn't reach far enough to strike a blow.

While we shuffled around and laughed, the bantam broke out crowing and swept down right into the middle of the fray. Little Lenny screwed up his face, shut his eyes, and yelled, only exciting the bantam more. The bird flapped around Little Lenny's legs, pecking at his laces. And what a sight it was! I doubled up laughing as Little Lenny stumbled back and then broke for the house, the bantam maniacally running along after on absurdly short, wrinkly orange legs. I'd never seen a bird go that fast without flying.

Lenny screamed. That wiped the grin off my face. He needed my help. Clutching my side, I ran in front of the bantam and tried to kick him back. Cripes, did that ever rile him up! That mad bird grabbed my loose lace and gave it an almighty tug. I pulled back. He tugged again and it snapped in half. He pulled it right outta my shoe, knocking me over.

The tables had turned! Now I was screaming and Little Lenny was the one laughing his head off. I reeled around and sat up. And you'll never believe what I saw. That bantam was gulping down one of the only two shoelaces I owned as if it were a wriggling worm!

I lunged, but quick Little Lenny beat me to it. Without thinking, he stuck two fingers down the bantam's gullet and grabbed the end of my shoelace. He pulled it right back out; wet, mangled, and half its original length. The startled bird retched, then streaked back onto the fence. It should have been funny but I was close to tears, just imagining how boiled Dad would be, what with the shortage of laces during the war.

And as if things weren't turning out bad enough, my little brother had boxing gloves and a wonderful birthday dinner to look forward to. All I had was a broken lace and a two-month wait for *my* next birthday. Would any boxing gloves even be available then?

Little Lenny ran inside while I sat there sniveling. Before Dad knew what had happened, Little Lenny came back out, dangling one of his own shoelaces, and offered it to me. He'd already replaced it by snatching another from a hand-me-down old shoe that no longer fit him. Lucky for me, he didn't care if his laces were mismatched.

Over dinner, Lenny got all the attention, bragging of his attempted rescue of the shoestring. But something inside me smothered my feelings of being left out. A new and growing pride in my little brother's accomplishments began to take root. I could see plain as the nose on my face that Lenny was no longer afraid of the rooster. And we all had a good laugh when I pointed out that we'd stopped calling him Little Lenny.

And our Lenny took his growing confidence to heart. He even stood up to the older school bully on the very first day. And in defense of a younger boy. The other kids all cheered when Lenny up and bopped Nasty Nick right in the nose. Quick as a wink, Lenny bounded out of reach, nimble as the neighbor's cat dodging "our" rooster. And not so much as a whimper emerged from my newly brave brother. Even when the headmaster smacked the back of Lenny's skinny knees with a ruler. Unjust punishment, I might add, as Nasty Nick started it, but Lenny was no snitch.

And from then on, Lenny joined me and the bantam outside. I'll always remember that year as the time a new Lenny emerged. And not just at school. We brothers transformed from our old family roles into true compatriots in our many shared games of kick and fly with the rooster. The rooster always hopped onto my shoulder first and took a quick "love bite" of my ear lobe, knowing that I'd push him off. He'd alight on my shoe, worrying its lace until I'd lift my shoe and gently kick the rooster up into the air. Then Lenny would glide up alongside me when the rooster landed, ready to nudge it with the toe of his shoe. The rooster would then give Lenny's laces a good riling up until it tuckered out. And that's when I'd notice the old Lenny hadn't completely disappeared. Whenever the rooster wanted to rest, the new-and-nimble Lenny always dodged back, just to make sure that my shoulder and earlobe were handy, not his!

—— CAROLINE WINKLER ——————————

Caroline is a former corporate tax director with a knack for researching and condensing complex information into an easy summary. She applied those skills to co-author *The Pocket Parent,* for busy parents of two- to five-year-olds. Caroline is working on a YA mystery novel, which also draws upon her childhood in Britain and Ireland.

A Story About the Body

by Laurel M. Ross

On the long dark drive home from the distant suburbs, I began to feel queasy. The pleasure of giving a talk was replaced by a roiling in my gut.

Home later in my city flat, lying on smooth sheets, I waited for the quiet. Two attentive cats arranged themselves against my folded torso. This arsenal of comforts could not drive out the demon, though. Sleep would not come.

The night dragged on and the sickness took form—a malevolent throbbing in the belly. Each story I told myself to explain it away failed. Supper on the run. Nerves about public speaking. Gas.

My mind replayed parental dismissals—"it's growing pains"—of all nocturnal childhood suffering.

At morning light I phoned my office to say, "I am sick and haven't slept. I'll stay home and wait for it to pass."

"So foolish. Get help. Why wait?" my colleague chided.

Was my body betraying me? Aha! I needed help.

And then I entered the Bardo of the ER where there is little tolerance for ambiguity or existential angst. Triage nurses considered my symptoms, measured my vitals, and dispatched me to a darkened waiting cell.

The pain increased.

No answers to my persistent examiners satisfied them. "Your pain on a scale of one to ten? Are you hungry? …thirsty? …pregnant? …constipated?" How many doctors passed through I cannot say, but many gloved fingers poked hard into my tender belly flesh.

Hours passed in that cell while a television droned on about violent crimes and threatening weather and miraculous household products.

Between interrogations, I eavesdropped on other bodies acting out compelling dramas nearby. ["That will need stitches."] ["Let him sleep it off."] In that hyper-real atmosphere I overheard my neighbors' woes—tales of gunshot wounds and car crashes and altercations. ["She says she fell."] Conversational snatches revealed a cavalcade of victims, perpetrators, innocents, and lunatics. ["Does anyone want to deliver a baby?"] ["How long have you been bleeding?"] At least one person died.

Questioning, probing and pain were my world until, at last, nine hours after my arrival, surgery was ordered, granting me the blessing of unconsciousness.

["Bloody murder!"] Startling words from a blaring television woke me. I found myself in a dim, unfamiliar room. A doctor materialized at my side and, without a smile or a greeting, began to describe the grotesqueness of my now-excised offending organ. "It was severe and almost burst. A ruptured appendix is a very serious matter."

The hysterical television voice from above distracted me. ["Slashed to pieces!"]

"We should have operated sooner," my critic intoned, oblivious to my grogginess. "You didn't complain enough." Patting my hand. "Next time, help us out. Be clear."

I looked away from him in shame, my eyes drawn to the screen above. Speeding cars and wildly vivid words. ["Head almost severed!"]

The beginning of the OJ drama unfolded as my own episode of the body ended with lessons learned.

— LAUREL M. ROSS

Laurel is a former professional photographer, a political activist, mother, retired conservation ecologist, chorister (alto), birder, prairie steward, crossword puzzler, tai chi practitioner, world traveler, and ordained Zen Buddhist priest. She is finally pursuing her lifelong dream of writing and has found OCWW to be better than an MFA.

Flamingos

by Lisa Sukenic

The wait in the room is anonymous. Fifteen women. I look down at the green carpet with brown leaves inside tiny squares, inside brown leaves, inside slightly larger squares. I notice these details.

This is a quick test. I've had it at least 17 times. The year my mother died, her mammogram was clear. A stroke of good luck.

It's Monday, MLK Day, a day off. They can fit me in. This time I waited a year and a half and this could have been a mistake. I wait. The women are unknown but the worries are the same.

When my mom was first diagnosed they moved from the family suburban home to a condo by the woods where she fed the birds and watched the deer in the fall and fawns in the spring. The woods led to a small pond that made my dad afraid. When he was 10 he had nearly drowned under a dock at his family cottage on Woodhall Lake. But he bought this condo for her to scare the cancer away.

No one talks in the waiting room. Everyone reads, or turns pages and fake-reads. Each ignoring that they are all waiting, hoping for the same outcome. The women barely look up, as if a glance could ruin their luck and cause them to get a positive diagnosis. Some are there because they need additional pictures. Weak smiles are passed back and forth.

"Sheila." The nurse calls my name and walks me back to a smaller waiting room.

"Put on your gown. Open to the front. Take the key. Lock up your belongings." The nurse walks away.

The women sit in dark pink smocks in the smaller, heated waiting room. The smocks tie to the side like a fancy kimono robe. A woman comments that this design is better than hospital gowns. We all look up briefly.

We sit like a flock of flamingos, waiting our turns. My mom always loved flamingos.

We are anonymous, like in an elevator, but with less conversation and no eye contact. Why would you? We're nameless to each other.

Flamingos' wingspans are five feet across.

I am five feet vertical.

This small waiting room, with its deep sighs, accidental open doors in changing rooms, and apologies. I wonder if anyone drinks the coffee here, so unlike a café.

She opens the door and calls me. I am next. I set the magazine back on the table and carefully straighten the flamingo smock and follow the technician down the corridor.

"Step up," she commands. "Look this way. Arm up. Move forward. Lean in. Face the wall."

An art print of two gigantic tulips, one of thousands hanging in rooms like these. I wonder who the buyer is for hospital art. My mother was a painter and my sister took after her. Every year our family went to the Tulip Festival in Holland, Michigan. These flowers are too big to be real.

Today my body does not listen well to her directions.

"Move to the right. Head to the left. Turn in."

This woman has little compassion. Last year's technician kept apologizing as if I was a child getting a shot; consoling me. This one is business as usual. Spends all day pressing breasts flat. This three-dimensional shape, turning into two, reminds me of the chipmunk that flattened itself under the door in my first house and became wedged between the wall and the toilet. The house, with only one closet and no basement, where we made love so loud that the men living next door taunted us, and we became silent, and worried about retribution.

"Step back," she repeats.

If I step back far enough maybe I won't have cancer. She needs to do an extra one.

"You must have breathed when I said not to," she scolds again.

Today I will wait twice, once for the mammogram and again for the ultrasound. The test is six months late. When mom was diagnosed, she swore it was the hormones she took and wouldn't take the test to see if it was genetic. How could she? She had three daughters. How responsible would she feel? Better not to know.

"Your doctor will contact you. The letter will arrive in the mail," the technician says robotically.

It will come in many days—so long that it is easy to forget and then I might be renewed for another year. It is equivalent to the Jewish New Year. Will I be renewed for another year?

I have the family history: my mom's lumpectomy, her sister's radical mastectomy. Mom refused to see there might be a connection, told her own sister their cancers were different.

"She's your sister. You're genetically related," I said.

"It was the hormones," my mom told me with certainty and turned her head and energy to her newspaper crossword puzzle. When she was diagnosed the second time, 15 years later, she came to visit me in Kalamazoo. My oldest was four and she brought her a doll. I don't remember much of the weekend. Food tasted wrong, hellos and good-byes were lopsided. Mom was given about a month to live. She lived for seven more years.

Flamingos are tough as hell. They can survive in high-altitude salt flats and alkaline lakes. If humans were in a hypersaline solution our skin would strip off.

I bury myself in my phone, like we buried the small photo of my mom in dad's lapel pocket as he lay in the casket.

My mom's bank checks had the pink ribbon on them.

Flamingos gradually turn pink because of the dye called canthaxanthin. It is in brine shrimp and blue algae. It is poisonous to most animals.

She wore pastels that washed her out. She was too pale and blended in with the bed sheets in the end. Dad only ate fried shrimp at the Chinese restaurant. We kept kosher at home.

Two years in a row we walked for breast cancer research. I have the picture of the girls sitting next to Buckingham Fountain. The last time mom was in Chicago it rained. She was so weak she couldn't participate in the walk. We sat in a small coffee shop off Michigan Avenue. The TraveLodge, with the little bear in bedclothes, a downtown dive. Rain dripped down in continuous beads like those oil lamps.

"No one wants to listen to my story. I'm not a survivor," my mom muttered.

The night mom passed, deer glided silently over the black pavement, dancing in the fog.

Flamingos only fly at night.

"Have a seat across the hall." I am waiting for the next test. The two other women flamingos say hi to me, mindlessly turn the pages of their magazines. Unread words. This woman is much more hospitable than the earlier one. I'm always told my breasts are too dense to tell on a mammogram. So why do they even do that test?

The second technician arrives and asks me if I had a nice weekend.

She is much nicer. Small talk at the Russian Roulette hospital. This time I do not get to keep the pink kimono smock on. I disrobe. The room is unheated. The nurse apologizes.

"One more time, hold your breath." Beep. This is a new ultrasound machine.

I am getting goose bumps waiting. Chicken skin. Beep.

"This is one of the latest techniques, different than 10 years ago."

She uses a spatula and paints on the gel.

"Sorry, it's cold." She continues painting the contours of my breast.

"This procedure lasts 20 minutes." She hands me a towel.

I will try to find where my car is parked in the lot where the levels are labeled with the fight-songs of the universities.

That night, I wake to the sound of the dog's tags jingling. I can always sleep, but today's appointment keeps me awake. My mom and sister suffered from sleepless nights. My dad and I could sleep through anything. The joke was that he and I could sleep standing up.

Flamingos can turn off one side of their brains when they sleep.

Tonight, my mom's insomnia sings to me.

LISA SUKENIC

Lisa is a 4th-grade teacher at the University of Chicago Lab Schools. She is a poet and an author. Her historical middle-grade novel in verse, *Miles from Motown,* will debut Spring 2021. Her poetry, haikus and short stories appear/are forthcoming in a variety of anthologies.

Goodbye

by Malik Turley

"It's time to go."

"No."

"Cleo, please."

"No."

Paul looked around, hoping someone would appear who could reason with his wife. Everyone had left, either to give them privacy or to distance themselves from the pain. There was no one within sight, and he knew they wouldn't have had any more success. This wasn't something anyone should have practice in or have tricks for at the ready.

"Cleo, we have to leave."

"No."

"I promise to bring you back in the morning. We'll come back, first thing. They open the gates at six a.m."

Cleo looked up at Paul with eyes full of anger. He waited, looking at his wife folded up on the grass, refusing to shrivel under her gaze. The two of them stayed locked in silence as the wind picked up around them. Paul shifted into a crouch and stretched out his gloved hand, offering it to Cleo. It wasn't until the predicted raindrops started to fall around them that Cleo accepted his offer and placed her naked hand in his.

"Thank you. I promise—we'll come back as early tomorrow as you want, as long as it's after they open the gates."

As they walked down the winding path to the car, Paul fished in his mind for the details of the last conversation he'd had with Cleo where she'd said something more than "no." If he'd known it to be an important one he would have paid more attention. They had been sitting at their kitchen table. He could, oddly enough, remember their plates and what was on them better than he could recall the content of their conversation. She'd had the garish orange plate that she loved and he hated, and it was piled high with hummus

27

and vegetables. His plate had been one of their everyday china pieces from their wedding, and he'd had an array of cheeses, meats, and fruits. The food didn't matter, and Paul had tried time and again to push it out of the foreground to get at the conversation they'd been having.

He tripped to a halt when Cleo stopped. "What?"

She didn't answer, but this time she didn't need to. They had found their way back to the car while he'd been thinking about dishes and food.

"Right. Sorry." Paul unlocked the door and went around to the driver's side. Cleo yanked her door open, threw herself into the car, and slammed the door behind her. With sagging shoulders Paul followed her into the car, silently sliding into the driver's seat, resisting the urge to look back up the path they'd just followed.

Driving out of the cemetery after dark required his high-beams and all of his attention. Paul didn't bother putting music on and kept his hands at ten and two. He hadn't liked driving before and it was painful now. Cleo used to be the one to drive whenever they were together. Having her in the passenger seat just added to the wrongness that surrounded them. He snuck a glance at her once they got to the driveway. Her anger filled the car, as it had filled the entire cemetery. That little glimmer that allowed her to take his hand was gone.

Paul missed her. He missed their conversations and how deep they often got. He missed her reaching out to touch him voluntarily. He missed her smile. It had been two weeks since his world had any normal in it, and it felt like a lifetime.

The drive home was mercifully short and uneventful. Paul had barely put the car in park when Cleo unbuckled and pushed the door open. He didn't follow her inside right away. After making sure everything that was supposed to be off was off, Paul unfolded himself from behind the wheel. Cleo was already back inside, and he was in no hurry to join her.

"Will you come downstairs?"

"No."

"The pastor is here. He just wants to check on us."

"No."

"It might help to talk with him."

"No."

The upstairs hallway was dark with only a sliver of light coming from under their closed bedroom door. Paul hadn't felt welcome inside their bedroom since they returned from the hospital without their daughter. Cleo spent all of her time in there, alone, only emerging to go to the cemetery. Paul slept in the guest bedroom and spent his time downstairs, doing his best to give Cleo the distance she craved.

Paul grabbed his hair at the temples and let out a silent sigh before attempting to smooth it down on his way downstairs. Cleo was the religious one. Cleo was the one active in the church.

When the house had been full of people coming to pay their respects, Paul was sure they were disappointed that he was the one receiving them. His presence made them uncomfortable. All the questions were about Cleo, how she was doing, what she needed, how they could help her. He didn't know how to satisfy their curiosity any more than he knew how to get his wife to open up.

When his friends came by, things weren't much better. The looks of pity, the questions not asked, the forced small talk. All of it pointed a glaring spotlight on how he shouldn't have been the one to survive, as if he needed anyone else to point that out to him.

Paul waded through it all, alone, taking on the solitude as another part of his penance. He couldn't undo the past, he understood that. He longed for the ability to do something to fix the present. Maybe the pastor would know, and maybe he'd be willing to share.

"It's time for lunch."

"No."

"Will you come down to the kitchen?"

"No."

"I could sit with you."

"No."

"Cleo, you need to eat."

"No."

Paul stroked the bedroom door, giving it the caress he wished he could give Cleo. "I'm going to go put something together. Maybe you'll change your mind."

Paul was careful to look at the floor as he passed the empty room between their bedroom and the stairs. Talking to his wife through a closed door day after day was painful enough. He didn't need to look inside Crystal's room to feel the sharp twist of pain from its stillness.

Memories were everywhere. He went to the refrigerator and paused to take in everything displayed by their magnet collection. Nothing had changed. The out-of-date field trip flier hung there, and the invitation to the damned birthday party. Their home felt frozen in time.

Inside the fridge was a different story. Paul opened the door and was assaulted by the change. Before, there would have been a variety of foods lying in wait for Cleo to combine into delicious meals that the three of them would eat together at the dining room table. Now there were stacks of Tupperware, holding meals for two, that had been dropped off by friends too uncomfortable with grief to stay longer than the hand-off required.

Paul took the top container off the stack without checking the contents. Food barely had any taste anyway, so there was no point in deliberating over which plastic box would serve up lunch or dinner.

Paul had gotten good at setting up plates to serve up the gifted food. He had figured out how long different things took in the microwave and how to stagger the reheating so he could end up with everything at an edible temperature at the same time. He'd gotten used to eating alone after having brought food up to Cleo.

Paul stood at the threshold of his daughter's room, tears streaming unchecked down his cheeks and onto the hardwood floor. He looked at Crystal's unmade bed and saw flashes of their last battle over cleaning her room. He saw the books, open and face down, on her desk and felt the pang of discussions they'd never have about plots and characters. He had talked himself into opening the door, telling himself lies about how it wouldn't hurt, promising himself it was just a room, that he was strong.

Everything hurt.

The clock showing the hour that would have been right when she left but was wrong now, weeks later, after daylight savings ended. The outfits left discarded she'd promised would be put away "when she got home." The tousled bed clothes tossed over the three teddy bears she still had at the foot of her bed.

Everything was left as if she were going to come back and set it right. As if she'd be back after the party. Five weeks. Paul's fist tightened around the party invite he'd pulled off the fridge. The scrap of paper that changed everything. The proof that he should have said "no."

"NO!" The word tore from Paul and filled the room. He stepped through the doorway and crumpled to his knees. "No no no no no no…" He repeated the word until his sobs took over, masking the sound of his bedroom door opening.

Paul's sobs slowed and he swiped away the tears as he pushed himself up to stand and face the truth. He approached the desk and touched one of the books. With a final shudder, he turned to leave the room.

Cleo stood in the hallway, her arms wrapped around her middle, holding herself together against the pain. Paul rubbed his eyes and pulled his hands down his cheeks, ending with them pressed against each other in front of his mouth.

Paul, broken and raw, approached his wife.

"Cleo?"

She hesitated, then stepped into his embrace. "I know."

MALIK TURLEY

Malik started writing four years ago in honor of Jen, her sister-friend who was taken too soon by cancer. It turns out she has a lot of stories to tell. When she's not writing, you will find her instigating change for women and the world as the founder of Hip Circle Empowerment Center.

The Coffee Shop

by Ellen Pridmore

The Coffee Shop sat on the corner of a quaint suburban downtown outside of Chicago.

Harry knew almost everyone who came to his coffee shop; a warm and cozy place where folks young and old came to eat, sip a cup of joe and visit. Today, Harry opened The Coffee Shop for the very last time.

"Good morning, Florence," said Harry, forcing a smile.

"Good morning, Harry."

"I'll get you a cup of coffee. I just brewed a fresh pot."

"So, where are your waitresses?" demanded Florence. "It's nine o'clock sharp."

"Lou Ann is finishing her cigarette outside. She'll be right in. Tracy will be here shortly."

"I'll take a donut," said Florence.

"Sure thing," answered Harry as he brought over her hot coffee and donut.

Raindrops spattered against the window on this chilly October day.

The décor hadn't changed since it opened in 1955. Once a year, Harry would close the restaurant for one week to clean and paint. The Coffee Shop was known for its colonial style—forest green trim against creamy white walls. The cushioned vinyl chairs and booths matched the trim with tables for two and four in the small shop. All sorts of pictures hung decoratively on the walls: past presidents, a framed Coca-Cola puzzle, a lighthouse painted in the distance and historic homes from colonial days.

The clock—still working after all these years—sat above the cash register telling perfect time.

Lou Ann walked in and put on her apron. "Morning, Florence. Want a warm-up?" asked Lou Ann.

"Yes, please, Lou Ann," said Florence as she rearranged the place setting.

As a retired librarian, and widow, Florence spent hours giving her opinions on all the conversations. Harry glanced at Florence and felt great sadness for

33

her as he knew she would miss The Coffee Shop the most. This was her first stop every day, meeting her friends for coffee.

One of the reasons the townspeople loved The Coffee Shop was the camaraderie and consistency.

The Coffee Shop was open 9-7 every day except Sundays.

The "Specials of the Day" board stood directly over the kitchen counter. Monday through Friday—the specials were always the same.

Florence sat quietly with her coffee and half-eaten donut watching the clock. Tracy finally arrived at work. When you're a regular at The Coffee Shop, almost everything is your business.

By 9:30, the breakfast crowd started to file in. Tracy and Lou Ann were busy hopping from table to table taking orders, refilling cups and talking with customers they would never see again.

The morning crowd was a mix of regulars and floaters—people that popped in once in awhile. John Springer took a seat next to Florence. They often sat together at breakfast.

Sometimes breakfast lingered until lunch.

"Morning, John," said Florence.

"Hi, Flo," said John.

"John," said Lou Ann. "Ordering the usual?"

"Yes, please."

John retired—and became a widower—two years ago.

One of the cooks rang the bell from the kitchen to let the waitresses know an order was up.

Lou Ann served John his scrambled eggs, bacon, white toast and coffee. Once in a while he would venture out on the wild side and order a waffle.

Florence ate another pastry while she and John talked about the latest books and how to solve the town's problems. Other regulars joined in and three tables were pushed together, followed by many coffee refill requests.

"We need to pass the referendum on updating the library," said Florence.

"I agree," said Joe. "My wife and I use the library almost every day—great programs for us seniors, as well as for families and children."

"Absolutely," replied John. "They also need to figure out this town's parking configuration."

"It's so difficult to find parking these days," said Lillian.

Florence shifted in her chair. It was time to talk about the inevitable—the conversation no one wanted to have.

"Harry," Florence interrupted everyone, "you haven't said a word about today being your last here."

Harry swallowed hard with a lump in his throat. "It's hard to let go of this place," said Harry, his voice cracking.

"It's unbelievable," said John.

"They're going to reconfigure this whole area," said Joe.

Lillian's eyes brimmed with tears. "We will sure miss you, Harry."

John, Joe and the others nodded in agreement.

"I will miss all of you as well," said Harry. "Let's enjoy the rest of the day."

"What time is the farewell party? I hope those developers don't think they're invited," snapped Florence.

"Be here at seven tonight, Florence. The developers will not be here," said Harry. "I would never invite people who are forcing us out."

Harry glanced at the clock. Already 11:30—where had the morning gone?

Right on time, the lunch regulars paraded in.

Florence and John stayed while the others dispersed and moved on with their day, but told Harry they would be back at 7:00 for the farewell.

Ida came in with her sister, Helen, and niece, Evelyn. The trio would sit at their regular table, say hello to everyone they knew, and order coffee and lunch.

"Hi, Tracy," they said in unison to their favorite waitress.

"Hey, there," Tracy replied. "I'll get your coffee." She placed down the cups. Ida ran her finger over the top of her cup.

"Tracy, my cup is not smooth on top. May I have another?" Ida asked.

"Of course, Ida." Tracy had a lot of patience.

"Ida, there's nothing wrong with that cup," snapped her sister, Helen. Ida gave her a look.

Tracy poured the coffee listening to the sisters banter like they did every day.

Ida and Helen were in their early 80s. Evelyn was Helen's daughter. The Coffee Shop was their first stop before a busy afternoon ahead.

After Ida got her fresh cup of coffee, she ordered tuna salad on toast with a peach.

Helen wanted her usual grilled cheese and coffee. Evelyn loved Harry's Bar-B-Que Beef Special. It was a favorite at The Coffee Shop.

"Tracy, is the pie fresh today?" asked Ida.

"It is, Ida," answered Tracy. "What'll it be?"

"Pumpkin," answered Ida, folding her napkin.

Harry walked over to the ladies to greet them like he had always done.

"Oh, Harry, we are really going to miss you," said Ida.

"Today is tough," said Harry. "I'm going to miss everyone, and coming to work."

Ida gently touched his arm.

While they ate, in strolled Victoria Foxwood dressed in her typical attire; black cape, black hat with matching purse, and bright red lipstick.

"She never says hello to anyone," whispered Florence to Ida and Helen across the aisle.

"I don't even pay attention," said Helen.

"I wonder what her story is," said Florence.

Harry overheard the conversation. *I'm going to miss this,* he thought.

The Coffee Shop was buzzing. Businesspeople came in for a quick bite and families with their children for lunch. The Stevens family came in regularly and today was their son Jonathan's birthday. He was five years old.

Harry came out from the kitchen where he was helping the cooks. The kitchen had a wide-open window, close to the tables, and all conversations were within earshot.

"Happy birthday, Jonathan!" said Harry. "What dessert do you want today?"

"Cake roll with whipped cream and a cherry!" exclaimed Jonathan.

Harry, Lou Ann, and Tracy came out with a slice of cake roll exactly the way Jonathan wanted it, with a single candle. The whole Coffee Shop sang "Happy Birthday" to Jonathan and clapped after he blew out his candle.

After The Coffee Shop slowly emptied there was a peaceful silence in the air.

John and Florence paid their bills separately. No credit cards. Cash or check only.

They decided to go to the library together and sign up for the Fall Adult Book Club.

"See you later tonight, Harry," said Florence.

Helen pried Evelyn and Ida away from another cup of coffee; there was so much to do that afternoon.

"We'll be back later," said Ida, waving.

Victoria Foxwood sat for quite awhile and looked out the window while she ate and drank. When she finished her lunch she paid the check. "I'll see you tonight, Harry."

"Thank you, Victoria," said Harry, so quietly it was almost a whisper.

Time went quickly and the dinner crowd came in. Some were the same people that were at lunch. Others were passing by, shopping or on their way someplace, and wanted a simple meal.

The dinner crowd stayed later that night.

Victoria Foxwood was the first to arrive before the rest of the regulars.

The breakfast and lunch regulars came back at 7:00 sharp.

The bakery delivered the cake. Harry opened the box and placed the cake on the table. Lou Ann helped Harry lift the cake out of the box.

"Harry, this is beautiful," cried Lou Ann.

It was a white buttercream double-layer sheet cake trimmed with forest green and cream-colored flowers. THE COFFEE SHOP, 55 YEARS, was written across the cake in forest green buttercream. Harry and Tracy took pictures of the cake and all the guests.

The Coffee Shop was full of endless chatter. Harry sliced the cake and Lou Ann and Tracy poured the coffee.

Florence was still angry at the whole new development plan. John and Joe tried to explain why this was happening, again.

Helen, Ida and Evelyn conversed with Lillian. When Ida motioned to Victoria Foxwood to join them, she did.

"The cake is beautiful," remarked Victoria.

"It's also delicious," said Ida.

"You can't go wrong with Morningfresh Bakery," agreed Victoria. "The cake is moist and the raspberry filling is perfect."

Harry stood back for a moment and looked around the room. What great friends he had made over the years.

Harry clinked a knife on a water glass to get everyone's attention. The Coffee Shop was silent.

"I'd like to take a moment to thank you for supporting me all of these years." Harry's voice paused for a moment. "We spend every day together for breakfast, lunch and dinner, and have become family. Here's to moving forward and a new chapter for all of us."

Everyone raised a coffee cup, glass of water or soda, and cheered.

The Coffee Shop—where there was always someone to talk to, sit with while enjoying a cup of coffee and slice of pie. Friendships were formed and bonded; birthdays were celebrated with a candle in the middle of a slice of cake roll or hot fudge sundae as every customer sang "Happy Birthday."

Decorations were hung; kisses and good wishes for the holiday and New Year were given.

When someone died, everyone paid his or her respects.

This had gone on for 55 years.

There was a big cake. There was delicious hot coffee. There was a lot of laughter. There were many sad tears as the townspeople said good-bye to Harry and The Coffee Shop.

After Harry wiped down the tables and counted the money in the register he sat down in one of the booths. He looked around and reflected back on all of his customers. Florence never missed a morning coffee at The Coffee Shop. John, Joe and Lillian attempted to solve the town's problems every day. Helen, Ida, Evelyn enjoyed their daily lunch and Victoria finally joined the ladies. The Coffee Shop celebrated a lot of birthdays like Jonathan's. Local business owners came in to eat or carry out food. Other people stopped in for a slice of pie, a cup of coffee, and visit with Harry. He recalled decorating for the holidays with Lou Ann and Tracy. Warmth enveloped the shop; it was like home.

No one felt alone at The Coffee Shop.

A place that was small and simple, yet it meant much more to so many people. Harry took the clock off the wall and turned off the lights for the very last time.

ELLEN PRIDMORE

Ellen is a children's writer whose non-fiction appears in *Boys' Quest, Hopscotch, Once Upon A Time...The Magazine for Writers and Illustrators, Greek Circle Magazine*, and *Fun For Kidz*. She was a bookseller for Barbara's Books. A member of OCWW for nearly 25 years, this is her first work of adult fiction.

Porch Pirate

by Susan Winstead

Tailing the delivery van into the modest, working-class neighborhood, Mark pulls over and waits. He observes the driver make the delivery, return to the vehicle, input some information into a device, then drive away.

His senses on high alert, Mark steps out of his car and visually scans up and down the street. Other than two very run-down cars—one of them his—the entire length of the street is quiet and empty. There are mostly single-story aluminum-sided houses in the neighborhood. He focuses on the house with the newly delivered large brown cardboard box sitting at the top of its cement staircase. Hopefully, the box contains a new microwave or maybe a printer.

Darting up the steps to the house, Mark snatches the box, shoves it into the back seat of his car, then slips into the driver's seat and gets out of there. He drives to another neighborhood and after being certain no one is following him, he exits the car and removes the rags obscuring the license plate. If he were ever to get stopped, his excuse would be the rags had been unintentionally left while hand-cleaning his car. Fortunately, he's never been pulled over.

Throwing the rags to the floor of the car, Mark slips behind the steering wheel again. He drives to where he lives, never exceeding the speed limit, signaling every turn. He pulls into the driveway until the back of his car is parallel to the door leading directly to the basement. He observes the neighboring house on his left side, making sure no one is peering out a window or watering flowers. All seems to be good, so Mark carries the box inside without being seen.

When Mark first started looting parcels left in vestibules of apartment buildings and on steps of single-family homes, he went to the higher-end neighborhoods, but they became tricky when people began installing security cameras. He had always stayed away from really fancy "boutique" buildings with doormen. Instead, he opted for the places where you could get away undetected during the day when residents weren't at home.

Whoever left the delivery trusted it would be there for whoever ordered the items in the boxes and bags when they arrived home. The ordering customer would eventually contact the business to find out what happened to their purchases. In the meantime, Mark had new merchandise he could sell. By the time the purchaser, the delivery service, or the business realized the merchandise had been stolen, it was long since out of his possession.

Mark hadn't meant to become a porch pirate, it just happened through a series of missteps. Though he graduated high school, classroom learning had been torture. So college wasn't for him. Instead, he had gotten a job in the stock room of a department store where he worked for six years before the entire chain of stores went out of business. He managed to get a similar job at another store and within a year the same thing happened. He was a good worker, but he bounced around from job to job, each of them drying up, too. He eventually faced a choice of a crappy minimum-wage job, attending community college to qualify for better jobs, or boosting packages from front porches.

Inside his home, Mark pulls the newly acquired box to the far corner of the dingy basement. He sees the return address of an Army post office overseas. He wonders if there is military merchandise inside and if so, why it was sent to a private family residence.

Using a box cutter, he cuts along the taped crease of the closed flaps before opening them. The odor of motor oil greets his nostrils. He slowly lifts out worn pants and shirts, some civilian and some military fatigues, and sets them on the floor around the box.

Mark shoves the box away, wondering, "What's this about?" Every box he has ever pirated contained actual new merchandise. No way can he profit from this smelly mess of worn drab colors.

He leans back against a coffee table, perplexed as to what this stuff could be. Everything had come out of someone's closet and bathroom. And why had it been put in the mail?

Mark picks up a cap from the bottom of a box and gasps as he suddenly realizes what he's seeing. It's a camouflage cap with a military rank pinned into the center. He drops the hat and picks up one of the camouflage shirts. A cloth label with a last name was sewn above the right breast pocket. Something makes him want to find out who owned the stuff in the box.

He opens a search engine on his computer and types in the name on the shirt. Though he hadn't paid attention to the house number, he knew the name of the street and typed it next to the name along with the city. Hopefully, the combination of the last name with a street, city, and state would yield a clue. After entering the information in the bar, he taps his keyboard.

Several links to local and regional newspapers pop up. Mark opens the links and reads several stories about a soldier who died in Iraq a month and a half ago.

Mark feels a lightness in his head, as if he is going to faint. His heart begins to race, perspiration releasing from every pore of his body. His hands fumble as he tries to figure out what to do. He hates to think of himself stealing the personal property of someone whose life has been sacrificed.

His mind conjures an image of the soldier who died. Someone who faced similar challenges as Mark, but chose a more honorable path than Mark's. In that moment, in his heart of hearts, Mark knew he'd become nothing more than a common thief.

Standing in the desolation of his basement, the silence seeming to magnify his guilt, Mark decides to do what every porch pirate knows not to do. He will take the box back to the address where he got it. First, Mark carefully folds each item of clothing and organizes the non-clothing items back into the box. He replaces the packing tape he cut through and seals the box to appear as if it had never been opened. He places the box back in his car and returns to the street in the neighborhood where he had been a few hours before. His mind is telling him he's taking a stupid risk, but his heart tells him he can't stoop so low as to steal the last items worn, touched, and used by someone lost in a faraway war. Mark places the box at the exact spot where it had originally been.

Mark returns to his car, still only one of two on the quiet street. From behind the driver's seat, he glances at the box with its sad contents sitting on the porch of the family home. Then he drives away.

With the box returned to where it rightfully belongs, Mark descends into deep soul-searching, thinking long and hard on his drive home. He will find a respectable job, even if it means working for minimum wage. He will do volunteer work to boost his résumé. He will take college classes even if he can only afford one at a time, even if studying is still a torture for him. He will be better. He will do better. He will find a better way. He will not be a porch pirate anymore.

SUSAN WINSTEAD

Susan has numerous publishing credentials, writing awards, and scholarships. She is past summer program chair, program chair, and president of Off Campus Writers' Workshop and currently a board member for Jane's Story Press Foundation. She is a veteran of the U.S. Army.

UNEXPECTED OUTCOMES

It seemed like a good idea at the time

Caught in the Net

by Moira Sullivan

Something is staring at me. I force my eyes open to see a little girl in a white dress looking down at me from the ceiling. My breath catches in shock. She is a creature from a Bosch landscape with feral face, pointed chin, cat's eyes, beak-like nose, and sharp teeth and claws. But it's her expression, between a smile and a grimace, that unnerves me, sending convulsive chills down my spine. I try to blink her away. Am I dreaming? No, because the creature starts to hiss and my cat answers, hair standing on end, tail beating against my body.

My God! What is it? I spring out of bed, rip the cross from the wall and hold it in front of me, just like in the movies.

"Get out!" I yell, threatening the creature with the cross. Eyes glowing, she retreats, still grimacing, and skitters backward from my bedroom into the living room, where I see her melt into the wall.

Will she be back? Cold terror is making my hands shake uncontrollably. What do I do? I scoop up my terrified cat and walk into my living room. My scalp prickles. Could I be responsible? My breathing is shallow and ragged. Is this fallout from the argument with my sister? My brain is frozen. Where's the creature now? I can't stop my teeth from clenching. I have to get out of here.

From my living room window, I can see into the café across the street. Kurt is there. At his table. As usual. Kurt will know what to do. This thought is enough to slow my heartbeat and calm my racing thoughts.

I stumble into the dining room toward the bathroom as Miss Kitty starts to yowl. I can't just leave her in my apartment with that thing, so I'll keep her with me until…until. I check the ceiling. Nothing. I grab the cat carrier from the hall closet and bring it into the bathroom, place it on the toilet seat, and close the door. "It's okay, Miss Kitty," I say over and over to comfort her as much as myself. But Miss K is inconsolable and continues to yowl. In one continuous motion, I open the carrier door and shove her inside despite her frantic cries.

I scan the ceiling. Nothing. We're safe. But what if she's crawling around the floor? I pull the shower curtain aside. Nothing in the tub. I look up into the mirror, noting the dark shadows under my eyes. No time to fix my face. I'm still in yesterday's rumpled jean skirt and madras top. No time to change clothes. I splash perfume on my chest and arms, hoping it will suffice.

Hands shaking, I pick up the cat carrier, leave the bathroom, slip into my sandals, and grab my knapsack from the closet, checking behind me the whole time. I leave my apartment and lock the door. I run down the stairs, looking behind me once more to see if anything is following me. Nothing.

Outside, I feel immediate relief and the warm sun on my face. Miss Kitty is too quiet, so I peer into the carrier to make sure she is alright. Then I hurry across the street toward the café and Kurt. The morning rush is over, and a second wave of customers is outside, waiting for tables to become available. I'm grateful to live across the street from the café, which has become my extended living room.

What just happened? Could the creature possess my cat? What would I do then? Are there cat exorcists? What if it's a ghost? Will anyone believe me? I imagine telling my boss about my supernatural encounter later, even though I know I'll be too distracted to go to work.

As I enter the café, I see clusters of coffee klatchers solving the world's problems before work. I recognize the bald head of Slava, my apartment manager, among the group of city workers and apartment managers that gathers every morning at the big table. Although they have often invited me to join them, I never have.

Kurt is impeccable in a tweed jacket and matching cap covering his graying crew cut, an ensemble he found at the Hadassah resale shop, where he bought me a fur hat with flaps. On the table is his usual pile of articles for me—edited, condensed, and repackaged little booklets about European politics and spirituality. Head down, I walk directly to Kurt's table, hoping to evade the retired locals eager to talk.

"Kurt," I say, but he already senses my approach and turns toward me.

"I see you've brought Miss Kitty, your fair feline," Kurt says, smiling through the carrier screen. Then he looks at me more closely, his pale, blue eyes showing concern. "Sit down, Maya. You look like you've seen a ghost."

"Maybe I have," I say, putting my knapsack on the ground and the carrier on the chair beside him. "Would you look after her? I need coffee."

"Of course," he says. "Miss Kitty and I will have a nice chat."

Although my stomach is churning, I want that cup of coffee. Approaching the counter, I see a poster advertising a lecture by a Canadian professor titled, "Only Connect." Funny, I've heard the café described as a place where you can be alone in public. I've spent many such evenings here, writing stories I never had the courage to submit.

Someone taps my shoulder. Slava is standing right behind me. A small swarthy man, Slava walks with a limp, which he claims was sustained during the running of the bulls in Pamplona.

"Maya!" Slava bellows. "Darling, what's wrong?"

I must look terrible!

"Tell Slava." He gives me a quick appraising look before putting his hand on my forehead, checking my temperature. The somewhat unhappily married Slava is protective of all his single female tenants of a certain age, so it's necessary to appreciate, but evade.

"Bad dream," is all I can manage.

I am beyond banter, but he doesn't want to waste his chance to discuss my leaky kitchen faucet that he has failed to fix and inform me of how much more repair time he will need. I let his bumpy speech roll over me, nodding when appropriate, unsure what I'm agreeing to. I will deal with it later.

"I need to talk to Kurt," I blurt out as soon as my coffee is ready, inclining my head toward Kurt.

"That, that..." Slava stutters. "We talk later." His upper lip wrinkles in distaste. Kurt has made him feel small on more than one occasion. The worst was the time he challenged Slava's Pamplona story, debunking this harmless fiction, and humiliating him before his friends. Kurt suffered a wave of ill-will for what he would describe as his unwavering dedication to truth.

Kurt and I have known each other for more than five years, during which he has shared personal things with me. Maybe this made me slower to judge his difficult personality. Maybe I'm used to having difficult people in my life. To me he was always compelling, encouraging, even kind in his way. I sometimes felt he was a little sweet on me.

As I walk toward the table, I call in sick to work on my Virgin flip phone.

"Sit down, Maya. Tell me what happened. Maybe I can help," says Kurt, as I take my seat at his table. He brings the heavy beige coffee mug to his lips.

No doubt he can, as he has a deep interest in spiritual matters and has dabbled in the occult. His almost-handsome face is creased with wrinkles that age him well beyond his sixty years.

"Here's the short version," I say, proceeding to describe my unsettling experience.

He takes in every word with the utmost gravity, staring at me as if trying to detect something. Then he folds his hands and pauses, before slowly saying, "You know I belong to a dream group at my church—"

"—the Woods Unitarian Church?" I interrupt, fidgeting in my chair.

"Yes," he says, still staring. "To understand the meaning of a dream, we focus on the odd details that often prove to be the most significant. Use your mind's eye as a camera to pan your dreamscape. Tell me—what is she wearing?"

"Kurt," I say, irritated, "the odd detail is that a hideous creature is smiling at me from my ceiling. Isn't that enough?" I glance at the clock, ticking its way toward nine, and try to drink my coffee, but...I'm thinking about the horrible thing on my ceiling...and the next thing I know, there's coffee on my skirt.

"Careful, Maya," says Kurt sharply, handing me a napkin. Then, in a low soothing tone, Kurt urges me to take deep breaths, as I blot the coffee up.

"Thanks, Kurt," and after inhaling once or twice, I continue, "She has claws and an animal face. No one I recognize. She faded into the wall. Do you think I'm in danger?"

He looks down at the table without answering and I start to get nervous. For someone who never tires of opining, he is much too quiet.

My hands are shaking again. I need to do something, so I walk over to the café window to look up at my apartment. A small white figure is peering right at me.

After an involuntary intake of breath, I whisper, "Oh my God, she's there. Still there."

I whirl around and walk toward Kurt who seems distracted. Customers are starting to turn around to look at us.

"Kurt, do you know her?" I gasp.

"Well, Maya, I don't want to alarm you unnecessarily, but..."

"Alarm me?" My voice rises to a hysterical pitch, "Kurt, I have a thing in my apartment that's not human! What do you mean?"

He sighs and looks down, unable to meet my eyes.

"Look. At. Me. Kurt," I say. He can't look at me. As if he's feeling guilty, but why? What's the matter with him? It makes no sense. I hear impatient rustling from the table nearest to us and I feel stares of annoyance.

Then he sighs again and reluctantly looks up and into my eyes. "My spiritualist godmother would say that you have a, a, a, um, a spiritual infection of sorts."

"A what? But how…"

"I'm getting to that." He tries to take my hands, but I shake free. "We all have auras, but sometimes if a person has a large aura, like yours, things can get trapped, you know, caught. These entities travel…they pass from one person to another, like little hitchhikers, they…they…"

I can't decide if he's crazy or if I'm in serious spiritual jeopardy. If this is true, then who passed her on to me? I think about my recent contacts. Nothing stands out.

"What do I do now?" I whine in a high, thin voice, trying to ignore the curious stares.

"I don't know." Kurt has lost his calm demeanor; his face is pale; his eyes are wide.

I had never heard him say those words before and I feel a wave of anxiety pass over me.

"And I thought *you* could help me!"

Does Kurt have anything to do with this? But he looks more scared and mortified than guilty. Did *I* invite the creature in? I revisit my relationship with my sister. Is the creature feeding on my bad energy? I don't think that's it. Is it the ghost of a former tenant? A lucid dream? Stress? Kurt's face is in his hands. He seems to know what this means but isn't telling me.

"Maya, Maya," Slava says.

I didn't notice Slava's approach.

"Maya, does he bother you?" Slava smirks, more interested in upsetting Kurt than protecting me.

Kurt recovers himself, face red, eyes flashing, and stands up quickly, towering over his challenger. "I don't appreciate your interference!"

Slava draws himself up, chest out, looking larger and fiercer than his small frame would suggest. He is compact and catlike despite his limp. His features are fine, despite his rough manner. I imagine that his and Kurt's ancestors must have battled one another in the past.

But my attention is drawn to my window where the creature is clapping her claws.

"Quick, Slava! Look at my window—do you see anything?" I ask.

He looks over—but she's gone.

"It's okay, Slava," I say, "we're discussing a problem in my apartment." To Kurt, I say, "Please sit down. Slava is trying to help. And maybe he *can* help us." I defend him instinctively. Slava is a man of action, but not always efficient action.

"Slava ALWAYS help," he affirms as he pulls up a chair.

I describe the situation and ask about past tenants. At first, he's a little hostile, advising me not to talk about ghosts in his building, but quickly dispels the tenant ghost theory. Then he stands.

"Slava go now. We fix. Come."

"I'm coming with you," Kurt says, getting up from his chair, carrier in hand.

"I assumed you would," I say, trying to mask my irritation at his apparent inability to help. "But is it safe for Miss Kitty to go back to my apartment?"

"I'll take care of her," Kurt says, unwilling to relinquish the carrier.

I throw my knapsack over my shoulder and we both follow Slava across the street to my apartment.

"Building is clean," says Slava as he opens the door to my apartment stairway. He could be referring to either pest extermination or his enthusiastic if not always consistent maintenance.

"Maya," Kurt asks, as we ascend. "Did you smudge your apartment when you moved in?"

"Dammit, no. My friend even gave me sage bundles, but I never used them."

"In that case, we'll do it now," says Kurt.

"Please excuse the mess," I say as Slava opens the door to the chaos within—in my case, the paper and book variety. "It's been quite a morning." I sling my knapsack on the couch in the foyer.

Kurt steps into the apartment right behind me and puts the carrier next to the knapsack. Closing his eyes and clearing his throat, he says, "Something is definitely disturbing this space. Did you bring anything new into the apartment recently?"

"Just your box of library sale books that I never got around to donating. I'll get the box from the hall closet."

"No, I get it," says Slava, rolling his eyes as he brushes by the silent Kurt on his way to the closet. He pulls out a large box of books, and easily sets it on the couch. "But where monster is?"

"That...cretin," mutters Kurt.

"I don't see the creature now," I say loudly. "Would you look for it, while I check the books?"

"You got hammer?" he asks.

"Follow me," I say, feeling his eyes on me.

He follows me the short distance to the kitchen utility drawer and I hand him a hammer.

"Just in case," he says, grinning and winking at me. He doesn't believe me. He walks into the living room toward the bedroom, hammer upraised. I know this will be tomorrow's café gossip. I turn to Kurt.

"You look a little pale, Kurt, are you feeling alright?" I ask. "Want some water or a little fresh air?" I point toward the kitchen door that opens onto the back porch.

He startles, opens his eyes and says, "Thank you, but that won't be necessary. I'll start smudging the place and keep an eye on that lunatic."

"More of a clown," I say, and hand him the smudging materials, also from the utility drawer. Before I tear through the books, I try to coax Miss Kitty out of the carrier, but she is motionless except for her thumping tail. The creature is still here.

The smell of sage suffuses the small apartment, making me feel better, but I stay in the foyer near the kitchen, afraid to venture further into the apartment.

Then I start tearing through the books. The answer must be here. Tucked into *Dark Night of the Soul,* I see a letter addressed to Kurt in a feminine hand. The return address tells me it's from his estranged cousin.

I scan the letter's wild claims about swindling his parents, living a criminal existence, and even rumored consorting with demons. According to Kurt, a guru had exerted an unhealthy influence on his cousin. He had not only stolen her money, but worse, had damaged her family relationships. Kurt had only learned of her death when reading the obituary section of the paper.

Slava doesn't believe me, but he is here helping me anyway. Kurt is still smudging, and I've just ripped up the letter.

"No, no monster there," Slava says, walking into the foyer. "I check."

"Thanks, Slava," I say, wanting to believe him. "Please burn this letter in the sink, but don't tell Kurt. Okay?"

"Just our secret, yes, Maya?" Slava takes the papers from me, eyes gleaming with delight.

After he burns the letter, he putters with the sink fixture and announces that he'll buy a new one, necessitating his return. I'm only too happy to have him stay, because I'm not confident the creature is gone.

"Can you feel it? The bad energy is gone," announces Kurt as he enters the foyer. "Gone forever," he says, handing me the smudging materials. He walks over to the couch and, without asking, opens the carrier door and releases Miss Kitty, who runs into the kitchen to her bowl of food. She usually likes to be near Kurt, but today she will have none of him.

"Thank you, Kurt and Slava!" I say, but I'm still uneasy, unable to detect an energy shift.

Slava walks toward me, ready for a full body hug. "Our secret, no?" he whispers in my ear.

"No, I mean yes," I answer, grateful to have a Slava in my life.

"I coming tomorrow. Fix faucet," he says, very pleased with himself as he exits through the kitchen door.

"Okay," I say, waving at his back.

Kurt nods, barely acknowledging him, and hangs back after Slava leaves. "Well, that's the end of that," he says.

"I hope so!" I say, but the end of what? Slava? The creature? How can he be so sure? "Anytime you want to talk about difficult things—or people—like your cousin…"

He winces. "What made you think of her?"

I shrug. "I had another argument with my sister last night."

"Don't get stuck on her flypaper," he says.

"You know best," I say, unconvinced. Is it possible he wore out his welcome? Is that what happened with his cousin? Robert Frost defines family as those who must take you in. I had taken him in when he was evicted from his apartment a few years ago. Am I Kurt's family?

He asks to use the bathroom and a minute later I put the carrier in the hall closet opposite the bathroom. I hear him talking softly. "You have to leave now. You shouldn't be here."

I don't hear a reply, so maybe he's talking to himself or someone on the phone. I go to the kitchen, where Miss Kitty is calmly eating her food. Who is he talking to...?

Then Kurt calls out, "I'll be going now, Maya. No need to see me out."

The door slams.

"Take care, Kurt!" I call out to the closed door.

I must know for sure, so I run to the door and pull it open in time to see them descending the stairway.

The girl is on his back.

She looks back at me.

Smiling.

MOIRA SULLIVAN

A voracious reader and professional translator (PT>EN), Moira Sullivan writes poetry and short stories. She hosted a community open mic at the former Café Express and served as an editor for the *RHINO* poetry journal. Her short story "The Pawnbroker's Deal" appears in the collection titled *Further Persons Imperfect*.

Winter Painting Party

by Gerry Souter

We were chums at the Chicago Art Institute school: Clink, Flick, and me. Clink was from Irish stock, clean-shaven, ex-Air Force and an illustrator more like LeRoy Neiman than the explosive Expressionist, Wassily Kandinsky. Flick was a bearded Vincent Van Gogh channeling Jackson Pollock. Clink styled himself as a free-spirit artist clone of Gene Kelly from the movie, *An American in Paris*. Flick—a brooding genius—dealt in real estate on the side and was the scion of well-off German parents. I was a South-Side Chicago lad, twenty years old, and an only child trying to excavate some painting talent from fallow ground. My parents kept lowering the bar of their expectations.

It was 1962 and winter in Chicago, a time of gray days and never-ending pewter skies, mounds of sooty snow and bone-chilling cold. Even the classes had become a sequence of sullen rituals. In our fourth college year, we were now facing emergence from the protective cave of higher education into the bleak and treacherous demands of earning a living.

Clink stared into his muddy coffee and muttered, "This is a bad scene, let's bug out."

Flick, who always slouched in his chair, raised his eyelids as if they weighed a ton, nodded, and lifted his forearm that ended in a clenched fist.

"Right on."

I remembered out loud that Flick talked last spring about his parents' cabin up at Crystal Lake. Flick regained consciousness once again. He muttered the magic words:

"Cool, I got a key."

Our road trip would be an amped-up lunge to preserve our artistic integrity before the inevitable lock-step march into job search and the gray world of employment. We would experience nature in the raw. We would have a painting party.

Flick's real estate dealings had earned him enough to buy a third-hand car. We'd drive up to that rustic shelter on the lake with our watercolors and spend the weekend sketching, painting and drinking—experience a real Beat Trip. Talk rude. Scoff at convention and scratch where it itched. Flick even had a stash of weed and some Zig-Zag cigarette papers.

Our paints, brushes, pads of paper and tackle boxes went into the 1948 Plymouth's trunk. We cut our Friday afternoon classes to get an early start. Flick drove his beater through the grim cold day. We paused only for a quick bowl of chili at a roadside beanery. When we finally bounced and skidded down the dirt road to the white clapboard cabin near the lake's edge, the sun was still above the tree line. We figured we'd dump our gear, grab a beer, our paints and pads, and take advantage of the beautiful light on the snow that had gathered in undisturbed hillocks at this shallow end of the lake. Cattails poked from the snow like arrows; and clumps of brown, hunched sawgrass dotted the ice like huge, white-frosted spiders.

Exhaling puffs of breath, we clomped into the cabin, dropped our stuff, and lugged in a case of beer from the trunk. I seized a can, popped it open, and held it to my mouth, but that first cold mouthful of chilled brew remained stubbornly in the can. I was holding a beercicle. Rather than risk forgetting the beer, Flick had loaded the case into the car on the previous evening and it had frozen solid overnight, swelling the cans and wedging them tight in the case.

"How can beer freeze?" Flick asked.

Frugal by nature, he had purchased a case of the cheapest, most watered-down lager known to man: Bullfrog Beer—guaranteed to produce a long line outside the toilet at any party. Lost in thought, Flick drummed his can on the edge of the dining table that took up a third of the kitchen. Sitting on the sink was a galvanized wash tub. He grabbed it and plunked it down on the stove.

"We'll heat 'em up until they thaw," he said, turning on the gas.

Nothing happened; no rewarding hiss came from the burner. He bent down and sniffed. Still nothing.

"Shit," he muttered and clomped through the exterior doorway. We listened to him crunching through the snow along the kitchen's outside wall. "SHIT!" came through the wall, followed by more crunching. With snow clinging to his boots and pants, Flick stomped into the kitchen and scowled at Clink and me.

"My parents must have returned the unused propane for a refund. There's nothing connected to the hoses outside."

Trained for military problem-solving, Clink pointed at the large fireplace in the living room, a soot-blackened hearth strewn with wood ash beneath its stone arch.

"What's that fireplace good for?"

Flick did not seem encouraged. "We can try," he said and headed back outside to see if he could find something to burn. Using a tire iron, he flogged and pried at a few cut logs and gouged them from the stack in the back yard. We stuffed the fireplace with anything flammable. Using an X-Acto knife designed to sharpen pencils, I managed to slice some bark and slivers into respectable strips of kindling.

Our fingers were numb, our noses were red, and beneath our heavy coats we were damp with sweat. Using wooden matches brought along to keep my pipe lit, I coaxed the kindling into spreading flames. The room became animated with our shadows crawling across the walls. Beyond the windows, night had sealed off every view and we were isolated in that Stygian blackness. And then we couldn't see each other—or the furniture—because the air had turned thick with smoke. We had forgotten to open the chimney flue. The fireplace had become a smudge pot.

Naturally, the rusted flue was frozen in place. Attempting to move it up or down was futile. We pried open a window to provide an inch of relief to our hacking and wheezing. We now had two choices: suffocate or freeze. We chose to eat. A can of sardines was broken out, opened, and passed around using one fork found in a drawer beside a dead mouse. That accomplished, we discovered there was no running water to wash down the salty fish, nor was the toilet working and the last one to use it had low hygienic standards.

That absence of water also had a chilling effect on the "painting" part of our party. We had chosen watercolors for their simplicity—just brushes, water, colors, and our keen, creative eyes.

Outside, that diminishing sunlight skimming the edges of snow-capped cattails and snow-sculpted shore shapes, glimpsed when we arrived, had flattened out into the evening's luminous but unrewarding gray as the sun tangled itself in a distant curtain of trees. All that wonderful metamorphosis had been lost on us as we stomped about, gloves thrust into winter coat pockets, watching our breaths crystalize into puffs of steam. The cloak of darkness had descended.

Even though the lingering smoke produced sporadic coughing fits, no one considered trying to drive back over that pitch-dark, deserted dirt road to the highway. Instead, we wedged ourselves into a large utility closet that doubled for storage of frozen jam, frozen tomatoes, frozen chili sauce and groggy spiders. We took turns peeing out the cabin's front door and retired into our vinegar and dill-impregnated tomb. With rags stuffed along the threshold of the closet door, we kept out the remnants of smoke from our terrifically successful fireplace blaze. Then, we tried to find comfortable positions to put legs, arms, leaning torsos and heads that were starved of inspiration.

Suddenly, Flick had one of his "Eureka" moments. Stuffed in a jam closet, sealed in a house filled with wood smoke, surrounded by sub-zero cold, he decided there was "smoke" and then there was "SMOKE." He snaked his bag of weed from his parka pocket and held it up with the packet of Zig-Zag cigarette papers. That produced a choral exclamation:

"Ahhhhhhhh!"

What better sleep inducer than the numbing buzz of pot? We bent to our tasks in the dim glow of Clink's flashlight. Clink and Flick each rolled a rumpled, but workable cigarette while I carefully packed the crushed dried leaves into the bowl of my briar pipe. This was more like it, three men on a match, thumbing our collective nose at bad luck and petty illegalities. I fired another wood match and everyone touched off their paths to blissful paradise—or in our case, paradise lost.

For anyone who has not smoked oregano, put off your desire to experiment. Flick had been scammed by the pot pusher. The pizza seasoning sizzled down the length of the cigarette papers like a fuse. My puff produced a gag reflex that forced air back down the pipe stem, generating a volcanic eruption that almost torched the group. After much brushing, coughing, batting out sparks, sneezing, and choked curses, our only hope was that Flick's parents would find our remains in the spring.

When rosy streaks of dawn finally pierced apertures in the rags and crept beneath the door's threshold, we stirred and eased open the door. It was like unsealing an ancient vault and releasing air that had been encapsulated for centuries. Collectively, we wished with all our hearts that we had not assaulted our upper and lower digestive tracts with those bowls of peppered chili and cups of hot coffee at that beanery on the way up to the lake.

Like released prisoners, we stumbled into frozen freedom. Exhaling clouds of breath, we brought with us a toxic effluvium of charred oregano, roasted tree bark, and nuclear chili-bean farts into the dawn's pink purity. Flick lurched out last from the cabin, carrying six cans of beer he had taken into the closet with him. Like a mother hen cuddling her chicks, he had thawed them with his body heat overnight. Without thought for our internal organs, we chugged down the beer and added it to the remnants of the chili, coffee, sardines, and fake pot. Our spirits soared. With much shoulder punching and rude talk, we climbed into the car and Flick keyed the ignition.

At this point, is it really necessary to describe the infinite depth of silence that greeted that key click? With old-world weariness, Flick creaked open his door, pulled the hood lock, crunched around back to fetch a screwdriver from the trunk, marched to the front of the car, and hoisted the hood open. He seemed to have aged thirty years as he contemplated that cold engine block. Clink, who had been riding shotgun, slid behind the wheel.

Flick shouted back at us, "When I say 'Now!' turn the key." He reached inside the engine compartment with the screwdriver to short something in the starter motor and shouted, "Now!" Clink turned the key, and with blue sparks arcing like a mad scientist's laboratory, the engine ground to life: *grind, grind, grind, grind, varooom!* The car shook, Clink worked the gas: *varoom! varoom!...Varoooom!* Flick slammed down the hood and dove in through the passenger door.

"It's alive! It's alive!" I shouted, searching desperately for some humor.

"Drive straight and turn left!" Flick shouted to Clink. "There's a gas station and restaurant up the highway!"

Clink obeyed and we jounced up the frozen rock-hard dirt road with much wheel spinning and engine-racing. We finally ka-bounced around a corner and rumbled onto the edge of slick pavement. Clink goosed the gas, and we swung, cheering and fish-tailing up the deserted blacktop.

"Hurrrah! Yeeha! Whoohoo! We're on our way!"

And then...the radiator hose broke.

A white tumult of steam exploded from beneath the hood and flooded into the front seats through the heater vents. In a surge of self-preservation, Clink stuck his head out the driver's side window.

Flick shouted into Clink's ear, "That gas station is on the other side of the hill!"

We wheel-spun up the grade as the plume of steam engulfed the car. The hot wet cloud turned the interior into a boiling sauna. As we zoomed over the top of the hill, the engine started sounding like pots and pans inside a clothes dryer, *clangity-bangity-clangity-bangity-clangity!*

In the restaurant connected to the gas station, a couple of truckers and some early rising locals enjoyed their second cup of coffee, mopped up the last of their scrambled eggs on toast, and added a final splash of syrup to their pancakes. Then someone must have shouted, "Looky there!"

Blasting over the ridge and heading straight down the road toward the diners was a Kamikaze Bomb, swirling billows of smoke and clanking like a runaway tank. Food was left to cool on the plates as the early risers evacuated in a stampede into the surrounding woods.

"Into the garage bay!" shouted Flick as he eased open his door.

When Clink saw the gas station rushing toward us, he killed the ignition, stomped on the brake, and aimed the car for the station's empty repair bay.

"Hang on!" he yelled, but Clink was alone. Flick and I had bailed out and were rolling ass over teakettle in the unplowed snow that flanked the station's driveway.

With the engine off and the brake pads glowing red, the old car exhaled a deep gasp, shuddered, and rolled into that repair bay slowly to rest against a stack of Quaker State oil cans. It coughed and the last of its mighty steam cloud piffled out like a canary fart.

Brushing off caked snow, Flick and I limped up to the bay as diners and mechanics approached, some with napkins still tucked in their shirtfronts, or carrying the tools they had been using at the moment the Kamikaze Bomb exploded into their morning routine. Flick opened the car's back door, took out three cans of steam-warmed beer, and handed them around. Flick then offered his checkbook to the gas station owner, a large slope-shouldered man wearing a stained gray coverall. He had gone purple in the face beneath thinning hair and he grasped the checkbook with dulled, slack-jawed comprehension.

Flick said, "Give me a number that will get us out of here."

Outside, the sun was full up, heralding a beautiful morning. We sat on the curb, sipping our warm beer and listened to the hi-low, hi-low ululations of an approaching siren. In our heads, we composed explanations for our crimes and thought about the great story we could tell for the rest of our days. My thoughts lingered on the single thought that might comfort my parents when they considered their investment in my pricey art education: "He can always teach…"

— GERRY SOUTER

Gerry has authored with his wife, Janet, 56 non-fiction traditionally published books in genres ranging from U.S. history to fine arts to business. Gerry has also written an adventure-romance novel, *Thread of Sand*. With degrees from the Art Institute of Chicago and the University of Chicago, he is retired from the careers of photojournalist and documentary/video producer.

The Toucan Cape, the Cornered Cat, and the Cardinal Outside

by David Alan Pelzer

Spence parks his handyman's pickup outside Coco's house, his nerves still jittered by her break-up note, followed by that triple round of coffee with the guys. He does not see the remnant box of clothes in her driveway that she said would be there. Did she forget to pack it? Or maybe some package thief made a drive-by heist on this misty May morning that threatens rain.

He had swung by her place earlier, after finishing the trim on the house around the corner, and thought maybe he had arrived too soon. To kill time, he then stopped at the Brew Ha Ha, where his coffee klatchers convened. They listened to his sad story all over again and told him to head back over, pound on the door and reclaim what was rightfully his. But what if Coco's daughter is in the house? The last time he disturbed her like that, there was hell to pay.

Spence sends Coco a text but gets no reply. She must be in session, counseling a client. As he ponders his next move, his mind wanders into the medley of jazzy blues playing on the FM. What began as a New Orleans-style funeral march has morphed into a funky Motown beat, reminding him of last year's neighborhood Halloween party, a few months after his divorce went through, and two months after Coco lost her husband. Spence dressed as a swarthy pirate, with a black silk cape and a stuffed macaw strapped to his shoulder. Coco appeared as Catwoman in black spandex, her eyebrows furrowed and joined, like Frida Kahlo's. After years of being just neighbors, she flirted. As the stereo pounded and the guests cheered, the two of them crouched and snarled and circled each other; then she pounced, pretending to devour his bird in three big gulps, as if she had channeled the power of a jaguar. The hostess told him it was the first time Coco laughed like that since Jake suffered his fatal stroke at the breakfast table.

Spence was out of town when the tragedy happened. He barely knew the guy. Jake was a reclusive sort, a birder, pleasant enough, and oh-so-patient with Coco and their daughter Nella, who was numbed by the loss. As Coco and Spence parted ways that evening, she asked him to drop by sometime, to inspect the flickering lights on her chandelier, and the late-night thumping in her dryer. She joked maybe it was Jake, checking in on her.

Spence rewired the lights in the great room and replaced her dryer drum. He helped her re-paint her rooms: the kitchen pure white, the great room bright rose, the bedrooms sky blue. It felt good to be needed, to help restore order. After his divorce, he, too, needed someone to help him heal.

Eventually, they started sharing meals. Then nightcaps, as they reclined on deck chairs in the sunroom. Then lounging on her sofa, munching popcorn as they watched nature shows on TV. Once, she dimmed the lights and asked for a five-minute shoulder rub before it was time for him to head home. She said she would be his teacher; his first lesson was about patience.

So, she was driving with one foot on the brake. Did she just want a hands-on masseur? The men at the Brew Ha Ha, who had heard all about his escapades with divorcees on Match, said lonely widows were much easier prey. Just give 'er time. They crooned, "Hey baby, I'm your handy man."

The curtains past the picture window are tightly drawn, the hedges overgrown. Is anyone home? If Spence drives off now, he may never see his clothes again. Okay, the shirts, the underwear, the socks, the spare painter's pants could all be replaced. But not the toucan cape.

Coco bought it to commemorate their get-away to Costa Rica that past winter, when her daughter returned to college. Their trip started as a vacation, but they ended up volunteering at a tropical bird refuge near Montevideo. Coco said it was something Jake, the birder, had always hoped to do. During the day, the two of them chopped fruit, cleaned cages, and made playthings from twigs, leaves, and cloth. At night, they slept in separate hammocks. Of all the birds, the toucans were the messiest. Intelligent, but hyperactive, and needful of toys and togetherness. Monogamous for life, they tossed fruit goop back and forth before mating. When stressed, they did not bite, they pecked.

"Poor neurotic things. We should adopt a couple to take home," she said.

"Are you crazy?" he said. "They belong here. We can visit some at the zoo."

By then, he liked hearing her say the word "couple." He had not been part of one since long before his divorce.

When they returned home, she went online and bought him the lime-based cape, showing a painted pair of toucans perched on a limb. It made him feel comfy and carefree, then emboldened. He began staying over, sleeping on her couch at first, then beside her in bed. She became more receptive, saying he had reawakened her feminine power, her inner radiance. They began to find niches for making love: on the bear rug in her nearby office, on mini vacays to woodsy retreats, in the deck chair on her patio at night, where the cape became a cushion. But never in her house.

"Oreo might act up," she explained, stroking the arched cat's fur. At least she had it declawed.

Even with the limits imposed, Spence mused maybe she now wanted a lover in her life. The Brew Ha Ha boys, newly enthused, sang, "I wanna be your lover lover loverboy."

Spence sees something crimson stirring in the overgrown bushes. It's a male cardinal flittering about, as if searching for his nest. The previous spring, while the daughter was still at school, the cardinal pair had made their home there. The male called purdy, purdy, purdy, then whew, whew, whew, then who-eet, who-eet, who-eet. The female sang cheer, cheer, cheer and birdie, birdie, birdie. One morning the male peered inside the picture window, his crest raised, thinking his reflection was an intruder. Coco said the bird might be Jake, checking in again. Ha ha, Spence said. But the flickering lights and late-night thumping in the dryer made him wonder if she was right.

Coco told him that, when the daughter returned from college in May, she found the toucan cape stuffed in her mother's closet, and Coco had to assure her Spence was just a friend. He was sent packing, at least until the daughter traipsed off to summer camp in July. He and Coco had to confine their trysts to noontime lunches and walks in the park.

"You're keeping me at bay for two months?" he protested.

Yes, she said. It had to be this way. Did he ever consider her daughter's feelings about all of this? While she was still at home, with her dad gone, the poor girl needed company. Coco said she might buy her a bird.

Poor girl, losing her dad like that. He did not like to say the daughter's name aloud; if he saw it her way, it might lead him to capitulate to the demands she made on her mother. Coco told him, "Nella needs time. Grief has its own clock, you know." Coco needed time, too. Maybe she just wanted a friend now. But it was too late to just be friends.

The klatchers agreed. They warbled like Stevie Wonder. "Full-time friend, part-time lover." He should just stay calm and wait it out. It was either that or return to Match.

Perched on his ladder each day, stroking his brush onto soffits and gutters, Spence mulled over his unanswered calls and found her haziness unbearable. He had to know, one way or the other. When he drove by her house, her car was never in the driveway. He phoned once, twice, three times. Each time, his calls were ushered into her voicemail.

The next night after work, he dropped by the house unannounced. The daughter answered the door. She stood there staring at him, as if she had seen a ghost. No, her mother was not home. Yes, she was doing fine, thank you. Simply fine.

Spence wondered then if she might be the real perpetrator. He called again and left Coco more messages, some long and rambling, others pleading, "It's me. We need to talk."

The next day, Coco fired off an email. "Keep Nella out of this! Can't see you. Sorry. Hope you'll understand."

Was she breaking up with him? Was this how she counseled her patients to dump their lovers? The next day, another note came. "I do miss you." What did that mean? Did she now want him back again?

A few days later, Coco texted, "Please pick up yur things on driveway while im at work. Drop keys in the slot. Don't come before 10."

So, she was shipping him off with just his clothes? Did he even want them anymore, when each article would only echo how she had slighted him? He tried phoning to say don't even bother, but it went right into voicemail. What he wanted to say was, "What did I do?" Or, "Is this all about your daughter?" What came out was, "Don't forget the cape."

When he relayed this to the men, they urged him to ditch the toucan cape and break away, once and for all. They all sang, "Just drop off the key, Lee, and set yourself free."

That's right, he thought. No more Mr. Nice Guy. He imagined himself backing into the driveway, loading the box, and squealing off, peeling rubber. So long, Cat Lady. It was fun while it lasted. Good times, good times.

As Spence sits in his truck, a vein of tenderness pulses through him. He pictures how she probably washed, folded and packed all of his things, then placed the cape neatly on top before closing the lid. Maybe she left the box by the front door? Following her orders, he pulls from his pocket the white envelope containing her keys, steps onto the porch, and prepares to drop it through the mail slot. No package there either. Maybe, in her rush to work, she left it inside? He lifts the keys from the envelope and tries the door. The key refuses to turn. Did she change the locks? Maybe he should try the back door, just to be sure.

He slides alongside the house to the patio, where the deck chairs that once served as mating beds have been folded up and pushed against the brick. On the patio deck sit two black Hefty sacks, a note clipped to one. "Moved your stuff. Didn't want it stolen. Bags work better in the rain. Sorry."

So, she's sorry she can't see him, and sorry she crammed his clothes into trash bags, like Sal Army giveaways? It's not even raining!

He tears into the bags, checking inventory. Everything is there, except for the toucan cape. Did she forget to pack it? Or did she withhold it on purpose, just for spite?

He tries the keys in the back door. No luck there, either. He hefts a bag over each shoulder, retraces his steps alongside the house to the front driveway, then heaves his remains into the bed of the pickup.

Now he sits and stews, half listening to jazz, until he finally flicks off the radio and cuts the engine. The only sound is the chattering of birds in the bushes, causing him to recall the tick-tick-ticking the toucans made when stressed. She had bought that cape for him, so that made it his. In his rage, he fears she might drape it around the shoulders of another man, then tie it tightly at the neck before opening it again, so she can devour him whole. He can't let that happen.

It's starting to drizzle. Droplets splatter on the windshield, forming rivulets that wind down the glass and into the cowl. Coffee break is over. Time to get to work. He rummages through the glove compartment for a flathead screwdriver, pulls a step ladder from the truck bed and skulks toward the house.

Feeling stealthy now, Spence crawls into the cedar bushes that have pushed against the brick and rests the ladder by the window. He works the edges of the flathead to pry open the base of the old casement fixture so he can push it up and out of its track. He sets the pane on the ground and climbs through the opening.

A hissing sound is coming from deep inside the house. It must be the cat. Over the course of their time together, Spence and Oreo had come to, well, a mutual understanding. Spence agreed not to uproot Oreo from Coco's lap, and the cat, in turn, would not pee in his loafers that lay around. When he came by, she dove under the red sofa, then later reappeared, extending her paw and batting at the toy bird-on-a-wire he dangled in front of her. But her owl-green eyes never stopped staring at him.

Spence stands by the picture window. The curtains are tightly drawn, shutting out the light of day. He flicks on the switch, but the chandelier lights start sputtering again. The kitchen, dining area and living room are all one big mess. Junk mail and papers lie scattered on the floor, along with bits of fruit splattered from the bowl the cat must have tipped over. Torn pillows sit on the saggy sofa where he and Coco used to cuddle. Underneath them, a scattering of bird toys: a bright felt ball, pink and turquoise tassels, rainbow-toned rubber blocks on a stringed chain. Narrow wooden beams are angled high across the room. The shocking pink wall shows scuff marks and nicks from furniture being shoved around. The great room has become an aviary, recently ransacked. He inhales the odors of overripe fruit, stale patchouli, and an untended litter box.

In the kitchen area, the gray light of morning seeps through the window, illuminating a pile of pots and pans that have torpedoed the sink. On the counter, a cutting board, strewn with peels of banana and papaya, lies in a puddle of juice. On the fridge, a photo of the Dalai Lama, smiling with universal sympathy. Below that, where there had been a photo of a happy couple with the toucans, there is now an empty space. So, has she now whited him out of her life?

His first impulse is to tidy up. Clear the table, wash the pots, vacuum the rug, clean the clutter. Anything to quell his anxiety about being there. But, if he touches anything, Coco will know he has been there. What might she do then? Call the cops? He cannot allow that. What would Robert Bly do? Would he stay and stand his ground, or pound the djembe drum that rests angled against the TV stand? Spence considers scribbling a note to flag his presence, to say sorry he can't stay longer to play Mister Fix-it. No, he shouldn't do that either. He must act like a ghost who leaves no trace.

He hears a low hiss under the red sofa. Squatting down, Spence spots two glassy eyes staring back at him, prepared to pounce. He gathers up the bird-on-a-wire, one of its wings now broken, and calls, "Okay, witty kitty, you can come out now." But Oreo inches farther under the sofa. While he cannot see her, he knows she is measuring his every move.

Silent as a spider, Spence slides down the hallway in search of his cape. As he passes the daughter's room, his eye catches the full-length poster on the closed door. A soaring eagle, its talons extended, bearing the caption, "It doesn't get easier. You get stronger."

A tick-tick-ticking sounds from inside the room. Then, a tick-tick response. When he opens the door to investigate, he sees the room has been transformed. In the corner, a single cot. In the center, a giant cage, draped by a black fabric sheet.

Then he spots it, plain as day, on top of the cage. Did Coco have second thoughts and pull it out at the last second, to freeze the memory of their time together? Yes, that's a better story to embrace, even if it's fiction. Suppressing a sneeze from stray cat hair, Spence runs his rough painter's hands over the shiny silk, the clasping claws, the black and white feathers, the smooth orange beaks. He curls the cape into a ball and presses it against his chest.

"Sorry, Coco, this cape is mine!" he pronounces. He will need to hand-wash the hell out of it or take it to a cleaners that specializes in silk.

The inhabitants inside the cage become quiet. Perhaps they are sleeping. Spence peeks under the shroud, and finds a toucan pair, coupling.

Keeping the cape no longer feels right. He closes the flap, unravels the baby-size bundle in his arms and splays it back across the cage, pressing out the wrinkles with his bare hands.

"No worries, Nella. It's all yours now," he whispers.

As he slips out Coco's bedroom window, he hears a thud against the picture window in the great room. Returning, he tears open the curtains and spots a flash of red, flitting away. He cups his hands and calls, "I'm sorry I couldn't give her what she wanted. Maybe a knight, or a bodhisattva. Or a chameleon, always changing colors. Were you all of those for her?"

But it's too late. This bird has already flown.

DAVID ALAN PELZER

David, a recovered agricultural journalist, has published several short stories, including a selection in the 2019 volume of *Hemingway Shorts*. His upcoming novel, *The Blue Guitar*, about gypsy jazz and lifelong friendships, is now in the editing stage. He has been a member of OCWW since 2018.

Outfit of the Day

by Kelly Q. Anderson

You would think that the seats at Roast & Grind would be warm, given that the shop name is reminiscent of warmish things like toast or steam. But the seats are not warm and certainly not toasty. They are a jolt of stiff, lacquered wood that chills my back.

They are the perfect chairs for penning newspaper articles. Yes, nobody reads newspapers anymore (thank you for mentioning that). Yes, they still pay newspaper reporters, although the amount is pitiful (thank you for mentioning that as well). In my next life I'll have a job that captures your attention. I'll do voiceover work for cartoons or publicity for a major fashion house. Or one season on a terrible reality show—and I'll be so awful I'll get a spinoff, and then turn myself around right when America is ready for a comeback story.

I cuddle my hands around the mug of mint tea. It's so hot that it scalds my tongue but I welcome it, ice-cold chair be damned.

I like writing here and I hate writing here. I like what Roast & Grind used to be: cozy, well-worn, and dated. Slumpy leather couch in the corner and seats encircling a rustic fireplace. But I hate how everything changed when Awake opened across the street.

Expertly curated by a well-known designer (very blonde, very smug), Awake is cloud-white, airy, and has the most expensive avocado toast in town at $15. It's everything we are told to want: locally sourced, locally owned, organic, environmentally conscious, and committed to community (very trendy, very smug). Naturally, everyone wants to be awake at Awake.

Roast & Grind held its own for a little while. The jingling door gave way to its regular crew of pleasant retirees, garden club members, fussy librarians, thirsty cyclists, post-yoga chatterboxes, tweens fresh from school, and yes, even local reporters. Usual patrons ordered their usual coffees and sat in their usual seats. As I crossed off deadlines and pecked at my laptop, the background noise began to noticeably shift. Gone was the usual chatter. In fact, all I heard them talk about was Awake.

"They have gluten-free donuts. GLUTEN-FREE DONUTS!"

"They don't take cash over there. Everything is done on iPads. Even tips."

"I heard the praline brew is phenomenal—my teenagers are obsessed."

My heart ached whenever I drove past the two stores and witnessed the painful new era: empty patio at Roast, line out the door at Awake; a folding sign collapsed on the sidewalk at Roast, pots of chrysanthemums at Awake. Slowly, quietly, a new narrative emerged: a small town could have many things, but not two thriving coffee shops. But hey, at least they attempted to keep up.

A few months back, I stumbled up to Roast & Grind with sleepy eyes but the darkened door wouldn't budge. *Closed for renovations. Thanks a latte for your patience!*

Renovations did not go well. I would describe the new Roast & Grind as "Well, we tried." Part of the charm of the old Roast was feeling as though I was hanging out in my favorite aunt's living room. A person could exhale in that space. It was never too stuffy or pristine. The leather couches were worn but cozy in all the right spots. The air was soft and sweet, like cinnamon. Though the layout was cramped, the walls were welcoming as if offering up a hug.

At the new Roast, things (i.e. the chairs) are stiff.

No more sofas. No more cozy. No more delightful aromas tickling my nose. For crying out loud, the hugging walls have been painted chartreuse. Chartreuse! (Let us cringe in horror together.) Someone had the audacity to not only rip out the old fireplace, but replace it with a wicker basket stuffed with decorative logs. Who has ever needed a decorative log?

This Roast & Grind—newly renovated, freshly lacquered—tries too hard. I loathe it, yet I keep showing up. I'm also cheap. "Locally sourced avocado toast" is code for "not in a reporter's budget."

"Iced latte with caramel drizzle for London. London!" Still the same old bellow in this weird new space. At least the barista's voice hadn't changed.

I watch a pretty woman (London, I suppose) step forward to grab her drink (latte, I suppose). I'm irked when she sits at the adjacent table. I mean, seriously? Right next to me? The place is empty.

She fusses with an enormous mauve-colored tote bag. The pattern looks designer but I couldn't tell you the brand. I glance down at the lump of green canvas at my feet. I'm stuck with my grad school backpack because people don't buy newspaper subscriptions anymore, they just scroll Twitter.

I write a bit but I also can't help but be distracted by Latte London's look. She's wearing artfully ripped jeans, some kind of furry sneakers, and a comically poufy scarf. Her hair is golden and shimmery, crown-like. You know the sort—beautiful in a way that's unfair. In this dull space, she's a walking exclamation point.

The shop door swings open with a screeching jingle.

A grandmotherly type walks in, clad in linen and herding two little boys. Her face is kind and stays that way even when the boys start shouting.

"Nana, I don't wanna come here." The larger boy points across the street to Awake. "I wanna go over there!"

"They don't have rainbow bagels here. You promised rainbow bagels!"

The baristas stand with strained enthusiasm. No doubt they've heard this spiel before. Nana, who has brought the boys to her usual spot, doesn't realize that this is now the old spot. The bad spot. The without-rainbow-bagels spot.

"Nana, you promised!" The smaller boy whines, stomping his foot and pulling on the woman's arm. She wiggles him over to the register and a long pause follows. I can tell by the accessories on her wrist what will happen next.

You see, Nana wears an expensive Swiss watch with a sapphire crystal face. Next to it, a handful of exquisite gold bracelets with tiny charms. But the real kicker is the cheap elastic wristlet with plastic beads. This sloppy handmade wonder is clearly the creation of a preschooler and Nana wears it with pride. Grandparents are easily ruled by the tiniest dictators. It's obvious who will win this bagel battle.

"I'll just do a small black coffee, please." The pity order.

Everyone knows that this lady is going to grab her $2 cup and hightail it over to rainbow bagel land.

Pour. Cover. Serve. It's a simple order but it drags on for far too long.

"Small black coffee. For Nana."

Latte London stands and scoots around the table, swinging her mauve tote bag over her shoulder. She holds the door for Nana, who thanks her, and drags her complainers outside. When the boys' sneakers hit the sidewalk, they break into a sprint. Rainbow bagels await. Latte London follows them out, but not too closely. I watch her sashay down the pavement, poufy scarf bouncing.

I'm on a deadline so I get back to work. I write up a brief on the local Fancy Cat Costume Parade. The winner was a wizardly feline from Hogwarts dubbed "Catty Potter." Second place went to Ruth Bader Ginspurr. As I draft headlines, I can't help but shake my head. The whole event (and my covering it) feels beyond trite. In J-school, I dreamed of breaking news and reporting live from angry protests, devastating car accidents, or joyous ribbon-cutting ceremonies. The whole deal with thumping heart rates and flashing press badges to tell the stories that needed to be told.

I craft a call-out box and attach photos, feeling like the animals are judging me with their eyes. Why are costumed cats so perversely amusing?

The event raised $8,000 for cancer research.

Eventually a barista walks around to start re-arranging their meager display of trail mixes. It's not needed.

I sip my tea and send emails to confirm appointments next week. I'm late on pitching story ideas, which were due this morning. Damn it. I shift in the cold chair.

The door jingles open with a screech.

Latte London is back. I purse my lips and cock my head as she breezes through the entrance and toward the restroom.

I wonder what rainbow bagels taste like. Are they like that fruity kid cereal, with all different flavors? Or is it just clever food coloring? For the next several minutes, I get lost in dumb thoughts and my laptop screen. My shoe kicks at my backpack, which flops over, revealing an ink stain from an old pen.

When Latte London reappears, she heads to the bar top where all the stirrers and sugars are arranged. She grabs a plastic cup and fills it from the water pitcher, placing the lid and straw just so.

She sits adjacent to me again, and buries her face into her cell, which is coated in an adorable black-and-white panda bear phone case. After a few minutes, she is methodically shifting. Standing over her ice water, then squatting low at the table, angling the panda phone to her liking. Did she just photograph her shoes?

I hear her fingernails softly tap and swipe the screen. But even through my periphery, something is different.

She's changed clothes.

Gone is the loud, exclamation-point outfit of furry sneakers and poufy scarf, replaced by a demure milky-white tunic, leather leggings, and ballet flats. She's tugging a cherry-red beanie onto her head, and pulling her long curls around her face. The tendrils are bouncing.

What. The. Hell. Is. Going. On.

She applies red lipstick using the camera on her panda phone as a mirror. When she appears to practice sipping from her straw with puckered crimson lips, I feel like I may burst out laughing so I stifle a cough into my elbow.

London's out the door again. I wince at the screeching sound.

I lean back but the chair is too stiff for me to see past the cars cruising by. I readjust my seat. The crowds at Awake are staggering. They may as well be hosting a block party on this Tuesday morning. A server appears to be handing out free cake pops that look like miniature sunflowers. This seems both adorable and delicious. I try to spot Small Black Coffee Nana and her boys, wondering if they got swallowed up in the crowd of caffeine-hungry bodies.

I hit *send* on my article.

After closing the laptop, I sit and stare ahead. A bitter aftertaste settles in my mouth.

I tug on my jean jacket and shuffle notes into my backpack.

The door swings and I brace for it.

Holy Sunflower Cakepops.

She's heading to the restroom. Again. Panda phone and all.

I just sit, brewing on it.

The clothing changes, the pouty lips, the frills of pouf and fur. The outfits that were just a bit much. The golden curls and flattering angles. Holding items as if she were showcasing them: handbag, coffee cup, sunglasses, etc. My brain stewed and stirred up a big bowl of rainbow bagels, trendy restaurants, and sparkling outfits until a clear-as-day realization emerged. It was so obvious even if it was completely weird to acknowledge in broad daylight. The evidence was right in front of my face.

Latte London is not a sociopath.

She is not in the Witness Protection Program.

Nor does she seem to be researching a dramatic theater role.

She's a fashion blogger.

An "influencer." A tastemaker. Someone who takes photos for a living: the leggings, the lipstick, the handbag, the bracelet, and even the cup of coffee. Those photos get linked to social media and practically scream, *buy these leggings! wear this lipstick! style this bracelet! sip this coffee!* She's a driver of consumption, the ultimate setter of trends. She's a person who uses failing coffee shops as dressing rooms.

She's working right now. Her enormous mauve tote bag is her traveling closet of props. Professional blogging, professional photography, professional existence. It's suddenly very clear that the outfit changes are meant to mimic a week's worth of content: poufy scarf Tuesday, leather leggings Wednesday. She is documenting the experience as if she were a different person on different days.

I tap Instagram on my cracked iPhone screen. Journalistic habits kick in, so I search for Roast & Grind, whose account is practically dusty and hasn't been touched since 2015.

Then I search for Awake.

The account is clearly professionally run. It looks just like its store: cloud-white, airy, and aspirational. I hate myself for enjoying its aesthetic right away. I tap the geo-code and up pop the little tiled photos of every patron documenting their coffee, lunch, rainbow bagel.

Awake is easy breezy. The toast is never burned, the avocados are never brown. Ceramic bowls hold tidy pats of hummus and technicolor crudités. Sandwiches are plated with sweet strawberry garnishes festooned into hearts. Tiny curls of steam rise above coffee mugs held by neatly manicured hands. There are teens cheers-ing with ice-coffees and toothy smiles. A toddler holding rainbow bagels to her face as if they were glasses.

I sweat a little under my jean jacket, my T-shirt growing damp. I keep scrolling through the photos. I note all the little hearts and emojis. I don't know how much time passes, but it does pass.

And there she is. Latte London is actually London Michaels of *Lovely London Time* blog fame. 79,000 devoted followers, including some celebrities (reality show ones, but still). There is a photo of her, time-stamped now, posed at Awake. Against a crisp white wall, she is gripping a sunflower cake pop, gigantic smile on her unfairly pretty face. She's wearing the poufy scarf look from earlier. Before she changed. Before she became someone else.

Flowers so good you can eat them! #eatlocal #LovelyLondonEats #ootd

She doesn't even eat the cake, I think to myself. She doesn't even eat the cake.

Those hashtags take me back to last Spring when I penned a feature on a teenager who wore the same dress every day for a year. She chronicled all the ways she made it unique. "The most basic fashion hashtag, the most overused, is OOTD. Outfit of the day," she explained as I furiously copied her words. "It's too popular but at the same time, I can't *not* use it."

My writing slog has come to an end but suddenly a switch is flipped in my brain. I fumble with my phone but manage to fire off an email to my editor. I'm smiling wide as I type fast, the rush of a story idea pouring out. I envision the photos, the headline, the subject, the receipts. Something that could save this place. Something that could save me from costumed cat parades.

All morning I had watched London swiftly reinvent herself in a coffee shop unable to do the same. We sipped from the same cups. We wrote our own stories. We sat in stiff, lacquered wood chairs, the kind that chill against one's back. Two parallel lines on the same piece of paper.

I like writing here and I hate writing here.

—— KELLY Q. ANDERSON

Kelly's favorite things are yoga and writing. She served as a longtime columnist for *The Glencoe Anchor*, and wrote regularly for *Chicago Parent* Magazine and 101.9FM The Mix. She holds a Journalism degree from the University of Iowa, studied at StoryStudio, and does handstands regularly. (KellyQAnderson.com)

No Harm, No Foul

by Nora Naughton

"Jeez, it's cold. No way we can get our coats?" Elaine asked Beth. Grains of icy water blew across the deck and bit at their exposed skin. Elaine lay in a fetal position on her lounge chair. Her blue eyes intense, her mouth a thin, flat line.

Beth shuddered. The cold wind ballooned her cotton shirt, sending goose-bumps up her spine. She reminded herself, once again, that any reservations she had about Elaine as a traveling companion simply did not matter. Elaine was the only friend in her circle with the inclination and money to backpack through Europe this summer. Beth hoped their differences would be complementary.

"No. I asked a crew member," Beth answered. "Our backpacks are stored in the hull until we dock." Beth sighed, "We are shit out of luck." Other cheap-seat passengers, protected by blankets or coats that they had sense enough to keep with them, hunkered down on deck chairs, now damp with icy remnants.

The overcast sky began to dim into darkness without the fire of a sunset. Beth tried not to think about how bad the night would be, sleeping on the open deck, without even a sweater. Elaine had been concerned about money. So they bought deck tickets, instead of a cabin, reasoning that sleeping under the stars of a European sky would be a memorable way to begin their adventure.

The day had been hot, with the sun out in full force. They had imagined a lovely boat ride across the channel to France, their first real destination since flying into Shannon airport. But clouds moved in. The weather had cooled—as they should have imagined it would.

"Do you hear that music?" Elaine asked, suddenly enlivened, her straw blond hair sweeping her shoulders as she turned.

"I guess so," Beth said, feeling, rather than hearing, a tempo of vibrations rattling the boards of the deck. "Where is it coming from?"

"That's the disco on the main deck," one of their fellow passengers answered, her blanket opening into a tunnel to reveal two dark eyes. "You can go there to get warm, but you'll lose your spot."

"C'mon," Elaine said, sitting upright. "Let's go."

"But you can't sleep there," the tunnel girl warned. "They won't allow it."

"Better than staying here," Elaine said. "Let's go!"

"But we'll lose our chairs," Beth said. The chairs she had saved, tight in a corner and partially sheltered from the wind.

"We're freezing our butts off!" Elaine was through the doorway to the main deck before Beth had a chance to think. She hesitated. She did not want to leave the corner and its relative shelter. Still, the two should stay together. Groaning at Elaine's impulsiveness, Beth ran after her.

The disco was warm with body heat. Beth soaked it in as if she were sunbathing. Outstretching her arms, she waited for the small of her back to warm up.

Elaine and Beth had just graduated from college. This trip to Europe, unstructured and unsupervised, would mark the beginning of their adult lives. College, even with all its opportunities for growth and independence, had been merely an extension of school. Good students, each had easily navigated college's familiar rules and structures.

A mirrored disco ball randomly flashed squares of light onto the room's occupants, creating a kaleidoscope of faces revealed, and then cloaked. Brass and glass railings edged a sunken dance floor, offering a perch for those less-inclined to dance to watch those who were. The watchers, mostly older men with drinks in hand, scrutinized the dance floor, ignoring the women beside them who moved to the beat, silently seeking partners. The men reminded Beth of the large black crows that sometimes sat on power lines above the alleys of Chicago.

Beth spotted Elaine at the bar. Again, Beth hesitated. Elaine was so blunt and single-minded. Traits Elaine attributed to her east-coast upbringing, where people ran up escalators instead of riding them like Midwesterners.

Beth both admired and resented the way Elaine got her way. Case in point: going to the disco with no discussion. Until the contrast of Elaine, Beth had never realized how ingrained it was in her to be easygoing and cooperative. That in the Midwest, how one behaved—even in a big city like Chicago, even if contrary to your nature or desire—was governed by rules of conduct that Beth had once believed immutable.

Still, Beth was pulsing with excitement. Everything would be new in this Old World and she would be far away from parents who loved her but sometimes suffocated her with worry. She joined Elaine at the bar.

Elaine and the bartender were discussing American politics, but Beth couldn't really hear. Beth ordered a Brandy Alexander, a drink that tasted like dessert. Sipping it made her feel warm and special, no longer a third-class passenger destined for a night of shivering. She watched the dancers, observing the other women. Beth considered herself average-looking. With brown hair and pale, freckled skin, only her large gray eyes were ever noticed.

Before long, Elaine, and then Beth, were out on the dance floor. Nominally with the guys who asked them but each in her own sphere, laughing at the movement of the boat, the tug of gravity and the challenge of maintaining balance.

Beth enjoyed the way her movements became fluid, like the sea, and the way the boat lurched, and her body followed. She accepted the swells and depressions; the loss of control, so foreign. Some dancers were not up to it, flailing wildly with an unexpected drop of the dance floor underfoot, frustrated or fearful that their dance didn't go to plan, surrendering instead to the stability of tables or bunks.

Gradually, the disco emptied out, the rough crossing ending the night early for most. Beth and Elaine danced on, sometimes out on the floor by themselves, sometimes with another hardy dancer, killing time. With that flush of youth that brings the power to attract without even trying, without even great beauty, the two moved fluidly with the music.

A waiter named Brian, about their age, leaned over the brass railing of the dance floor and asked the two if they were tourists. His Irish brogue put Beth at ease, reminding her of her Irish grandparents. Nice looking, with blue eyes and dark hair, he had a friendly smile.

Elaine told Brian that they were from the States and explained why they were hanging out in the disco. Brian sympathized but warned them that he'd have no choice but to kick them out when the bar closed at 2 a.m.

Beth said they understood. Not to worry. They'd manage.

Brian told them about the pubs and towns in Ireland they should visit on their way back around. About his band, and his dreams for it, the fiddle and the tin whistle, and playing in pubs till closing or a lock in.

Beth told him that her mother made her study the accordion and how she hated it, it was so old-fashioned.

"The accordion is cool," Brian said. "You should have given it a go."

"Maybe," Beth said. "But it was embarrassing where I'm from." Beth looked away and tried to remember why that had mattered so much then. She took a sip from her drink and offered, "I'm 100 percent Irish."

"No, you're not," Brian contradicted. "You're American!"

"I'm *from* America but my parents, my grandparents, all my ancestors are Irish," Beth insisted. "100 percent."

"No," he said, shaking his head and laughing at Beth.

Beth laughed too but she thought, "Alien." A retort that routinely came to her mind whenever she could not comprehend someone, particularly a man. An internal mantra, "Alien," was both a comfort and a fear.

"I'd love to go to America someday," Brian said.

"You should visit us!" Elaine jumped in.

"You should," Beth agreed. Beth could see the offer pleased him. That made up for his thinking she wasn't Irish. They exchanged info and she imagined showing him around Chicago.

Later, Elaine and Beth waited at a table. Expecting soon to be kicked out, they watched staff wipe down spills around them. Brian approached their table.

"I've been thinking," Brian said. "The ship is deadly empty this time of year." Lowering his voice, he continued, "And there's a slew of cabins that aren't being used. If you want to wait for me, after we close, I can take you to one you can use for the night." Brian's eyes were on the bartender, drying glasses at the bar

"That'd be great!" Elaine said, jumping in her chair.

"But won't you get in trouble?" Beth whispered, having followed his gaze.

"Nah. If the boat was full, that would be an altogether different kettle of fish. But we're running practically empty so no one will be botherin' you. Besides, it's pure cold out."

"Thanks, that's so cool of you," Elaine practically hummed.

"Now, Brian," Beth said, holding her hand up, silencing Elaine. "Your offer is really sweet but there's no strings right? Because we're not looking for anything like that." Beth examined Brian's face, trying to read him, noticing for the first time a line of faint freckles across the bridge of his nose, so like her brother. He smiled.

"Nah. No strings," he said, reaching out and squeezing her shoulder, tentatively, as if he too were surprised that he had touched her.

Elaine and Beth looked at each other and nodded.

"You have a deal," Elaine said.

"And thanks, we really appreciate it," Beth said.

When the disco closed, Beth and Elaine followed Brian to a staff elevator. Inside, he turned a key into a round keyhole next to the button array and pushed the L5 button. The elevator descended. With each floor, a soft "ding" sounded as the elevator slipped past a level, a jarring noise in the quiet.

"Boy," Beth said. "We really *are* going into the bowels of the boat. Now I get that expression."

Brian laughed. "Well, this voyage, only Levels 1-3 are being used. I figured, Level 5 is safe. No one is going down there. The elevator locks out the levels not in use."

"Oh!" Beth said, startled.

"But you can always go up to the deck," Brian said. "You'll not be trapped."

"Yeah. That's good. Safe." Beth chuckled awkwardly. "I can't imagine anyone venturing this far down."

"Actually," Brian said, "there's less movement below. Less seasickness. Some people prefer it. When we're not crowded, though, it is easier on the crew to keep the passengers up top."

Elaine shifted her weight from one foot to another. Her discomfort seemed to rise as the elevator sank, level by level. She pressed closer to Beth. Unnerved by Elaine's silence, Beth searched for small talk.

"It didn't occur to me there'd be an elevator on a boat," Beth said at last.

"Technically, this is a ship." Brian said.

"Oh, larger than a boat?" Beth asked, but the elevator door opened, interrupting her.

On Level 5, Brian walked ahead, stopping at a cabin close to the elevator. Elaine and Beth held back. Emergency lighting strips on the floor and ceiling cast conical shadows on the hallway walls, like traffic cones, marking the path. Maybe they should turn back to the elevator, but Beth was afraid Brian would be offended. And that the act of doubting him might precipitate something.

"This is it," Brian said. "Nothing fancy, mind, but you'll keep warm." He opened the door for them. "You can lock it from the inside, see?" He demonstrated by flicking the bolt.

Beth, relieved, thanked Brian again. Elaine waved goodbye. Once in the cabin, with the door locked, they laughed.

"God, I was thinking we made one big mistake, going who knows where with him," Beth said.

"I know!" Elaine said. "I mean, we kept going further and further down. I couldn't say anything, I was so scared. I kept thinking, two against one, two against one."

"Yeah, you were practically in my lap!" Beth chided. "And I'm thinking, what if they never find our bodies, thrown out through a porthole or something into the sea. My parents would *kill* me!" And the two laughed again.

"But why take such a chance?" Beth imagined her mother asking, as she rubbed her hands together, creating that dry swishing sound that signaled a blow-up, full of anger and anxiety. Beth sighed, unconsciously saying out loud, "Better to be lucky than smart."

"I'll say!" Elaine laughed.

Comfortable, they got ready to go to sleep, hanging their sweaty clothes on the hooks across from the bunkbed, keeping their underwear on. Elaine in the top bunk, Beth below. They slept deeply in the warmth of bedding, the smell of the sheets, clean but stale.

An hour or two later, Beth woke up, groggy. Voices. Loud. On the other side of the door. Her nerves suddenly crackling, she strained to make out what the voices were saying. How many voices—two, three? Were Beth and Elaine discovered? Stowaways, that they both were.

"Cris-sake!" said a man's voice, slurring, his brogue prominent. "They're *Americans*, you eegit. Course they want the ride. They're as-kin' for it. And we're going to give it to 'em."

Beth heard growling laughter, whooping.

"Give 'em what they want. Pleadin' for it, they are. Getting flahed tonight!" the last shout accompanied by pounding on the door. Beth heard a response but couldn't make it out.

Beth tried to still her breathing. Stay quiet. Maybe they'll get bored and go away. She waited. Elaine, in the top bunk above her, quiet.

And then Beth heard what she didn't want to hear—the sound of a key in the lock. Beth's skin flushed. A master key? Why hadn't she thought of that? How stupid she was. Her mind now seeing possibilities she'd only vaguely considered.

"Alright, alright," Brian said. "I'm agreeing with ya. I'm an eegit."

Beth squeezed the hem of the sheet like a rope, tugging it to her neck. She thought of her mother, at the sink, wringing out the natural sea sponges she insisted on buying, looking out the window, the water dripping down her elbows, her back to Beth.

"Elaine, are you awake?" Beth whispered. No sound came from the top bunk.

"Go on," Brian's friend urged. "They're right in there. Waitin' for ya."

The door opened a crack. The dim light from the hallway now blinding, except for two dark silhouettes. The hum of the hallway lights, so immediate.

Beth pulled again at the sheet which settled heavily on her legs and torso, encasing her in its coolness, chilling the heat rising from her breasts. There was no time to grab her blouse and pants, hanging on the hook only a few feet away. To grab them would mean getting up and exposing herself, being seen in the triangle of light from the partially opened door.

Calm down! Beth told herself. Get a grip. Think. No sense screaming. No one would hear the screams. Obvious on the elevator ride down—when it already seemed too late to turn back. And what if Brian's friend was turned on by her screams? Beth rubbed the flesh between her eyebrows. No. Normalize it. Chat.

"Brian, I thought we had a deal. No strings, remember?" Beth tried to make her voice reasonable, without any pleading. "C'mon Brian, be that guy I know you are, the one who was just being nice, helping us out." She waited. No response. And yet, no further entry into the room.

"Go on, go on, already," Brian's friend said.

"You know, Brian," Beth said, "Your friend has got us all wrong. Elaine and I weren't looking for anything other than to sleep down here." She paused. "You know that, right?" Hearing nothing, she added, rushing, "Not every American girl is...asking for it."

Beth sucked in her breath. Had she made a misstep? To acknowledge the possibility? Brian's friend grunted. She stared at the mattress of the bunk above her, its foam bulging toward her, constrained only by stripes of metal bars.

"Some sort of misunderstanding, Brian? Right? Because, you promised, remember? We had a deal." The door hinges strained. Brian's weight heavy on the doorknob. "And Brian, you're the kind of guy that keeps a deal, right?"

Abdomen tight, Beth waited. The shudder of the cabin's ventilation, suddenly loud in the silence. A lyric, long buried, wove around her mind in the quiet of her waiting; like the rows of a basket wind downward to a center base, turning back again to the rim.

"...Force follows, if reason fails; reason fails...when the bonds that bind, break..."

"Right," Brian said, abruptly. "Just a misunderstanding. We had a deal." Smacking his friend, he said, "I told ya they weren't like that. You almost had me breaking my word." His friend's response, low and unintelligible.

"Sorry, Beth," Brian said, slurring the "s." Then, too loudly, "Like you Americans say, 'No harm no foul,' right?"

"It's okay." Beth said softly, like a lullaby. "It's okay. It's alright."

"Me and this big oaf will be leaving you alone tonight." Brian continued. "We won't be bothering you again." He pushed his friend down the hall. "Who's the eegit now? Get on with ya." His friend grumbled something in response, but his voice was indistinct, his words without shape or meaning, retreating.

The door closed. The triangle of light disappeared. Beth waited in the dark until she could hear the elevator doors close before she got up, grabbed her clothes and turned on the light. Once dressed, with the light on, she felt less vulnerable, but the enormity of it hit her in waves. Not an auspicious start to adulthood. But they had survived, if not unscathed, at least better than she had hoped, or had reason to hope, lying in her underwear in the dark quiet depths of the ship.

"Elaine, are you awake?"

"Yes."

"Did you hear that?"

"Yes."

"Why didn't you say something?"

"I'm sorry," Elaine said. "I was too scared." She shifted in her bunk bed, dangling her head so she could face Beth. "Besides, I would have told them off, not made nice. You were great, though." Elaine paused. "But it was *not* okay." Elaine said. "Nothing about this was *alright*. You shouldn't have let them off the hook."

Beth turned away. Her abdomen, still tight. She had forgotten. She *had* placated Brian, saying it was okay. No harm done. But she said it only to appease him, to pacify him. Her face flushed red. Brian was drunk. The bond she had formed with him was precarious. Wasn't that actually smart of her? And what had Elaine done to help? Nothing. Elaine was supposed to be the assertive one: the bad cop to Beth's good cop, not quiver silently above her. Scared? They *both* had been scared. Elaine had left it all to Beth to figure out what to do, how to respond. On her own, in the lower bunk, closest to the door.

Beth had an impulse to kick the mattress above her with all the fury that she would have used on Brian and his friend. Instead, she took a deep breath and forced her stomach muscles to loosen, fiber by fiber. She needed to let it go. Her fear, so long constrained, had exploded into rage. All the possible twists and turns, overwhelming. Elaine's criticism, infuriating. She needed to focus on the outcome. Elaine was free to judge because they had survived. Beth made decisions. Perfect? No, but at least she had made them! She had not condoned Brian's actions. Or his friend's. She was not somehow complicit. Elaine was simply being Elaine.

Beth's rage and fear began to dissipate. She began to feel giddy with the release, almost like she was drunk. Finally, after some time had passed, she was calmer.

"Do you want to stay?" Beth asked.

"No, let's get out of here," Elaine said, looking grim. "I won't be able to sleep here."

Elaine dressed. The two cautiously rode the elevator up to the deck.

Once surrounded by the safety of other passengers, Beth breathed slowly and deeply, the sea air still cold and damp, the dark sky hazy with clouds. She had quelled her own panic and talked her way out of a bad situation, even as Elaine, for all her Eastern brusqueness, lay silenced in the quiet fear of that top bunk. Beth felt pride in her resourcefulness, her exercise of control.

Still, she had taken an enormous risk—all for a cabin she readily abandoned. Her judgment about Brian, while essentially correct, had too meager a basis. She had failed to contemplate the complications of a persuasive friend, easy prejudices, and male blindness in the face of desire. Failed even to conceive of possible unknowns. And, yes, at some level, she had also failed to stand up to Brian and his friend, choosing instead to appeal to Brian's pride, to pander to his sense of honor.

"Aliens," Beth thought, suddenly severing delicate fibers of connection, so difficult to weave. She would not talk to Brian again. He would not visit her in Chicago.

The cold wind off the deck now felt bearable, welcome even. The icy spray, splashing from the bow, as the ship pushed forward into the dark, a tingling reminder both of her vitality and the unknown dangers to it. She leaned into the wind, as if she were the bow's figurehead, facing the unknown. She imagined that the mist on her skin froze. In the future, she vowed to remain safe by avoiding the unsafe.

Her body felt depleted, drained of adrenaline. She knew she would soon sleep easily. But before succumbing, she considered whether her mom had been right. As resourceful as Beth had proven herself to be, perhaps she was still too young to go on this trip, too young to know what she did not know.

NORA NAUGHTON

Nora is an avid gardener and a recovering lawyer who is currently working on her first novel. With the generous support of writing communities like OCWW, she is learning to openly embrace and develop her formerly secret passion for creative writing.

A Faint Scent of Roses

by Roberta Albom Liebler

Just be patient a little longer. She's as calm as could be expected. Wait until her cradling arms transfer her terrier's body. Ceremoniously, lower the still slightly warm animal known and loved as Plummet into the white and beige box. Pause to catch Mildred's nod. Not nearly as long as expected. Close the box gently. Walk slowly with shoulders slightly hunched.

After sixteen hours of caring for thirteen dogs, seven cats, a potbellied pig, two pet birds (plus their distraught caregivers), and a migrating Mallard duck that crashed into a newly washed picture window, all Dr. Thomas Andrews wants is to go home, eat a simple dinner, and lie down to sleep beside his gentle wife.

Instead he watches Mildred retrieve a bouquet of brittle yellow roses and untangle a length of ivory ribbon from the wire wastebasket in the far corner of the animal hospital's Tranquil Room. Only a few petals fall on the pebble embossed linoleum floor as she ties a bow around the flowers.

"Death is also beautiful," she mutters, laying the wilted flowers on the boot-size box containing her long-time companion.

Tom places the embellished coffin on the white satin-covered platform near the exit door he dearly wants to open to go home.

Having lost their pet, most people shed a few tears—hand them a few tissues from one of the many strategically placed boxes. They pat their eyes and blow their noses. Take a few deep breaths. Give thanks for the sensitively provided service. Leave, courageously. Ten minutes at most, frequently under five. Not Mildred. She's stalling. Leaning on her parrot-head cane, she sits down on the long bench farthest from the door, points to the facing bench. Give her a few minutes of human comfort before she returns to her silent house.

A thunderstorm is predicted to arrive before nightfall. Still time to get home to his wife's embrace before dark. Don't want Clare to worry. Even as a young wife, Clare warned against giving into "the pull" of accepting responsibility for every creature's well-being.

Displaying neither tears nor brave acceptance, Mildred the thinker, the finally retired life insurance actuary, asks, "Why do veterinarians know when a life is complete but medical doctors don't?"

Dinner is going to be late tonight. This question will not be quickly answered. Oh, to be like the psychologist who responds to the question the elusive patient asks 47 minutes into the session, "How could my husband fool around with a younger woman when I have been such a devoted wife?" with the professionally sanctioned response, "We'll open next week's session on that topic." No, the veterinarian profession doesn't offer scripts to sustain boundaries. Try a short, compassionate answer.

"Veterinarians often care for animals from before birth to after death. We get attached to our patients. Don't want them to suffer." If anyone else had asked this question—thankfully, no one has—they would pretend to be satisfied with this practical answer and leave. Not curious Mildred. She needs more.

His eyes wander sideward to see what he was intending to ignore. Sticking out of the French cuffs of Mildred's meticulously ironed shirt are yellow bony hands with scaly irregularly shaped dark brown lesions. Under her dark-banded nails, chalky white spots are evident. If he saw these symptoms in another mammal, he would diagnose the illness and acknowledge its fast progression. But his friend is pulling the sleeves of her sweater over her fingertips. Sometimes seeming to ignore the obvious is the most compassionate response.

They both startle at the rolling thunder, the flash of lightning. When the blinking overhead lights stabilize, her covered hands are peacefully cupped in her lap.

The rain is slow in coming. Still maybe time to get home dry, but she's not leaving soon. Don't be rude. Her question deserves a deeper response. "Veterinarians struggle over the paradox of desiring to preserve life and the ability to end suffering. Animals have neither the poetry of an afterlife nor the perception that life is meaningful under any condition. For animals, suffering is only pain. A peaceful death for a suffering animal can be a kindness to both animal and owner."

The sweet words don't comfort him, nor, he expects, do they comfort his old friend. If someone else were delaying leaving, it would be an imposition, but this kind woman is offering him the rare gift of a probing confidante. Accept. Graciously. Share what is festering on the mind, but until this moment, inexcusable on the lips. But be careful. "High achievers apply to veterinarian schools because we love being with animals. We enter conscientious, serious, and highly ethical. Then we're trained to think in terms of cost-benefit analysis." Never articulated that before, but it's true.

Mildred bends in his direction. This expert in calculating risk has been unselfishly supportive since their first meeting. Only years after she chaired the search committee that hired him as their small New Hampshire's town veterinarian did he find out her husband had died only weeks earlier. Would never have suspected what she had gone through when she introduced him and his new wife to the important townspeople along with most of the pet owners.

Wonder if anyone reaches out to her? Why only now this realization? The more she loses, the more she gives. Is her invitation to reflect on the profound an imposition on his time and his privacy, or a gift so rarely given that one doesn't even know how to accept?

In the stillness, a long-suppressed image overtakes him. A relief to share. "I examined a magnificent horse before a race. It was at the end of my second year in veterinarian school. Glorious animal with the heart rate of an athlete and the body of a Greek sculpture." Too perfect for this imperfect world? "An hour later, during his first race, the horse tripped, fell, injured. His owner determined that insurance money was a better deal than a stud farm. He ordered me to shoot his horse."

Tom exhales slowly. To stop now would be like a dog not allowing himself to lick an open wound.

"Back in my apartment I could still hear the crash of firm flesh on concrete. If my roommate hadn't taken his diabetic medication out of my hands…"

Mildred does not gasp in shock nor yield her direct eye contact.

After all these years of professional practice, finally a receptive listener. "Suicide has a strong pull when the future is filled with excruciating choices."

Realizing he has lifted the cover of objectivity to reveal his frailty, he relapses to the impersonal comfort of group identity. "Veterinarians have a high suicide rate. We work in an environment with low levels of support, high expectations, long hours, on top of professional and social isolation. A dangerous profession for perfectionists with more than a tinge of neurosis."

The thunder crashes louder than before. He jumps. "I became a veterinarian for pets at a time when their owners considered them more than a financial investment but less than a family member. The pet vet's ethical dilemmas used to be easier to resolve. Putting an animal out of his misery is one thing, killing a salvageable animal for financial reasons is another. Expecting an animal to receive the height of medical care, beyond the reach of most humans, is questionable. The boundary between the ethics of a veterinarian and a medical doctor is blurring." The revelation is astonishing. "I once could have answered your question more easily."

Mildred nods as if signaling for the next symphony movement to begin.

Say what has been rattling through your mind. "Last week, I advised a new patient that her cat's cancer was too far advanced to be treated and the cat's pain would be increasing. She threatened to report me to the professional board if I didn't refer to her to the best veterinary oncologist at the university hospital. I did. Reluctantly. Dr. Royal called this morning, chiding me for wasting his time on an animal that is obviously near death."

Tom releases his breath, slowly exhaling one of many life-or-death ethical issues still unanswered but no longer banging around in confidentiality confines. "I'm not sure of the demarcation between professional expertise and cautious placating anymore."

Don't selfishly take comfort without giving back—Mildred is still waiting for the answer to her original question about the difference between how veterinarians and physicians determine when a life is complete. She deserves an honest answer, but questions about death are never quickly resolved, especially when death of a loved one is so recent. Try.

"Most medical doctors consider death a professional defeat. Yet society sanctions veterinarians to put animals to sleep—a despicable euphemism." With the floodgates open, the repressed torrent escapes in a frenzy. "As a result, many vets come to look upon euthanasia as a positive when our own lives become insufferable. Death becomes a choice. A difficult choice, but one of the options. Plus, vets have ready access to lethal means and the knowledge of how to use them."

He slaps a hand across his lips. Articulating his wife's terror any further would be a breach of the trust scrupulously revitalized nearly two decades ago. Dear Clare is terrified of how the pull to end another's suffering can lead to the license to end one's own. Clare urges leaving the excavation of the forbidden before a pit is dug too deep to climb out.

But he can't abandon Mildred when she's gazing into the pit. "When we enter our profession, we're too young to understand how death will be an integral component. As a vet, I'm expected to decide when ending an animal's life is justified; as a life insurance actuary you determine how much a human is worth at different ages." Clenching his teeth, he stops before the next sentence he intended, the sentence that would mean Clare would certainly go to bed alone: "Has to be another way to value life."

Instead he deflects, "Where will Plummet's last resting place be?" Good choice, the veterinarian equivalent of: How old are your children? Another lesson from our psychologist, an expert in distraction, used when marriage therapy became too heated. Clare, even when upset, was too sharp to fall for that ploy.

Mildred knows he's trying to change the subject. He's already said more than he intended. He wants to go home. Can't blame him. Being greeted at the front door by your true love is sadly, for her, a fond memory of the distant past. Maybe her words will allow him to feel like they're trusted friends mutually disclosing.

"I will bury Plummet by the stump of a tree my father planted," Mildred replies. "During that horrible blizzard several Februarys ago, I watched as it tumbled down in a mighty crash. Not a squirrel nor a sparrow scampered out of the branches. They had already escaped like gulls that fly inland in anticipation of a hurricane." The view outside the kitchen window forever thinned. Losing that tree still hurts. The beginning of so many losses.

"This winter Plummet will join the decaying leaves to nourish next summer's wildflowers." No falling apart. You have nothing to give him but your truth. "Upon my death, my house goes to the senior center down the block because they promise not to rake the leaves except on the walkways." Good, no wavering voice. Push forward. "People now live never seeing decomposition. Never smelling the loam in the forest. Never watching a vulture feast on the carcass of a raccoon."

Her veil of aloneness is fraying with the sharing of intimate thoughts. "Some religions have an after-death narrative—a second existence, but one with no free will. An afterlife that is only the consequence of the first—what happens after the fairy tale is finished." Is too much emerging? "We are made of dust from distant stars. We return to mix with the particles of the past to grow the future. Death is only the end if your self-image is limited to your conscious self." Being profound or stupid?

The lightning flashes illuminate his widened eyes and gasping mouth.

After Tom performed his task with such compassion and exposed himself in ways that he might now regret, he could use help in returning to the ordinary.

She retrieves the backpack she gently slipped off her shoulder not two hours ago, so as not to disturb the whimpering dog in her arms. Withdraws the shoebox that had once held silver party slippers. "Would you arrange for a needy dog owner to have Plummet's things? Everything is clean."

"Very thoughtful, Mildred, but you know I can't give drugs I prescribed for one animal to another."

"Oh, I didn't include the drugs," she assures him. Might he compliment her trustworthiness? Doesn't matter. "Don't worry, I won't deposit them where they are a threat to the water system or unsuspecting living things."

A steady rain begins.

Her trembling hands scoop up the box. Move it in Tom's direction. He catches it inches from the floor. Places it unopened on the end table.

His ethical choices are crashing into each other. Mildred values precision, but accuracy depends on which formula is selected. His hands are twisting behind his back; his heart is pounding. Her voice is reverberating, transforming her question into his: Does anyone have the right to judge when another person determines their life is complete?

Fearing emotions will overwhelm him, Tom switches to a professional tone. "Plummet's last medication, the blue capsules, can be lethal. Wouldn't take more than half a bottle's worth to put an adult into a sleep from which there is no awaking. A whole bottle could end a life in minutes."

Mildred offers the tranquil smile of nuns in medieval triptychs. Impenetrable. If only thunder would break this unbearable silence.

Even better, a high-pitched barking beyond the examination rooms starts with one dog, followed by another, and another, until even the thunder is surpassed.

"They're unaccustomed to voices after dark," Tom informs her while standing, angling his body toward the front door.

"May I visit your kennel?" She doesn't wait for an answer before pushing on the armrest to hasten her escape from the bench, stabilizing herself with the cane.

Children and young couples, the newly single, and the always single often have hinted a desire to be invited into the kennel: "I hear puppies." "Your puppies sound like they would like a visit." "I love to see puppies." About as common as an expectant parent desiring to visit the newborn nursery. But never in his decades of practice has a person who moments ago experienced her beloved dog's death made this request.

Mildred takes slow, wobbly steps in the direction of the barking.

He wants to direct her to leave, but he's troubled, indecisive. Why did he confirm the deadliness of the pills? Why didn't he just offer to stop by tonight with pizza and relieve her of the pills? He'll take her to the backroom kennel. That'll cheer her up. Give himself time to think. Make himself feel less guilty.

An alive scent of excitement, fur, cedar chips greets them.

She circles the kennel path again and again. Energized by each of her passes, the dogs bark louder and louder. And yet she gives the same attention to the just-weaned puppies, the young beagle not embarrassed by the absurd cardboard collar around his shaved neck, or the whimpering collie still trying to stand up on a newly casted leg.

Pointing to a cage in the back, Tom breaks the human silence. "This dog is ready for adoption after surviving a bout of pneumonia. She can't return to a home with rambunctious kids. She's always been a bit frail. In a peaceful, dependable home, she'll be a calm companion for years."

Mildred glances at the dog.

Encouraged by her response, he reaches into the cage to offer her the placid spaniel.

She shakes her head "no."

Enough of this hypnotic circling. Time to circle back to the room that leads to his car, his wife, perhaps his son's phone call.

What does she want? After twenty-seven years of seeing Mildred often, always being greeted warmly, always showing an interest in his practice, his family, only by chance, when arriving too early for a burial, discovering the modest marker for her son killed in the First Gulf War. So much always remains unsaid.

Mildred keeps on walking. If she were of the same species as those in the cage, he could clamp on a leash and lead her out. If she were a child, he would distract her with a treat in the waiting room. If she were an adult with places to go, he would begin shutting the lights.

Despite distaste in feeling like a used-dog salesman, he opens another cage door. With soft clicks and tender stroking, he coaxes the occupant out, right into Mildred's path. "Apgar has been here since his owner died."

Mildred watches the small mousy brown dog raise his paws toward her woolen socks. Collapsing on his haunches. Approaching again. "How long will he live?"

A veterinary cardiologist would answer without hesitation, without queasiness. "He's old and frail, but he still has life in him."

"How long?"

"Prognosis isn't an exact science."

A tinge of impatience is audible in her repetition. "How long?"

Hate to be the steady leg of a drawing compass serving as the center point of the narrow circle of predictability or the arc of a life, but Mildred's struggling. Help her. "My estimate? Four to six months if cared for in a loving home. Less if he remains in the kennel."

"How sure can you be that it wouldn't be more? Letting nature take its course, of course."

"My experience tells me he will lie down in a warm corner this winter and peacefully die."

"Before spring?"

"Yes, before spring."

He pets the dog. Returns him to his cage. "Whining isn't going to make you more appealing, old dog."

With her cane clicking briskly, Mildred walks to the Tranquil Room, stops a few feet from the remains of her dog.

The kennel settles down.

She halts by the satin platform to arrange the bouquet. Takes half a step back. "If the wet leaves aren't too slippery, I'll return on Tuesday for Apgar." Turns around to Tom, "I need time to grieve."

He lifts the cardboard coffin.

She straightens the brittle bouquet. "Helping another creature enjoy the last whispers of life makes one's own end less frightening."

They pause at the open door, watching a triangle of geese head south.

"Tom, do you ever wonder which of the geese will be strong enough, lucky enough, to return in the spring?"

Their heads follow the flock as the last squawks rush into the future.

"I wonder if I will see them return," Mildred mutters.

They walk around the puddle in the muddy parking lot. Mildred stops to watch a chipmunk scamper across a waning flowerbed, stopping to gobble up seeds.

"Clare planted that garden years ago to celebrate our anniversary. I used to sit in the arbor every day to think. I seldom even notice it anymore."

The last raindrops soften the rose petals.

"Let's plan to sit together in this garden next spring when the bulbs push up buds and migrating geese return."

Almost in unison they breathe in deeply, savoring a faint scent of roses.

ROBERTA ALBOM LIEBLER

Roberta writes about the subtle changes that shape a life. In her debut novel, she explores the intersection of individual choices, public health, and the global environment. Having taught and developed curriculum in diverse disciplines, she continues to expand her perspective as a loyal member of OCWW.

Repeal!

by Della Leavitt

I turned 16 the day Prohibition was repealed: December 5, 1933.

I was poised to graduate Chicago's Marshall High School and blind crazy for my dreamboat, Billy Miller, Davey's cousin—yes, *that* Davey Miller, leader of the notorious Jewish gang that carried his name. I thought I knew it all.

Back then, I thought my oldest brother Solly also knew the score, unlike our Old-World immigrant parents. After all, he was the only one in the family who knew that Billy and I were sweethearts, and he kept his mouth shut, but I should have known better. Sometimes he waggled his finger at me, just like our pa did.

No one could tell me what to do. Then or now.

"Don't throw away your life, little sis," Solly said, towering over me. "You're smarter than any girl around."

He didn't give away compliments for nothing, but I sloughed it off and jabbed his arm.

"What do you know about love, big brother?"

My Billy had waves of thick black hair and flashing green eyes like I'd never seen on anyone before or since. I was smitten.

"Are you sure you're Jewish?" I teased on our first date to *Little Caesar* at Lawndale's Marbro Theatre, a movie palace designed like a Spanish castle where I went to worship the stars every Shabbos afternoon while Ma and Pa were in *shul*. Ma never rode the streetcar on Shabbos or on any holiday, but she looked the other way when we children did, because we were American-born.

"We came to this great country to be free," she liked to say, repeating again and again how the Cossacks rode through their *shtetl* swinging clubs and clobbering her on the head.

"My grandma is Irish. Does that matter?" Billy said, and tenderly took my hand.

"Not to me." My heart beat faster. *As long as Ma and Pa don't mind.*

We moved to Lawndale on Chicago's Great West Side when Ma found the bigger apartment she had wanted for years. Besides, she thought the old Maxwell Street neighborhood had become too dangerous, agreeing with Pa when he decreed, "I better not catch any of *my* children with hoodlums!"

Around the corner from our family's Maxwell Street deli was Larman's Gambling House. Everyone had heard about the man who the coppers shot dead during a raid that took place before I was born.

I asked Solly how Larman's stayed open. He put his finger to his lips, looked over his shoulder, and said, "Old Man Larman pays off the lieutenant at the Maxwell Street Station."

When I asked Pa if that were true, he turned as crimson as a bowl of Ma's thick borscht, shook his head, and waggled his finger at me. "*Sha!* A girl should not talk of such things! Nobody should!"

I liked watching the women go in and out of Larman's wearing short, fringed dresses and strands of pearls, masked by heavy face powder and rouge, looking like the flappers I swooned over in the talkies. Ma called them *whoors*. When I had the bathroom to myself, I tried to copy their glamorous hairstyles, desperately smoothing my unruly black ringlets and coaxing a stubborn curl in front of each ear.

It was my Billy who suggested the time was right for our family's business to take in liquor. "People are applying for licenses now," he said.

I shuddered.

"What are you worried about?" He put his arm around me. "It will be legal in no time."

What Billy Miller didn't understand was this could blur the narrow line Pa and his brother Louie had worked hard to toe. They prided themselves on never cheating customers, paying the rent on time, and taxes in full. That was why the Gentile pharmacist leased his building to them at the prime corner of Maxwell and Halsted Streets. In the Depression, times were tough. There were long lines at Al Capone's soup kitchens and our family's deli was failing.

I shared Billy's idea with Solly and he clapped his hands. "Yes! A tavern's the ticket. Uncle Jake can help. He's got connections."

I nodded. Everyone called Pa's youngest brother Jake "The Yankee," because he was only four years old when they came over from Russia. He spent several months in the slammer for bootlegging, but the family only spoke of it in whispers. *The Yankee's no hoodlum. He got in with the wrong people.*

"Solly, you should ask Pa and Uncle Louie. You know they would never listen to me." And God forbid if they had a hint Davey Miller's cousin gave me the idea for a saloon. They would call me crazy. *A meshugenah!*

Solly went in early for his night shift. "Did you hear the news today, Pa? Illinois was the tenth state to ratify the Prohibition repeal amendment."

"What does that have to do with us?" asked Uncle Louie.

Pa put up his hand and said quietly, "Hear him out, Laban."

"I think we could see profits in the liquor business," said Solly.

Pa shook his head. "No, son, that life is for gangsters. All we have is our good name to last beyond the grave."

Solly argued. "When it's legal, Pa, the gangsters will be out. All we need are government licenses."

Uncle Louis spoke to Pa in Yiddish. "How can we complete those papers?"

Solly answered in their common tongue. "I'll do it. I learned enough in Business Law at Crane Junior College. Finally, my schooling will be of use."

Pa and Uncle Louie went all-in, funding the tavern by taking every cent they had saved since landing in Chicago twenty-five years earlier. They borrowed from the rich South Shore cousins who came over in the 1880s and even went to Ma's family to ask for whatever they could spare. Liquor licenses were expensive and the renovations were, too. I almost cried when they removed the ice cream soda fountain to build a long, mahogany bar, because I had always dreamed one day Billy and I would sip chocolate phosphates side-by-side with Pa's and Ma's blessings.

Pa saw my tears, but didn't understand. "There, there, Dena. If we're going into this business, we've got to do it right."

I asked Pa if our tavern could become a swanky joint like the Miller Brothers' M & E Restaurant, where Lawndale politicians sat in luxurious burgundy leather booths and gambled in the back room. I imagined myself a slinky cigarette girl, just like in a speakeasy.

Pa pushed his fingers through his steel gray hair and looked toward Heaven. "That's not for us, silly girl. We are a simple, honest family. Where are these wild thoughts coming from, Dena*leh*?"

"Call me Daisy, my American name."

"*Oy vey*! What is with this Daisy? Who's filling your head with such ideas?"

I looked away, remembering how Billy's kisses made me feel like Daisy, a real American girl, not plain Dena, the immigrants' daughter.

Pa was wrong about the Miller Brothers gang. They weren't all bad. Solly told me if they didn't patrol the streets we Jews wouldn't be safe. Sure, sometimes the gang showed up alongside Capone's killers, but they also beat up the roughnecks who threatened Jewish schoolchildren. When our Polish neighbors accused the community of stealing babies for blood to bake into Passover *matzah*, Davey Miller himself went to their priest to prove no Polish children were missing. How dare they use their libelous Old Country excuses to spark pogroms right here in Chicago! Didn't they realize this was the United States of America?

The sun poked through my blinds on that momentous December day, the day Solly predicted the final states would ratify the Twenty-first Amendment to repeal Prohibition.

He rapped on my door. "No more lollygagging, Dena! Let's go!"

I was slow to rouse because I had been out late the night before and only Solly had heard me sneak in. I was still dreaming of kissing Billy until I remembered this was the big day. I dressed quickly, buckled my shoes, and sliced a piece of Ma's good bread, adding a *shmear* of cherry preserves to eat on the long Roosevelt Road streetcar ride from our flat on Independence Boulevard out to Maxwell Street.

"No school today, Dena?" Ma called. But I didn't answer, trailing behind Solly, struggling to keep up with his long legs. Before we reached the corner, I heard a familiar whoosh of a streetcar's releasing brakes.

"Wait up!" Solly shouted, pounding on the wooden side of the streetcar as it pulled away. When I caught up to him, I choked back a laugh to see Solly turn red. He must have been *plotzing* with worry about the new business, because he never got angry.

"What are you laughing at?" His tone was sharp. If Solly wasn't a gentle soul, he might have slapped me, but I didn't want to rile him.

"Don't be a *nudnik*! You'll see, the new tavern will be fine," I said. But the truth was, my stomach was tumbling, too. Before the next streetcar arrived, I gobbled my bread and jam, cramping my gut. Only three stops away from our destination at Halsted Street, my right leg got the jitters. Did Pa remember to put Solly's perfectly lettered signboards out front when he opened up in the morning? Soon Solly's foot was also tapping with the *shpilkes*. After a one-hour ride, we alighted, turned the corner, and gasped.

All the people! Lines stretching in both directions far away from the sandwich boards, north past Roosevelt Road and south down Halsted Street, throngs waiting to enter our new tavern at the moment it was deemed legal to take a drink.

Solly was silent, but sported the biggest smile I'd seen in weeks.

"Your signs did it!" I cried, hugging him tight.

REPEAL TODAY! BEER HERE!
10¢ a glass! 15¢ a schooner!

A mix of folks stood elbow to elbow, all waiting for the same news: Jews, Italians, Irish, Greeks, Poles, and Negroes who had just moved to Maxwell Street from Mississippi. Talking, laughing, yelling, and clapping each other on the back. Some dressed to the nines and others in everyday overalls. Not only men waited for their first legal drinks, but also women of all ages stood in line. Men wearing suspenders and women swishing flouncy skirts. Scents of cheap cologne mixed with the sour sweat of bodies pressed close together. Women flirted with the men next to them; others clutched babies to their breasts and had toddlers grasping their ankles. I was surprised to see Miss O'Grady, my sixth-grade teacher, who looked away when I tried to catch her eye. Women urged their husbands to run inside to buy sandwiches and soda pop to keep children calm and sated.

Who could have predicted the weather? A Chicago heat wave! The week before, on Thanksgiving Day, the temperature had reached 50 degrees. A second Indian summer. I had never felt anything like it.

Solly clasped my hand. "God must be smiling on us."

I laughed, gawking at the crowds for another minute before hustling inside for a shift at our busy sandwich counter. We were famous for the best corned beef sandwiches in town and Pa wanted to serve them with the beer. Uncle Louie sliced the juicy briskets paper thin. We always put the mustard directly on the meat, not on the rye bread. Everybody in the deli business knew that's how it's done.

Solly sent me to the office to listen to the radio. The minute I tuned in, the announcer interrupted *The Goldbergs* program:

"Just over the wires: Utah votes *Yes* to ratify! REPEAL! Ring-a-ding-ding!"

Happy Days Are Here Again! blared across the airwaves.

I thought my heart would stop.

Humming the snappy tune, I scooted past Solly and flashed him an A-Okay signal. Then dashing outside, I sang out the good news. People cheered, hugged, and threw their hats in the air. They rushed the door, but no one roughhoused or pushed anyone aside. Emotions were sky-high. Everyone had new best friends.

Uncle Jake arrived in time to tap the first barrel. He poured himself a glass, and then one for Solly. "How about me?" I demanded. I still remember how the suds splashed my lips, filling my mouth with a thick yeasty flavor, tasting nothing like the watery beer Pa didn't know we drank during Prohibition. The strong smell reminded me of Ma's kitchen every Thursday afternoon when she baked three loaves of bread.

The cash register rang and rang. I stopped counting how many barrels they brought up from the basement. People stood three-deep at the bar, toasting each other, our family, FDR, and the great state of Utah. Everyone was having the time of their lives.

Pa surprised me with a hug, saying, "We'll stay open all night!"

"Or, as long as our beer supply holds up," Solly whispered into my ear, laughing. "You sure got it right, kiddo! This will be a good business!"

My Billy came in around midnight and pulled me away from the bar. I put my arms around him and he pulled me in close, with a deep kiss I will never forget.

Pa saw. "*Nu?* Who is this?" and stepped between us.

"A friend from school."

Pa pushed Billy away from me. "I don't like the looks of him."

"Hey," Billy said. "She's my girl."

Pa got loud. "What are you talking about? She's my beautiful daughter. My *shayna maidel*."

Uncle Jake nodded to the other bartender and ducked under the bar, pushing through the crowd. "What's wrong, Harry?"

"My Dena is kissing a hoodlum."

"Leave it to me," Uncle Jake said. "I'll take care of this."

I didn't like the curl of Uncle Jake's lip. People kept calling for beer after beer. The sounds made me deaf.

"Solly, go to the police station," Uncle Jake shouted over the crowd. "Go, now! Tell the lieutenant we've got trouble!"

I knew what Uncle Jake was doing. "No, Solly! I screamed, blocking his path. "Don't you dare!" My brother stopped and looked into my eyes.

"What are you waiting for?" Uncle Jake roared. "Go on, Nephew!"

I tried to grab onto Solly as he headed for the door.

"Pa! Make him stop!"

Pa reached for my arm. "You don't know what you're saying, Dena*leh*."

I shook him off. "Don't call me Dena. I'm Daisy!" I saw Uncle Jake pull a pistol from inside his coat.

"STOP!" I screamed. I felt like I was inside a slow-motion moving picture. Alone in the silence.

Billy ran toward the door. Solly caught him by the shirt sleeve.

"Let him go, Solly!" I yelled.

Uncle Jake lifted his pistol over his head. When I heard the shot ping the tin ceiling, the sound pierced my heart. The room erupted. People turned over tables and hid beneath them. What had been boisterous fun turned to panicked chaos.

"Everybody, calm down!" Uncle Jake shouted. "We stopped a thief! The police are on their way." Solly handed my Billy over to Uncle Jake, who held him by the edge of his collar. Billy flailed and let loose with a punch, but his fist met only air.

I pummeled Uncle Jake's chest. "Let him go! Let him go! He's no thief!" I held tight to Billy's forearm. I looked up at the bullet lodged in the otherwise perfectly-etched tin ceiling. "He's my Billy! Billy Miller!"

"MILLER?" Pa threw his palms upward and then covered his face. "*Oy vey iz mir!* He *is* a hoodlum!"

Uncle Jake shook his head. "Harry, we *are* in trouble now."

Solly came back with two coppers, one tall and thin with a handlebar mustache; the other, short and fat with a menacing look, twirling his club. The tall one locked steel handcuffs onto Billy, while I grabbed Billy's shirttail, trailing behind as they pulled him toward the door.

"Don't worry, Jake. We've got him," the fat copper said with a wink.

"He's innocent!" I shrieked, still holding onto Billy, my feet scrambling to keep up, sliding over cigar stubs and cigarette butts, as they dragged him away. I twisted my fingers around a tiny triangle of material, trying to hang on. "Where are you taking him?"

"Get back," the tall copper said, prying my fingers loose. "Be a good girl and stay here safe and sound with your papa."

"Dena!" Solly called. "Over here! At the bar!"

Solly was no longer my favorite brother. Not after what he did.

"No more Dena. I'm Daisy!" I sobbed, snuffling tears back into my nose. How could they do this to my Billy? To *me*! I ran out, screaming, "Solly, I hate you!"

When they threw Billy into the back of the paddy wagon, he gave me a last forlorn look. I pounded on the back door of the wagon, trying to grab the handle, and then fell flat on my *tuchus* in the middle of the street. As the paddy wagon squealed away, I heard the rat-a-tat-tat of a truck's backfire. It made my heart lurch.

I couldn't bear to go back inside, so I walked around the corner to Larman's. A few women stood outside drinking.

"Have one on us, girlie," a pixie-like waif with a deep voice beckoned.

Another laughing siren's words floated out eerily in the dark. "Hey, what happened in there? Did they snatch your man?"

That was the night I broke with my family. For good. I remembered a recruiter from the Michael Reese Hospital nursing school who had visited Marshall, and I decided, then and there, that would be my escape. Room and board provided. Uniforms, too. I'd always admired nurses' starched white caps. I could move out of our family's flat right after high school graduation, and when I completed nursing school, I could live anywhere. I'd always wanted to see San Francisco or New York City.

It was high time to become Daisy.

All-American Daisy.

—— DELLA LEAVITT ————————

After careers in tech, teaching, and educational research, Della Leavitt passionately pursues the writing life. A 2021 fellowship from Chicago's Newberry Library supports Della's historical novel-in-progress, *Beyond Maxwell Street (1911-1956)*. Springing from her family's history, the multi-generational epic focuses on women's agency amid limiting economic and reproductive options. Della proudly serves as secretary of OCWW.

GREAT COMEBACKS

Stories about recovery

 Turnabout

by Doug Warshauer

Alexis waits in the back of the Uber until all the other kids disappear inside the house, leaving only Mrs. Cutler—it must be Mrs. Cutler, this is Kate's party—standing sentinel in front of the door. "Wait until you see me go inside," Alexis tells the driver, then tromps over the snowy driveway in her heels.

At the door, Mrs. Cutler flips to the second page of her legal pad. "Found you. Go ahead, darling." Alexis turns and waves the car away. From there she can see the list over Mrs. Cutler's shoulder, can see her name at the bottom, scribbled in a darker shade of blue than the others. A last-minute addition. An afterthought.

Inside, the heat of the home hits her like a flash of summer, and Alexis is aware of how endless the four months before graduation will feel. Too long to endure, too short to salvage high school. She tosses her coat atop the heap perched on the Cutlers' leather sofa, picks up two others that have slid to the floor.

The route to the basement is paved with melting slush. She follows the grimy path and checks out the Cutlers' art, a rococo scene of goddesses lounging in a meadow. She's tempted to linger, to delay her appearance downstairs as long as possible.

But three more girls have just flipped their coats on the pile, and the hallway is too narrow for Alexis to let them pass, and one of them, Hannah, puts her hand on Alexis' shoulder and spins her around. "Look at your dress! Where did you find that?" The other girls are staring, too, with the kind of surprised enthusiasm that reminds Alexis of the few times she's made a basket in gym.

The answer eludes her. The tight red dress is one of seven she ordered online. The other six are draped over the bed and the floor of her room in a scene vaguely reminiscent of the Cutlers' painting. It's an image not so different from how she imagines the kids will be posed in the basement.

In three and a half years of high school, tonight was her first dance. It's Turnabout, the event when the girls do the asking, and she arranged with a

111

guy she knows from English class that they'd go together as friends. But they went their separate ways ten minutes into the dance and she hasn't seen him since. She couldn't have gotten his name on the list for this after-party, anyway. And this is the best part of the night, everyone says. She floats downstairs with Hannah and the others as if buoyed by her held breath.

In the basement, four girls are playing beer pong. Two others are seated on bar stools, watching, their backs to the counter and the glass bar behind it that reminds Alexis of the setup at the Olive Garden. The Cutlers have done nothing to suggest that their stock of liquor is off-limits. Alexis never fully believed the stories that filtered down to her of after-parties gone wild, of baton-wielding cops stampeding through quiet suburban homes, of kids scrambling through half-open windows and mudroom doors. Maybe her life is finally beginning.

There are only two boys, seated on the couch playing Fortnite. She recognizes them from AP Bio. Part of her is a little let down to see them here.

Hannah pulls her behind the bar. "You want a White Claw?"

Alexis takes a sip. Melting ice slides down the seltzer can, but the drink is warm, like they forgot to chill it until twenty minutes ago. Somehow, this bothers her more than it ought to. She touches the can to her cheek, tells herself to relax. To try to have fun. This is supposed to be fun.

Someone bumps her from behind. She stumbles, hits her shin against something sharp and metal, and catches herself just before her forehead bangs into the fridge.

When she turns around, Jordan is bent over the ice bucket. Of course Jordan would be here. If cruelty were a sport, that girl could have had a D-I scholarship. "Excuse me."

Jordan doesn't look up. "What?"

"You just rammed me out of your way."

She rises with a mini champagne bottle dangling from her fingers, lets it swing like a pendulum. "Uh, do I know you?"

"You're kidding, right?"

Jordan shrugs.

"Seriously, Jordan. We've had like four classes together."

"Whatever." She spins out of the bar area and calls to Kate Cutler, "When are the boys getting here?"

Kate is pouring a bag of chips into a blue plastic bowl. "They said they were coming right after the dance."

"I'll text Tyler and see where they are."

Jordan was always the nastiest of the popular girls, but since this fall, when she began dating Tyler, she's grown worse. At lunch, Alexis and her friends sometimes dream up ideas for revenge, like filling the air-conditioning vents of her car with mosquitos or pouring Everclear in her water bottle. But of course no one ever did any of that. They're not that kind of people.

A few more girls stream into the basement. Alexis stays behind the bar. Everyone notices her as they come for a drink. The dress is a hit, maybe because of the way it hugs her figure, maybe just because no one's ever seen her done up before.

"Look at you."

"Where've you been hiding 'til now?"

I don't live in a convent, she wants to say. *If I told you the truth…*but she knows she won't say anything.

The basement is filling up, but other than the two weird kids playing video games, it's all girls. Kate peers up the staircase as if the guys might be gathering at the top, unaware the party is down below. "Jordan, what did Tyler say?" Kate asked.

"He didn't respond."

Alexis can tell that Jordan is peeved to admit this, as if it drains her reservoir of authority. On her way here from the dance, Alexis spotted Tyler's car parked at the McDonald's in town. Of course she recognized the car—anyone at their school would know it: a Jeep Wrangler with the license plate BYEOFCR. People said he'd gotten ten speeding tickets and always managed to talk his way out of them, but people say all kinds of things about Tyler.

She has the urge to tell Jordan she knows where her boyfriend is, to say it loud enough for the whole party to hear. "Tyler and his buddies are scarfing down Big Macs," she could announce. Her glory would be short-lived, though. It's not like she was with them, snatching their fries or sharing their shakes. Eventually she'd have to admit that she just drove by his car, and what kind of burn is that?

Alexis is still standing in the bar, listening to the music, and sipping her warm White Claw when the boys arrive. Their rumble makes it to the basement before they do, an earthquake of pounding feet that makes the liquor bottles vibrate on the glass shelves. Then the boys explode into the room, the odor of fast food clinging to them like a helicopter parent.

They move as one to the bar. It's too late for Alexis to escape, so she slides to the corner, as far from the ice bucket as possible. In seconds, the crowd fills every inch of space. She's pressed chest-to-chest, rock-concert tight against Darren, her lab partner from sophomore Chem. The song changes to *Break Up with Your Girlfriend, I'm Bored* and for some reason, Darren begins to dance. Only there's no room to move, so all he's doing is shimmying himself against Alexis, smushing her right boob, then her left, in an alternating sequence at 84 beats per minute.

"Get off!" She twists and pushes against his shoulder and manages to make enough space to slide away. She elbows her way through the crowd. You'd think people would get a drink and get out of the bar, but they're lingering—if anything it's getting denser—and her heart is beating faster now. Bodies thunk her from all sides. Sweat forms on her forehead and under the tight red dress. Her first after-party, and she is going to be trampled to death. There are two boys standing shoulder to shoulder, right in front of her. She jabs both arms into the space between them and pulls them apart like a swimmer doing the breast-stroke. Then she feels a splash on her face. She imagines she's actually in a pool until she recognizes the taste of cheap beer. It's soaked her cheeks, run down her neck, drenched the fabric over her chest.

A tall kid with a half-empty Solo cup laughs. "Sorry." Then he tilts his head back and downs what's left.

Alexis manages to make it out of the bar area and find a bathroom. The hand towel is already wet, so she takes a not-so-absorbent decorative towel off the rack and dabs her face. In the mirror, she checks the front of her dress. Splotches everywhere. No matter how much she dries it, the shape of her left nipple shows through. This is a sign she doesn't belong here, proof that they've disturbed the universe's equilibrium. It's the kind of thing that would never happen to Jordan. She thinks for a moment about making an escape, climbing out the bathroom window and sprinting all the way home. But they're in the basement so, duh, the bathroom has no window.

She closes her eyes, sits on the toilet. It's fine. It's like getting bird shit on your head. Yes, it's humiliating. But it's not *personal*. She'll make a joke of it if anyone says something. Who would, anyway? They're not in 7th grade anymore.

When she comes out, the boys have joined the game of beer pong, and the rest of the gang has crowded around the table to watch. She stands just behind Hannah, close enough to hide the front of her dress. It's Tyler's turn, and he's down to the last cup. When the ball lands inside it with a little splash, Alexis cheers with the rest of the group, maybe a bit too loud. Tyler seems to grin at her, to hold her gaze longer than she'd expect. He has the kind of smile that makes up for a lot of faults.

With the game over, the crowd shifts, and Alexis finds herself uncovered. From across the room, Jordan walks toward her. She's smiling, too, but it's an evil sorceress smile. As she passes by, she leans close and whispers, "Love your dress. But be careful you don't poke someone with that thing."

At this moment, Alexis would like to tear Jordan's top to pieces, shred it strip by strip off her body. Except that's what Jordan would do. Instead, she folds her arms across her chest. If she stays like this, she can cover the worst of the stain, keep her nipple from standing out too much. She's not going to let Jordan ruin her night.

She heads back toward the bar. It's less crowded now. Tyler is holding court around the keg, a couple of his buddies entranced by some story he's telling. He breaks off when Alexis arrives. "You need a beer?"

"Tito's. I see it back there." She turns her back on them, pours the vodka into a cup, adds Sprite from a two-liter bottle sitting on the counter. When she spins around again, she's re-crossed her arms. "How did you get so good at beer pong?"

"Pure, natural ability."

The boys around him laugh, and Alexis flips her hair. Her assigned seat is beside Tyler in Psych, but they've never talked in public. She's not sure what to say next. Social situations lock her up like a jammed zipper. It doesn't help that she's avoided them most of her life, so she has little idea what people talk about at parties. Instead of saying anything, she smiles and sways her shoulders to the music.

In the corner of her eye, she spots Jordan talking to Nicholas. Alexis is pretty sure they're talking about her, because both of them keep sneaking glances her way. In junior high, Nicholas used to hang out with Alexis and play card games like War, but he's way too cool for that now. It occurs to her that the kids are dealt into high school cliques by some cosmic version of War, and that some alternate shuffle might have landed her in the popular crowd.

Nicholas heads toward the bar. Alexis considers saying something to him, asking what Jordan said about her. But that would be stupid. He wouldn't tell her, and what difference does it make, anyway? She's just putting the idea out of her mind when Nicholas walks straight up to her. He stands way too close, and she's about to ask what he's doing when he wraps both his arms around her back and mashes his mouth onto hers.

She tries to push him off but, with her arms still crossed in front of her, she's trapped. She turns her head from side to side. "Stop it!" she yells. With his mouth over hers and the loud music and the crowd noise, she's not sure anyone will hear. Or maybe everyone is already watching, and the sound filling her ears is their laughter. She can taste the alcohol on his tongue, and for some reason it makes her panic, as if he's trying to poison her. She tries to thrust her knee upward, but even that doesn't work. His legs are too close.

Then there's a hand on her upper arm, gripping tight, pulling her apart from Nicholas. It's Tyler. Once Nicholas has been yanked away, he laughs like a cartoon villain.

She wipes her mouth, trying to remove what she can of his disgusting saliva. "It's not funny, asshole!"

"Seriously, dude. What the fuck?" The veins in Tyler's neck are bulging.

Nicholas points over his shoulder. "It's just a joke. It was your girlfriend's idea."

Beside the ping-pong table, Jordan and three other girls are cracking up. But what's worse is that everyone in the basement, even the boys playing Fortnite, have frozen in place and are staring at Alexis.

She bolts out of the bar, through the basement, up the stairs. It was stupid to come to this party. She's not friends with these people. In half a year, she'll never have to see them again. She can go to college and start fresh, go to parties where people won't think it's weird to see her, where she won't have to keep so many secrets. Later in life, her mother has often told her, it will not matter how popular you were in high school.

She picks through the pile of coats. There's so many more now. Where is that damn thing? Her tears make it hard to see.

By the time Tyler comes upstairs, puffy down jackets cover the floor like a path of rocks across a stream. "Alexis, you don't need to go. Nicholas is an idiot."

"I hate this. I don't belong here."

Jordan has come up behind Tyler. "Let her go. What do you care?"

Alexis spots her coat on the other side of the living room, under a coffee table. She grabs it, heads to the door.

She's half out when she stops. No. It ends here. It has to end here. She spins around and walks up to Tyler, until she's close enough to feel the heat of his breath. "Take me home."

Tyler glances over his shoulder at Jordan, then shrugs. "Okay. Sure." He grabs his own coat. It's right there, no need to hunt, that's how things work for Tyler. He follows Alexis out the door.

Jordan grabs his arm. "Are you seriously going to drive her home?"

Alexis imagines that, in the moment while she's waiting to see what he decides, the future of the human race hangs in the balance.

In the Wrangler, Tyler turns on the ignition, backs the car out of the driveway. The wheels crunch over the ice.

Alexis wiggly waves at the girls, who are half-lit by the doorstep sconce light. Jordan is screaming something, her mouth and eyes stretched like a bean-bag-toss clown face. "Your friends suck. I told you this was a bad idea," Alexis says.

Tyler's eyes are on the backup camera. "You were right. I'm sorry."

Just before he turns out of the driveway, Alexis places her hand on the back of his neck and strokes it in small circles, in just the way she knows he likes it.

— DOUG WARSHAUER

Doug's first book, *If I'm So Smart...Where Did All My Money Go?* won the Axiom Business Book Awards Bronze Medal in Personal Finance. His fiction has been published in the *Saturday Evening Post*, and he's currently working on a novel. He's been a member of OCWW since 2017.

Its Own New Thing

by Shanna Yetman

JUNE 22, 2056
Atmospheric CO_2: 250 parts per million

"How are *we* going to be?" My dad drones on, his red hair flopping wildly, his pale cheeks flushed. His eyes are bright; he makes sure to look many of us in the face, including me. I look at the ground. He makes me feel uncomfortable.

Both my parents are bigwigs in the environmental evangelist movement, and Earth needs them. But I need them too. I shouldn't say this, but sometimes I hate this stupid planet; I wish we'd all just wash away with it or it would just take care of itself. I sneak a glance at my cousin Britt and my Auntie Star. Auntie smiles and points forward, reminding me that I should pay attention to Dad. When he speaks, I try to listen, honest, but his voice is so boring and what's that word? Monotonous.

"We get to decide what's next. We get to be the founders of mankind's second act. Humanity needs new tenets." A few of his flock nod their approval.

New rules for humanity? Boring. I know I should pay more attention; they'll probably ask me questions at dinner tonight and I should say *something*. I look around. More than a hundred of us are gathered in our summer-winter clothes on the top floor of the greenhouse. I move from my chair onto the floor and settle my back against our lettuce bed. It's going to be a long night.

I feel better when I look outside. It's June and snowing. I love the way the snow falls on our glass dome, immersing us in an ice cave under a purple sky. According to my parents, it wasn't always like this. First it was unbearably hot, then it was unbearably cold. The planet's thermostat on the fritz. Once summers began to warm and the ice began to melt, Dad took this as a sign to settle. He decided he could do whatever Earth was calling him to do in one place: Chicago.

There's still enough natural light to see the thick white birch trees and dense forest that run along either side of our building.

119

I watch my mother. She sits next to Dad, taking notes, nodding or laughing at whatever marvel comes out of his mouth. She's so full of energy. She winks at me and I sit straight. Auntie says she's the heart of this operation, but I think she says that because they're sisters and they have to boost each other up. Mom is rail-thin with curly brown hair. She is glowingly beautiful. I think of her as a priestess. But, really, she's an ornithologist, and even looks like a bird sometimes, at least in my mind. Of course, I haven't seen any real birds ever, but I've stared at plenty of the dead stuffed specimens in her office.

Outside, the birches sway with the breeze and a few feral cats playfully assault each other. Inside, people are shedding their winter layers: snowpants on the ground, thick coats off, hats and gloves in disarray or hanging near our heat lamps. Everyone is settling in, getting excited. Many of them have spent their whole lives thinking about what we should've done to tread more lightly on Mother Earth.

Lee, the midget meteorologist (he did morning news in Maryland, way back when), mentions communal high-rise living. Boring. Others offer up plant-only diets, bartering, massive reforestation. Boring. They could talk this to death.

I inch closer to the glass. We aren't that high up, and because of the way the snow is blowing, most of it has accumulated on the top and front of our dome, but the other side is snow-free. This is the side I'm sitting next to. The forest to my right is vast and the trees are tall, like they've been growing for 20-plus years, though we only planted this grove eight months ago. Since then they've taken over our neighborhood. Growing faster than trees have ever grown before, our plant biologist reminds us.

I look for the cats and notice only one.

I turn to face my father once more. His whiteboard is full of lines, arrows, circles. He's numbering the best ideas. People are busy in their conversations; most of them have gathered at the front behind the tomatoes. I can only see the backs of heads.

There's a tug on my braid.

It's Henry. He's pimply-faced and fat and I hate him, which he knows. So, of course he's going to bother me. He's been looking outside, and his eyes are big, like he's seen a ghost. He points. "Did you see that?"

"What, Henry? What?" I'm annoyed but also a little bit interested. There's nothing out there. Henry's lips are blue, and open. His chest is heaving, becoming more erratic. If I didn't know better, I'd think he was having a heart attack. But that doesn't happen to kids, right?

He pokes my neck and shoulders, turns me so the window is in front of me, tries to make sure I see what he sees. His voice is barely audible. He whispers in my ear. "Look! Look, Lily!"

I follow his finger toward the forest. There's a bird-like creature, the size of a toddler, in plain sight. It looks like a grouse, or at least what I know of them from my mother. Even from this distance, I can see four long, sharp teeth protruding outside of its beak.

I look back at my parents. The adults in the room are still occupied with Mankind 2.0. Nobody is paying any attention to us. I take a step closer and learn quickly where the cat went. This thing is feasting on it, tendons and sinewy muscle hanging from its beak. It shakes the dead animal confidently and I watch as the cat's eyeballs dislodge, dangling from the lifeless body by the optic nerves.

Eww. I don't look away, though. There's something else. Every so often it stops eating and excitingly shifts its shape. Its back feathers go up and out and its orange breast feathers create an iridescent smiley face.

I've seen a version of this thing before.

It looks like one of my mother's wraggly-old early 20th century bird-of-paradise. The one she keeps trying to pin and prop up to get its transformation just right. To make it look real. Of course, her version is more twisted than this one. Her birds look like monsters. This animal is quite pretty when it struts its stuff, even if it does have guts hanging from its mouth.

Later, at dinner, I'm bursting to tell everyone what Henry and I saw. Even Dad notices my excitement. He pats the top of my head as we sit down at the wooden picnic bench that has been our dining table for the past year. But before I can say anything or even really sit down, Auntie gestures for me to get up and help serve.

I pour water into everyone's cups and think about those teeth and the way that bird ripped through the cat. Could it do that to a human? I watch as Dad passes around a bottle of whisky that must be a hundred years old. All the grownups take a sip and pretty soon the conversation flows.

"Things are really heating up." My mother shakes her glass in my direction. I refill her cup, but it kind of spills all over her and the table and she frowns. "There's been a few sightings."

Sightings? So they've seen it too. I move slower so that I can hear every word.

"Wolves, right?" asks Auntie.

My mom shakes her head. "Not wolves."

Auntie looks confused. So Mom tries again. "I mean there are wolves," she pauses and watches Auntie place a bowl of millet porridge on the table with a huge spoon. Britt puts down a plate of stewed eggplant and tomatoes.

I crinkle my nose in protest, momentarily distracted by the slop in front of me. Again? "Isn't this just leftover breakfast?"

"Breakfast for dinner, Lil." Auntie shakes her head at me. "Now sit down and eat up."

Dad chuckles. "I've got some crickets over here if you want 'em. Full of protein." He pops a few in his mouth.

Mom and Auntie laugh at what must be my grossed-out face. Auntie gives Britt a few high compliments on her use of seasoning. Herbs and spices are something we are just adding to the greenhouse, and Britt has become a wonder at mixing the flavors together. I love Britt—she's a year older and my best friend, but even she can't make these leftovers worth it.

I sit down and place a napkin over my lap and pick up my fork. I'll pretend to eat. "What do you mean, wolves?"

Mom looks at me and sighs. "Not wolves." She takes a bite of porridge. "You should probably know. There's rumors going around about animal sightings. New creatures."

I forget that I don't want to eat and stuff a bite of millet in my mouth. I can feel the grains stick in my throat. I cough and then cough louder, reaching for my water. It all goes down the wrong pipe and I spit out everything.

"Henry and I saw one."

Everyone stares at me. Oops. "It was big." It's really the only thing I can think of saying.

"Saw what, Lil?"

"It was a bird." I shake my head when my mom's face perks up. "Or birdish."

Dad pops a few more crickets in his mouth and looks at my mother. Both their faces are so serious now.

Mom turns to everyone else at the table. "We have to be careful; we don't know what's out there. Harmless, maybe, but we don't know." She looks at Britt and me and says it again. "Be careful. Travel in groups. Tell people where you're going." That one was directed at me, I'm sure, because I like to wander off and explore.

The warning shuts us all up for a minute and we clear the table and move to the living room. Britt's eyes are still wide from my revelation and I know she'll have a hundred questions.

Soon, Mom asks me to come up close to her and I figure she wants to hear more about my sighting.

"Your father and I have something to tell you, Lil, and we don't want you to be mad." She pats the sofa cushion and I sit next to her. They like to prepare me when they think they are about to tell me bad news. Usually it's not that bad.

"Things are changing. You saw for yourself, today. If there are new creatures out there, we've got to learn to live with them, study them. You heard the sermon. We get the chance to create something new."

I nod and look down at my feet. My toes are dirty.

"There's a few other communities out there like us and we think we can all band together."

"Okay, so?"

"Your dad and I have a lot of work to do." She pauses and looks to him for support, but he's deep in conversation with Britt. "We think it's best that you move in with Britt and your Auntie for a little while. So, we can focus on the work ahead of us."

Wait, what? This *is* bad news.

"You mean I won't live with you anymore?"

My mom shakes her head. "Just for a little while. Until we find a clear path forward."

I blink and stare at her. "Okay." I don't want her to see how I really feel.

Mom pats my shoulder. "Really? Is that it?" She smiles and hugs me. "We'll still have Sunday dinners. It's just that Auntie has more time to devote to you."

Yeah, because that's her job. She's the resident babysitter. I smile at my mother and fake total acceptance. But inside, I wonder how I can fix this.

What if I brought that bird back? The thought hits me like a ton of bricks. Mom says she wants to study them. If I caught one I could prove my worth. I bet she'd love to see those feathers up close. Maybe then, she'll let me stay.

"It's a monster, Lily. A real live monster." It's daybreak and Henry, Britt and I are outside the complex. We're going to find that thing and bring it to my mother if it's the last thing we do.

"No, Henry. It's a bird. A real live bird." At least that's what I hope it is. What if he's right, though? What if it is a monster? Do I have this all wrong? I wash the thoughts out of my head and decide to focus on how stupid Henry is. I roll my eyes at him and Britt laughs. I'm thankful I brought her along. I can't guarantee Henry won't run away like a sissy.

We've wrapped our feet and hands in heavy-duty layered plastic for protection. We crinkle as we walk, and this worries me. Will it hear us? Or worse, will it know we are coming and attack? I consider taking the plastic armor off, but then I remember those cat guts.

Today is what they used to call a spring day. The weather has turned, and the ground is dripping with snowmelt. It's slushy and muddy and I really can't tell what's been out here and what hasn't. It must be 40 degrees. It's hot.

Henry is oafish and stomping while we walk. I'm getting sprayed with mud. He doesn't respond well to the heat and begins to unzip the top half of his snowsuit. He shakes his head at me. "You're crazy if you think that thing is a real bird."

"Birdish."

"And we all know that Lily's mom loves birds." Now, it's Britt's turn to razz me.

"She studies birds," I say.

"Everybody just looks the other way while your Mom *studies*—" Henry uses air quotes. "—old stuffed museum birds." He pauses and turns to face me. "She's got an unhealthy obsession, you know."

"Does not," I say. "She definitely does not." I look at my feet. "They are specimens, and she likes them because they remind her of how things used to be." I shrug. "Or something like that." She'd basically said that to me once, way back when.

There's rustling in a nearby bush and both Britt and I jump.

"I wonder if it's close?" asks Henry.

"It's the wind, stupid," says Britt. "We aren't close to anything."

Henry turns to me and his face is white again. Has he seen something? "Listen," he says.

Everyone is quiet. A loud hum presses into my ears.

"Do you hear that?" I ask. Henry and Britt nod. I gulp. Is this it?

The chirp-buzzing is followed by a low guttural howl and then a *chicker-ee-chickeree-chee*. A few moments later the howl is back and so is the *chickeree*. This is clearly a call and response.

I can almost make out where the second sound is coming from. It's to my left, maybe a few hundred feet. I run in that direction.

"Lily! It ate a cat," screams Britt.

I don't respond.

My feet crunch on the leaves and sticks. I'm getting closer to that *chickeree*.

This forest is dense and birch trees are everywhere. It's dark. I listen to the sound to orient myself and realize that I'm walking in circles. I can't tell what direction I came from. I'm by myself. There's more noise. It's close.

I see a long, lone flicker of sunlight to my left; I decide that must be the way.

The trees clear and I step on top of a giant bird's nest. It's at least as big as our garden plots. The creature that Henry and I saw yesterday is nowhere around. Instead, there are two chicks the size of chickens, chirping. I stop. Their mother's got to be close. She wouldn't leave them. One of the chicks lunges at me, biting my leg. The beak feels like a razor. I'm bleeding. I hope the mom can't smell blood. She must be looking for food.

I should run. This is real. I'm in their territory. They eat cats!

But I don't want to leave. I'm taken by them. I've never seen anything like these babies. They have the same gray-and-brown-striped pattern across their body as their mother. They also have a long black strip of feathers running around their eyes and down their neck. Their beautiful bright orange plumage appears on the top of their heads and at their breasts and I wonder if these babies can do what their mother does. Can they shapeshift too?

I see Henry and Britt and I wave for them to come over. I hadn't actually thought about this part. How are we supposed to transport the animal back to our complex? Britt's brought her old tattered backpack. It's full of water and fruit. I grab it and dump out its entire contents.

She crosses her arms and gives me a "what the?" look. Henry gets my drift and he picks up a piece of fruit. "Maybe it's hungry?"

I nod. I want to tell him to put out his hand—that's what they really want. Henry waves the fruit in front of them and they respond. One of them even gets up and snaps its beak at Henry, almost biting his finger.

This is when I pounce. I grab the bird by the neck. I'm amazed at how light it is—five pounds tops. I've got it firmly by the neck and it is hissing and wriggling and pecking at me, but it's easy enough for me to place the backpack over its body. I then turn the backpack right-side up and loosely tie it.

"Mother Earth, Lily! Is it okay?" Britt asks. She's standing as far away as she can. She looks spooked. "Are you okay?"

Then Henry smiles broadly at me and slaps me on the back. I lurch forward, almost dropping the bird bag. "God, Lily. I didn't know you could move so quickly."

Neither did I.

I can't believe there's a weird bird-like creature wriggling around in Britt's old backpack. I can feel its sharp little claws and beak through the tattered bag and I hold it out in front of me as I run to my mother's office. I stop to catch my breath outside her door. I look inside the bag to check on our treasure and it's sleeping soundly. Something stops me when I open the door. I think about my father's rules for humanity, his tenets. *Let us all live side by side with nature. Let's cherish its richness and rejoice in its mystery.*

I look at my squirming backpack and feel guilty, but I'm excited by the idea of mystery. Mystery means exploration. It means uncharted territories. I worry for a second. What if Earth is producing new beings? What if Dad's right? Is this our second chance with nature? Should I let this creature go? But then I see my mom through the window. She's with that damn decaying bird-of-paradise specimen again. Maybe I can take it back after she looks at it. I know she's got the feathers all wrong and her model looks awkward and clumsy. She needs to see a real bird. More importantly, she needs to know I can help with the work they are doing. She needs to know I'm valuable.

I open the door. She isn't expecting anyone and her chin is on her desk as she tries to reconstruct her dead bird. I make a loud noise and she looks up. The creature has started squirming, cooing its soft chickeree sound.

"What you got there, Lil?" She's all scientist, yet still a priestess to me. I want her to be proud of my find.

The chick is moving viciously inside of the sack and I drop it on the ground at my mother's feet. My mom startles and pushes her chair back to give the emerging bird wide berth. Once it shakes itself free, it paces the floor. When my mother leans in to touch it, it snaps wildly at her and then runs underneath her desk. My mom moves quickly and tips over a card table, trapping it.

She and I kneel by the bird and watch it. She studies it from every angle. She gets excited; her voice rises with every syllable.

I'm pleased with her excitement. But she's also frowning.

"This is not okay, Lil."

I roll my eyes at her. "I just wanted you to know that I'm brave. I can help."

"Help? You're 11!"

The chick has calmed once more, and she moves the card table and reaches under the desk to grab it.

"This is a baby, right?" She looks at me and shakes her head. "I bet the grown one could really tear into something." She pokes my stomach. "Like you."

I back away, but only a little bit. She touches the inside of the beak and I do the same. "You can already see those little buds of teeth." I feel the bumps and ridges that will become those massive teeth. I shiver. Not so innocent.

"We should feed him." She looks around her office and finds a few tomatoes. "I'll cut these up." She cuts the fruit into small enough bites and slowly puts her hand out toward the bird. The bird responds; soon its feathers are up and out and that psychedelic orange smiley face is back.

We watch the bird eat. She shows some of its features to me, like its crown feathers and how the back feathers have a pattern that, when pushed up and out behind its body, create eyes. She tells me that birds don't have teeth, that their bones are hollow because they need to be light to fly. She tells me this creature isn't a bird at all. She also tells me that she knows that I'm brave and that both she and my Dad love me very much.

My shoulders slump. I know what's coming. She's preparing me for bad news. Instead, I interrupt her, I don't let her say it, at least not yet. "You know, it's like a bird-of-paradise."

There's a long pause.

My mom pulls the creature closer to her chest and it coos wildly, as if it knows we are talking about it. "No, Lily. This animal is its own new thing."

Amazing.

For a moment, it's just me and my mother and this creature in this new world and it feels so right.

SHANNA YETMAN

Shanna is an environmental writer and mother of two children. She loves the short forms. This work, "Its Own New Thing," is part of one of her novels in progress. She is a DCASE grant recipient, a New Millennium Writings award winner, and attended Bread Loaf in 2019. She works for Loyola University Chicago's School of Environmental Sustainability.

CēShel

by Cathy Chester

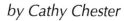

Turning off the main highway, the bus jostles onto a two-lane dirt road and the echoing screams begin, "We're here!" With still a mile to go, I sense the excitement growing. The bus stops and with one leap I am off, running around the meadow, inhaling the cleanest, most pine-infused air. This is my last summer at Camp Cedar Springs, and I want to make it the best by jamming everything I can into the next four weeks.

Without thought of anyone behind me, I stop dead in my tracks. I slowly tilt my head upward inch by inch, taking in the full height and width of sprawling limbs of the Guiding Tree. Several ropes hang from the lower limbs and kids are already swinging from one twisted line to another.

From across the field, I hear someone bellowing my name, "CK!" It's Mia. I streak wildly toward her. Mia and I met last year and became inseparable. Amid laughter and hugs, we topple to the ground. Mia screeches, "CK, we're in the same unit, and we just have to be in the same tent!"

Giggling mischievously, I respond, "Let's make sure we stay in the tent farthest away from the main house. Wouldn't want to run into a counselor on our midnight jaunts." We laugh and hug some more.

Cedar Springs is a camp sponsored by the local Community Center where I live. It is broken into seven areas called units, each having a main house surrounded by eight or nine tents. Mia fills me in on more details and some changes from last year as we walk back to where Joan, our counselor, is gathering our group.

Shaking my head, I ask, "Mia, how can you possibly know all this?"

Mia cautiously looks from side to side, then back at me. "CK, I can't share all my secrets, not even with you." We laugh out loud, not caring who hears our eruption.

We settle in, and Mia points toward a girl named Delaynie. "Look who else is back. I'm surprised they let her return after all the grief she caused last year."

Rolling my eyes in disgust, I respond, "I still remember when Delaynie pushed Brenda off the pier and watched her thrash around in the water. Delaynie told the counselors that Brenda tripped and then said, 'So it couldn't possibly be my fault.'"

Mia agrees. "Sure, and I suppose it was a coincidence when Delaynie tossed all of Brenda's clothes out of the tent, and everything got soaked in the rain. Delaynie's so mean! We better not be in the same unit! It will spoil everything." This is Mia's last year too.

Once everyone gathers under the giant tree, Joan begins talking. "For those who haven't been here, we know this massive tree as the Guiding Tree. Potawatomi lore speaks of tree spirits that help on a quest to find your true answer. The tale explains that its limbs spread under the weight of secrets shared and grows tall with possibilities." After a dramatic pause, Joan continues, "This giant walnut is also the center point of our camp. Follow any trail throughout Cedar Springs and it will safely guide you back here."

Shivering and brushing up against Mia, I whisper under my breath, "I get goose bumps every time I hear this story. Think of all the secrets this tree could share."

Next, Ms. Cole, the director, introduces herself, adds a few general announcements, and, before we explode from all the waiting, she sends us off to our assigned units.

Before grabbing my gear, I notice a little girl all by herself. She's sitting hunched over with her legs pulled in by encircling arms and her head hidden between her scrunched-up shoulders. She looks like she wants to disappear.

"Hi," I say. "What's your name? Is this your first time here?"

She inches away and twists around until all I can see is her back. She replies sharply, "I want to be alone."

"You didn't tell me your name," I say.

"Didn't think I had to."

"Only trying to be friendly." As I walk away, she murmurs, "CēShel. My name sounds like seashell but spelled capital C long e, capital Shel, with no spaces. My mama named me."

Turning back to face her, I say, "My name is CK. If you ever need anything, I'm in Pine Trail Lodge."

"Who's asking for help?" she replies angrily. "I'm fine. Leave me alone."

Wow! It sounds like the same attitude I had my first time at camp. Didn't know anyone, never camped before, didn't have any say-so about going. I figured my parents didn't want me around, so they sent me to the last place on Earth I'd ever want to be. The chip on my shoulder weighed me down for weeks.

I think I'll check on CēShel occasionally to make sure she is okay. The counselors are always talking about "paying it forward." This is my chance.

Days pass with boating, swimming, archery, hiking, and rope-climbing skills. I'm Katniss from *The Hunger Games*, with Mia playing Rue at my side. I relish every minute.

One afternoon, I see CēShel walking alone. I wave and call out, but get no response. I catch up to her and ask, "Hey, haven't seen you around. How are things?"

"Fine," she says, her head swiveling in all directions. "Go away," she pleads. "I told you to leave me alone."

Out of nowhere comes Delaynie's voice, "Hey Cē, who's your friend?"

CēShel's eyes widen with fear. She whispers, "Now you've done it. Go away."

I hesitate, but something tells me it's better for CēShel if I leave.

Most of the kids at camp are friendly, but it only takes one thriving bully to make someone's life miserable. Once again, Delaynie is the bully, and, since Brenda didn't come back this year, CēShel is her victim. CēShel's ripe for the role with her unusual name and inability to stand up for herself. The other girls avoid CēShel so they won't end up on Delaynie's nasty side. Incredible how much control Delaynie has. She's not much bigger than anyone else, but she's a whole lot nastier.

CēShel's group classes are back-to-back with mine. When Delaynie notices me, she taunts CēShel. "Hey Cē, isn't that your friend? Oh, can't be. You have no friends."

CēShel turns away from the group as they laugh. I start to go over, but CēShel shakes her head no.

Reaching down, Delaynie picks up some crushed seashells from the sand and shows them to the other girls. She points toward CēShel, and once again, they all laugh. This time CēShel walks away, but someone pushes her. She trips over a rock, stumbles to the ground, and cries. CēShel has no one. Sara, the unit's counselor, sits at a nearby picnic table watching. Why doesn't she care?

Striding up to Delaynie, I hiss, "Hey, what's your problem?" The group splits, leaving Delaynie and me in the center.

She mimics, "What's your problem?" Then adds with a thug-like voice, "I don't have one. But if you're looking for one, I am more than happy to oblige."

I take another step. CēShel blocks me.

Sara comes over. "What's going on? CK, you shouldn't be here; you're causing trouble."

No one dares speak up for me.

"But Delaynie was—." Before I can continue, Sara exclaims, "You need to go back to your group. Now!" To me, Sara's reluctance to confront Delaynie shows she is more than a little afraid of what other trouble Delaynie can cause.

Stubbornly I ask, "Aren't you going to do anything about the way Delaynie's treating CēShel?"

"I don't hear CēShel complaining. Mind your own business." Sara gathers the girls and goes back to the table where she had been sitting.

Helping CēShel will have to wait until tomorrow. I need to think.

Later that night, I hear Mia rustling in her sleeping bag. "Mia, are you still awake? This whole Delaynie and CēShel thing is really bothering me. Can we talk?"

Mia has other ideas. "Let's go for a walk. Maybe it'll help us come up with some ideas." Wickedly, she adds, "Time for us to cause some commotion. Let's have some fun."

"You sure, Mia?" I say. "I don't want to wash dishes for two days again." We giggle as we sneak out of the tent. Not wanting to wake anyone, we wait to turn on our flashlights.

We wander a short distance when Mia stops me with an outstretched arm and points. "Look over there! Why are flashlights darting all over the Guiding Tree?"

We creep closer. It looks like the counselors are hanging something on one of the ropes. "Probably a piñata," I whisper. "Tomorrow is El Día de Las Flores Coloridas."

"But why are they hanging it in the middle of the night?"

Suddenly the night becomes ghostly quiet. We turn off our flashlights and strain to see anything in the darkness. After inching forward a few more steps, blinding lights flash in our eyes. Shadows surround us and we hear hushed, angry tones.

"Who's there?"

"Why are you out of bed?"

"Don't come any closer."

We freeze and gaze into Ms. Cole's disapproving frown. "We couldn't sleep," I stammer. Mia's hair bounces up and down as she nods in agreement.

Through clenched teeth, Ms. Cole yells at Joan, "I thought you said everyone was asleep in your unit. They're your responsibility. Take them back to their tent."

Turning to the caretaker, Starky, she says, "Stay here and make sure no other campers get near this tree." Pointing to the rest of the counselors, she grumbles, "Go back to your units!"

In our tent, Joan warns, "Don't say anything to anyone about this. We were having a meeting, and the only time we can all gather is at night. Now, crawl into your sleeping bags, and don't get up again."

I'm frightened. I feel we saw something more than the counselors having a meeting. When Joan leaves, I roll over to talk to Mia, but she is already asleep. I guess I'll have to wait until tomorrow to talk about CēShel.

In the morning, Ms. Cole meets with all the campers at the Guiding Tree for the usual daily announcements. The piñata that Mia and I expect to see is not there. Mia shrugs. "Maybe they were just looking for a spot last night, and they'll hang it later."

Ms. Cole quiets everyone and explains, "We have visitors from the American Camp Association walking around today. They check the camp to make sure everything is safe. Nothing to worry about. Just go about your daily routine." I swear Ms. Cole is staring at Mia and me the entire time.

On our way back to Pine Lodge, Mia points to a long row of cars hidden by trees and bushes. Before either of us can say a word, Joan appears in front of us, blocking our view. "You're going to be late for swimming class. You better hurry."

We are busier than usual, and by nighttime, I am exhausted. More to myself than anyone else, I mumble, "I'll check on CēShel in the morning."

Mia answers, swallowing her answer in a yawn. "Okay, go for it."

The next morning I wander over to Isle Point to ask if anyone has seen CēShel. Each head slowly turns toward Delaynie. Taking her time, she replies, "What's it to you? You her mother, or something?" The girls laugh.

"No, I haven't seen her for a few days, and I want to find out how she's doing."

Delaynie snickers. "Yeah, we'll send out a search party right away."

The girls laugh even louder. I want to punch Delaynie right in the face.

I walk over to Sara's tent to ask her. Sara sees me coming and busily starts straightening out her clothes. When I get there she tries to ignore me, but I'm not leaving until I get an answer. I sit on her cot. She never looks me in the eye. Her hands continually move over the top of her shorts, picking at bits of shredded material.

"CēShel's gone," Sara says. "I didn't think she was having fun; CēShel was too much of a loner. She didn't want to be friends with anyone. I tried to help, but nothing worked. CēShel's taken care of."

I can tell Sara's not telling the truth. She's acting like I do when I've done something wrong. She never tried to help CēShel or step in when Delaynie was bullying her. Suddenly Sara grabs her water bottle and leaves. I walk to the Guiding Tree to think. I've always loved it here, but something isn't right. I'm glad camp is ending soon.

Standing around waiting for the buses to take us home, we share laughs and memories of the past four weeks. Mia comes over and stands by me. "Look who's coming with her little groupies." I turn to walk away, but Delaynie shouts, "Hey, CK, I want to say goodbye. See you next year."

"Not me. I'm not coming back," I answer. "You drove Brenda away, and for all I know, CēShel. Well, you won't add me to your list."

"What? I didn't do anything," Delaynie sneers as she looks at the girls surrounding her.

"No, you never do. It's always someone else who does your dirty work." I stare at each of the other girls, and one by one, they walk away.

Delaynie looks stunned. "Hey, where are you all going? We can still have some fun; it isn't over yet. C'mon, we can all sit together on the bus. Wait."

I yell as she runs after them, "Being left out isn't fun, huh, Delaynie?"

The ride home takes a lot longer than usual. I can't shake the feeling something is still wrong, and these are going to be my last memories of Cedar Springs. It wasn't the four weeks I had hoped for.

I arrive home, and forget about CēShel for a while. A few weeks later, I stop by the Community Center looking for CēShel, but she's not there.

I approach the lady at the main desk and ask, "Is there a way to find an address of someone I met at Camp Cedar Springs? I'm not sure of her last name, but her first name is CēShel. That's capital C, long e, capital Shel. She pronounces it like seashell."

"I'm afraid we're not allowed to give out personal information," replies the lady. "Try looking it up in the telephone book."

I laugh on my way out. Do they even print telephone books anymore? At least I have somewhere to start; I have CēShel.

When I arrive home, I type CēShel into my computer and hit "search." An article pops up grabbing my attention; *Death at a Local Summer Camp*. It's about a local girl, CēShel Hames, age nine, who hanged herself from a tree at Camp Cedar Springs. A suicide note stuffed in her pocket read, "I never feel good enough." I can't read any more.

My mind flashes to the night Mia and I came upon the counselors. They weren't putting a piñata up; they were taking CēShel down. It wasn't the camp association walking around the next day; it was the police following up on the investigation.

It feels like someone has punched me in the gut. Tears stream down my face. I rock back and forth in my mom's arms as she keeps repeating, "Not your fault, you didn't know." But deep in my heart, I know somehow I should have helped CēShel understand that she *was* good enough.

I have goosebumps again, but now it's because I know one of the secrets of the Guiding Tree.

— CATHY CHESTER

Cathy returned to her love of writing after 42 exciting years as a teacher. She is a member of the Society of Children's Book Writers and Illustrators, the Poetry Foundation, and various critique groups. Her interest in short story writing brought her to OCWW in 2017 and she hasn't regretted a day of writing since.

Seven Days

by Lisa Maggiore

started my new life with caffeinated coffee.

Thanks to congenital heart disease, I spent my past life drinking decaf. But after being on the transplant list for 10 months, I received the gift of a new life on my 32nd birthday from a young man killed by a drunken driver. My emotions seesawed between guilt and gratitude for my organ donor's death. When I was on the guilty side, I drank red wine and listened to Samuel Barber's "Adagio for Strings." When I was on the grateful side, I chugged energy drinks and coffee. I'd feel jittery, but I embraced a feeling that I'd never experienced with my old heart.

My heart finally had something to boast about as I welcomed my new life.

I decided to go on thrill rides that evoked fear in a normal man's heart. Mine did not even quiver.

After a few months of roller coasters, I decided to up the ante. I'd jump out of a plane.

My older sister eyed me as if I had said that I would stop taking my anti-rejection medication because I was *cured*.

"Oh, Mark," my mother said. "Weren't roller coasters enough of a challenge?"

"Seems dangerous," my father said. "Considering your lifelong surgeries; you've been sewn up more times than most humans."

After high school, I joined the family's stationery business for the medical insurance and to work hours that accommodated treatment regimens: oral antibiotics, puffer, and home infusion of IVs. From ages 29 to 30, I spent more hours in the hospital than in my apartment. At 31, I moved back into my parents' home. Before the transplant, I was unable to walk even a few steps without being exhausted and breathless. I was skeletal. Death and dying occupied my thoughts.

Now I was going to jump out of an airplane.

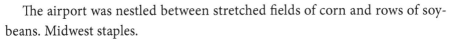

The airport was nestled between stretched fields of corn and rows of soybeans. Midwest staples.

I pulled into the lot on Friday afternoon. After two espresso shots, I turned off my cellphone. I needed a break from my family's endless messages.

"Hello, there," said a tall, athletic woman as I approached the hangar. She swung her blond braid over her shoulder, revealing the name *Kelly* embroidered on the shirt. As I advanced, her sky-blue eyes narrowed.

"Now, why would anyone want to jump out of a perfectly good airplane?" Kelly asked.

My breath shortened as I thought hard on my defense.

She tapped me on the arm and said, "Just kidding. Come on, let's get you suited up."

"Wow. Nice way to comfort a nervous jumper."

"You don't look nervous," she said, then added with a grin, "And I don't hug on the first jump."

Her banter made me feel tense and excited.

In the hangar, I watched a video about tandem skydiving. It seemed I'd be connected to a harness that was attached to Kelly. Thinking of being near her sparked adolescent excitement and derailed my focus on the jump.

"Best time you'll have in your life," Kelly said. "And if you do everything this video instructs, you'll jump without injury."

"Good to know I'm with someone prepared."

"I'm a professional," Kelly smiled. "I've been jumping out of planes since I was a kid. My dad started this business after Vietnam. He was an Army Ranger. It's mine now."

"You have an exciting career. I sell stationery."

"I heard paper cuts are on the rise."

I laughed. "The paper business is very lethal. I'm thinking about pursuing a new career."

"CIA? FBI?" she mused.

Before my transplant, my parents/bosses understood when I needed two hours for my morning session of medications, or when my cardiologist appointments lasted all day for my echo, EKG, defibrillator check, and stress test, or when I was admitted to the hospital on a long staycation.

I felt different then. I *was* different. I didn't attend college or parties or wait in a long line for the release of a new movie, or meet a girl in a bar. The last time I dated, or had sex, was in my mid-20s. I was afraid my heart would stop if I found someone and it didn't work out. I quit searching for love.

"I wanted to work in sports medicine, but I was sick for a long time and needed my family's help. I'm better now, and I'm here because I'm stretching out and doing new things."

"It sounds like you have a lot of living to catch up on," Kelly said. "So, let's get to it."

The harness gave me a wedgie, but before I could adjust, Kelly handed me goggles and we boarded the plane.

The engine made a thunderous roar, and my heart pounded against my sternum, vibrating my battle-worn chest. I savored the moment, closing my eyes to be one with the rhythm of the propellers. As the plane flew, we sat in silence for 10 minutes.

She patted my arm and yelled, "You ready?"

Before I could nod, Kelly snapped her harness to mine and together we waddled toward the closed door of the plane. My mouth became dry, maybe from all the espresso. I grabbed my harness by crossing my arms over my chest. Kelly reached around and pushed on my forehead so that the back of my head rested against her shoulder. She pulled open the door and pried me away from safety.

The blast of cold air struck my face and my heart thumped in my ears. Kelly leaned to the side from the open doorway several times. She tugged on our harness and yelled, "Welcome back to the living, Mark."

Then she shoved us both out into the open sky.

Kelly and I sat on crates in the hangar with our harnesses loose but not yet removed. I was too cranked up after the jump to take off my gear. The late-spring temperatures were hotter than normal and sweat ran down my back. Kelly finished her water. I sipped on my second energy drink.

"What else is on your adrenaline bucket list?" she asked.

The jump boosted my confidence, even though heat crept up my neck. "Going on a date."

"Anyone I know?"

This moment was proving scarier than the jump. "You know her well."

Kelly lifted her chin, "What makes you think I'd say yes?"

"You seem like a risk-taker and I'm a marginal risk at best."

Kelly laughed and shook her head, but that didn't stop her from suggesting that our date could be a hike the following day.

"The state forest has rock formations. It'll get your adrenaline pumping, but I'm drinking water, and don't even think about bringing energy drinks to rehydrate."

"What? Energy drinks won't hydrate me?"

"I swear, Mark, your heart's probably working 10 times harder and wondering when you're gonna show it some love."

"I show my heart love by doing adventurous things. It took me over two years to build my stamina to walk, let alone run and climb."

"If you don't mind me asking, what happened to you?"

I spilled out the story of my illness, surgeries, and recoveries. Kelly's face displayed a mixture of worry and hope—something my heart completely understood.

Saturday brought more worry and hope. Hope, because I was going on a date. Worry, because I was going on a date.

Those feelings soon faded as I beamed with pride at every mini-mountain I climbed, every grassy incline I navigated, and every hour being with Kelly.

I packed sandwiches and we ate on the peak of a hill and quenched our thirst with water Kelly carried on her back. Her gap-toothed smile closed as she lifted out the energy drink that I'd buried under a bag of chips. I grinned and shrugged. She shook her head and tucked the drink inside her backpack.

I'd noticed her setting a stopwatch before we left. "Tell me why you're timing yourself?"

"I'm hiking the Pacific Crest Trail next year, and I'm conditioning to get a 16-mile daily average," she said.

"I hear it's intense."

"Twenty-six hundred miles. Takes about five to six months."

Kelly kept talking, but my eyes wandered to the tank top emphasizing her small breasts and the cargo shorts highlighting her muscular legs. I felt a boyish infatuation; the usual women in my life were family, friends, and healthcare professionals.

"You're thinking about wanting to sleep with me?" Kelly's brazenness startled me. I shifted in my spot, formulating a witty comeback, but my cleverness abated, so I told her the truth.

"I haven't been with a woman in over 10 years. I miss being intimate with someone. And you're right, that is what I'm thinking."

Kelly remained still for a few seconds. She raised her sunglasses and stared into my eyes. "If you want me, you can have me. But body only. If you want my soul, that's gonna take a lot more work."

As my breathing sped up, my heart skipped in beats like the chaotic rhythm of jazz. She took me to her house.

Kelly unlocked the faded wooden door and swung it open. As I stepped over the threshold, she turned around to face me and pushed me against the wall next to a tall, lush, potted plant. She guided my arms above my head, yanked off my T-shirt and kissed me. She drew back and whispered, "It's been a long time for me, too."

I wondered why, but that fell to the background because I felt self-conscious about my surgery scars. Kelly held me firmly and we locked eyes as I tried to figure out how she felt about my imperfect body. I saw a familiar loneliness on her face. I slowly grinned. Kelly did the same. I caressed her cheek with my thumb, and she took my hand and kissed the tips of every finger.

She led me to her bedroom upstairs. My legs shook. I hoped my body would remember what to do. Our teeth banged while kissing, and I laughed out of awkwardness. I tucked strands of hair behind her ear, then flinched when her fingertips gently traced one of my scars. She whispered, "It's okay." Our eyes met again, but this time I saw a quiet fire. And I, who wasn't sure if I could perform, did so well the first time that I steadied myself for another round.

"You're insatiable," Kelly huffed, as she rolled away from me. "I won't be able to walk, much less jump out of a plane tomorrow."

I crawled over the sheets and kissed her, dragging my hands down her smooth, fair skin. "You're beautiful."

"I bet you say that to all the girls."

I intertwined my fingers in hers. "Only the ones I jump out of planes with."

The following morning, we sat on her back deck enjoying coffee as the sun rose.

"My mom died when I was six," Kelly said between sips. "She was my world with Dad gone; first in the military, then building his business. He tried so hard to take care of me, but I resisted because it wasn't the way Momma did it. One night he got so frustrated he flung dinner across the kitchen, fell against the wall, slid down, and started to cry. We were on opposite ends of the kitchen, eyeing each other like boxers in the final round. I missed the touch and love from Momma. But I remembered thinking that daddies loved their little girls, too. And I needed to let Dad take care of me.

"I crawled over to him through pasta sauce, and he crawled over to me through noodles, and we cradled each other. I never forgot how good it felt when Dad wrapped his arms around me. It's a feeling I've been chasing for a while now, because he died two years ago."

At work the following Monday, I struggled to concentrate. I kept replaying scenes with Kelly, in and out of bed. We'd left each other with the promise that we'd talk every day until I returned Saturday for another hiking date.

I left work early and purchased my first pair of hiking boots to impress her.

At the end of the workday on Tuesday, my mother called a "meeting."

The meeting turned out to be an intervention.

"You know how much we love you," my mother said with watery eyes. "But we're concerned about you."

"I saw hiking boots on your front seat," my sister said quickly, "and open tabs on your computer about backpacking trips that go from Washington to Mexico."

"What gives you the right to spy on me?" I demanded.

"Son, we're not here to judge every decision you make," my father said. "But we're worried you're pushing yourself too hard."

I stared into the green eyes that mirrored my own. "You mean pushing my heart."

"Yes, your *new* heart," he said.

"I jumped out of a plane last Friday and I survived. My heart's in great shape. I even went on a date."

There was a collective silence in the room that made my hands sweat, but I wasn't about to stop. "I went hiking with my jump instructor, Kelly. She's brave and adventurous. And beautiful. She's going to hike the Pacific Crest Trail next year, and I was thinking of tagging along."

My parents' eyes were wide. My sister was fuming.

"How long have you known her?" she sneered.

"Almost two weeks." I stretched our acquaintance just a little.

She choked on her soda while my mother's eyes darted toward my father's.

"Mark," he said, "we understand you're filling your life with things you missed out on, but it's not safe to just throw yourself into everything—"

"Or everyone," my sister snarked.

"Stop!" I took deep breaths to calm my racing heart. "I'm healthy." I focused on my mother. "Remember what Dr. Shah said?"

My mother dabbed the corners of her eyes with a Kleenex and nodded.

"She said to stay active, and that's what I'm doing. I'm strong, and the more I move, the more my heart will benefit." I glanced at each of them. Their comfort and love had given me motivation to cling to life. I knew that caring for me had been their full-time job. But now, I was ready for them to find new careers.

"Whether you agree or not," I said evenly, "I'm doing what I think is right for me. If that's hiking the PCT, then so be it. If it's taking a woman out for dinner, then so be that. If I ask that woman to marry me after a year, then so be that, too. I'm grateful for everything you did to keep me alive. But it's my life. Not yours."

Before anyone could respond, I walked out and headed straight to my car. I called Kelly to take her to dinner. She laughed when I said I'd be there in two hours. But she didn't say no.

We ate at an Italian restaurant that served as the meeting hall for the local Elks Club. Kelly loved the spaghetti and ate there twice a week.

I sat back and slowly drank my beer and I told her about my day.

"I don't want to come between you and your family," said Kelly.

"You're not. This is my choice, not theirs."

"I'm sure your illness made them feel powerless, and maybe making decisions for you was the only way they could help," said Kelly.

"That's true. My sister thinks I haven't known you long enough to be so involved."

"Oh, man, no wonder she's concerned. Jumping in the sack with your instructor after knowing her a day."

"I didn't share everything. What we did in bed is only for us."

"Discreet is good, but maybe we should cool it."

I thought about escaping and hiding in my car. But I didn't endure a lifetime of loneliness to slink away now. "I heard that the guy sitting with you would make a great boyfriend."

Kelly chuckled. With an arched eyebrow, she asked me back to her place for dessert. I figured that was code for "sex," so I greedily accepted.

I called in sick Wednesday, leaving a voicemail, then turning off my cellphone. We hiked another trail and talked and talked. I shared how painful it was to watch the world through a hospital window and my fear of dying before finding love. She told me about an ex-boyfriend who wanted marriage and children—just not with her. And how, after her father's death, she considered suicide. I grabbed her hand and squeezed it.

"This sounds cliché," said Kelly, "but I know you'll understand. Life is precious. That's why I chose life."

After lunch, Kelly left her house and drove to work. My eyes settled on a wall of pictures in her living room. Some were of her mother, judging from Kelly's age in the photos. They shared the same sun-bleached hair, freckled skin, and brilliant, gap-toothed smiles. But most photos were of Kelly and her father.

His stature surprised me. I thought he'd be muscular, but he was not much taller than me. His inky black hair lightened as he aged. His beard and mustache had streaks of gray that gave him the look of someone from the *Lord of the Rings* movies. It was clear from the pictures of them at deer camp, fishing in the mountains, and jumping out of planes, that Kelly's father was her world.

I checked my phone and had two texts. One from Kelly saying she'd be back around seven for dinner and one from my father saying he hoped I was feeling all right and he would see me tomorrow at work.

"My last boyfriend was a hunter," Kelly said as she grilled moose burgers that evening. "We backpacked in Alaska and Canada, and deep-sea fished in the Florida Keys. He should've been happy, but he wasn't. I think he suffered from depression. I tried to help him, but he wouldn't let me. I finally left him last year." Kelly flipped a burger. "I loved him, but I loved myself more."

In bed that night, Kelly suggested we play truth or dare, naked.

I cleared my throat. "Uh, I don't have much to tell. I've only been with one other woman."

"It's just for fun, to get to know each other better."

"I need an espresso shot."

Kelly shook her head and slowly leaned forward to kiss my lips.

Kelly was right. I bared myself without judgment. We finished by rolling around and laughing. Then we discovered each other's bodies in a way I'd never experienced before.

I interlaced my fingers into Kelly's and said, "I love you."

She didn't blink. "You've been without a woman for so long that I'm not surprised you'd feel that way. But don't go mixing up sex with love."

"I'm not. My organ donor gave me the gift of life, but *you* gave me the gift of love."

Kelly was quiet for a moment. "I accept your love, too."

I left Kelly's house on Thursday and drove to work to quit my job. I never did love stationery. And being with Kelly helped me realize that love, no matter if it's about a woman or a job, is most important.

"You're fucking insane," my sister said.

Tears streamed down my mother's puffy face.

My father lifted his 200-pound frame from behind his desk and lumbered to where I was standing. He held out his hand for me to shake. "We'll keep you on as a consultant, so you have insurance. Do what you need to do, Mark."

I phoned Kelly and asked her if I could move in the next day. She laughed and said I was crazy. But she didn't say no.

LISA MAGGIORE

Lisa is a native Chicagoan—reppin' the North Side—and former social worker. She is the author of the children's picture book series, *Ava the Monster Slayer,* an Illinois Reads pick for K-2 in 2017. Her adult fiction includes short stories and a novel. Lisa is an OCWW member.

Motorcycle Momma

by Judy Panko Reis

First day back to work after his burial. Ides of March. Jenny fights the urge to slump lower in her Amigo mobility scooter as she waits with the crowd. The train is late. She's an ice sculpture on wheels about to dissolve.

She heaves against gravity. Tries to stop thinking of Matt (again). Gulps and inwardly revisits the crash (again).

Jenny's scooter squeaks onto the hydraulic lift, which raises her onto the train. She positions the scooter's wheels in the passenger car. The train clangs forward, and the Amigo glides into its carved-out spot. Bulky parkas and pom-pom hats wobble in the aisle. A whimper escapes from her throat. It's a huge day, returning to work with her new disabilities. She's dizzy with self-pity, terrified she will fail to perform at her pre-injured standards. *No more loss.*

Despite her Oxfords, leg brace, lifeless left arm, and scooter, Jenny imagines herself fitting in, wearing hose and heels, as before her injury. She mourns her shoulder-length hair, shaved for surgeries. *The good old days.*

She is nestled in a black down jacket and her cherished Cashmink scarf, which Matt gave her during his medical residency. She loved the green that mirrored the hue of Matt's eyes and the way they gleamed when he and she belly-laughed about the Cashmink label and their secret love for knockoffs.

Trembling, she fingers the fringes of the scarf, recalling the horror. She envisions their cracked craniums leaking crimson. Swirling red light rushed them to St. Andrew's Hospital. Days later she was shuttled to an inpatient rehab where she learned to sit up, dress, feed and bathe herself with one hand. And then, as an outpatient, she mastered riding her Amigo. After limping through parallel bars while weighted with clunky braces on her affected left arm and leg, Jenny's walking was still shaky.

Matt was soon sent to his final home, a facility for complex-care patients. Primary colors brightened its corridors where '60s Muzak accompanied a percussion of clicks and hums coughed up from weary ventilators.

Images of her last visit to Matt's bedside cause an ache. She can still smell the wilting red roses on the table beside the hospital bed where Matt's skeletal six-foot frame lay tethered to tubes. She can still see his dark spiral locks sprawled on the pillow. She can still hear his muffled wheeze after her fingers planted a kiss on his ashen forehead.

The coma sucked him into Hades. *Is there room down there for two?* When the void claimed him, Jenny's temples throbbed in anger. *How dare you desert me?* She silently cursed him for getting the better end of the deal, leaving her alone to manage an alien world with a pulverized brain.

When Jenny unzips her pocket in search of a tissue, *wham*, her left ear is clobbered by a red backpack. It is shouldered by a lanky, somber-faced man under a thin comb-over. A 30-something. Like her.

Jenny's shriek pierces the din of commuters scrambling around her. No one notices. *Can my morning get any worse?*

Red Backpack pivots toward the flip-seat beside her wheelchair. He's so close that his shoelaces skim the wheels of her scooter. *What? Am I invisible?*

She ducks, clenching her shoulders to avoid getting slugged again. Oblivious passengers continue to clout her with their gargantuan packs. They don't see her and they don't apologize. Red Backpack is no different.

He releases a loud sigh, in harmony with the low squeal of his seat cushion. He stares into his cell phone like every other passenger.

Jenny sniffles, inching the Amigo back from his high-tops. *Get a grip, Jen,* she lectures herself and retreats within the balm of invigorating memories with Matt. They are straddling his BMW cycle along the Möbius strip of the Illinois River, cruising through the forested ravines of Starved Rock State Park.

A spasm in her left hand jolts her out of her reverie. When she applies pressure with her functional hand to calm the jitters, Jenny notices her companion's bloodshot eyes shift from his phone to her scooter. It is the first time he sees her.

"Nippy outside," he says. "Lucky you've got your wheels. Gives you a beeline into warmth, right?"

Her brows furrow above her pasted smile. "Guess so."

He leans toward her scooter.

She gets a whiff of his cologne. Musk. The scent sweetens the stale air of the crowded car. She studies his comb-over. She wears her own female version of a comb-over to hide scars that crisscross her scalp.

The sweetness of his Musk grows, and she wonders if he is headed for a job interview. Or a romantic rendezvous? He hovers closer toward the tiller of her scooter.

"Have you been using this long?"

"Almost a year."

"Can I ask why?" He catches himself. "Sorry, you don't have to answer that." His apology betrays a silent sorrow that blunts the intrusion.

"I had a stroke. It affected the right side of my brain. That's what happened to me."

It's the lie she has honed to explain her disabilities. The fib protects her privacy. She's tired of being treated like an object of public scrutiny who owes every stranger an explanation for her "condition." It also assuages her guilt for not pressing Matt harder to stay safe.

Her emotions are mangled like her brain. She barely recognizes herself anymore: lying to strangers, her disfigured, patched-up skull, her paralyzed limbs seizing into spasms.

Living as a brain-injured woman has become a wild ride of daily uncertainties. Her neurologist reassured her that this emotional and cognitive commotion would ease as she resumed familiar activities.

The fiction of her stroke seemed true enough; at least it credibly explained the effects of her brain trauma. It also conveniently airbrushes out the scenes of Matt and Jenny arguing over her insistence that they wear helmets on the bike.

"Come on, Matt, get the helmets before we ride. Please."

But Matt, seized with adrenalin, ignored her.

Worrying that she was too risk-averse for him, Jenny did what she always did, and caved into his charms. So, they mounted the bike sans helmets. Could she ever forgive herself?

Matt had a charisma that drew even foes into his aura. He would lock his green eyes onto yours and offer a reassuring handshake, his two hands cupping your hand with tenderness. Warm touch was important to Matt, as was treating his patients like close neighbors. Entering the clinic with a grin across his rugged face, dressed in his lab coat and sneakers, he broke the ice, greeting patients by name, asking about their families and jobs, before he addressed their clinical concerns. Matt's patients quickly learned that he delivered on his promise to partner with them on their medical journey. He was only an email or a cellphone call away.

The graveside service of 38-year-old Dr. Matt Cortez drew dozens of fellow physicians. As the coffin was lowered, Jenny spotted several of Matt's patients. She winced at the irony of Matt predeceasing many of the oncology patients he had guided into recovery.

Matt's expertise and winning manner earned him professional recognition. But there was this anomaly.

Matt's rebelliousness could work for him and against him.

When they first dated, Jenny was impressed with Matt's reverence for life and his dedication to medicine, but she grew perplexed when these values appeared at odds with his reckless thirst for adventure. During a canoe trip in Wisconsin, Matt refused to heed warnings about the river's rapids. His disregard got them stranded and in need of rescue; the debacle left Jenny humiliated. It also bothered Matt. "I messed up, Jen. No excuses." Jenny forgave him and eventually they both shrugged off the event.

In the first months after the crash, she was convinced Matt would rally to resume his work in oncology and their plans to marry. Today, returning to work, she decides it's time to let go and to rise from the mud, like a lotus flower opening its petals to new possibilities. *No mud, no flower.*

She reminds herself that Matt will never return to his beloved patients. She will never ice skate arm-in-arm with him again or dance the tango with a rose between her teeth in front of their fireplace. They will never again roar the BMW motorcycle through the open roads of the Rockies. Her gut convulses with grief.

While psychotherapy has helped to ease her survivor guilt and to refocus her anger on overcoming the obstacles to an independent lifestyle, Matt remains stitched beneath her skin.

The conductor's keys jangle. Tickets are flashed and punched. Red Backpack, eager to talk more, leans closer, his face tightens. *What's up with this guy?*

"Is that a Harley-Davidson sticker? How fast does this thing go?"

Once she re-entered the community as a scooter user, she slapped a Harley sticker on the Amigo to defuse the stigma of using a wheelchair. Despite the trauma, she preferred to be viewed as the passionate motorcyclist she had been, rather than the pathetic nobody she felt reduced to by her brain trauma. Plus, had Matt recovered, he would have loved the logo. The Harley sticker sparked scores of enthusiastic inquiries from strangers, a relief from the glances of pity that many tossed her way, if they dared to look at her.

Jenny counters Red Backpack's curiosity with a stock response.

"Yep, it's a Harley sticker. No, Harley-Davidson does not make mobility scooters. I keep it on 'turtle,' the slowest speed, because I don't want to mow anyone down. Not to mention tip over and end up, you know, *more disabled*." She tries to air-quote "more disabled," but with an impaired left hand only the fingers of her right-hand flash the air.

"These scooters are not designed for speed." Jenny's explanation is punctuated with a flirty giggle. *Where in the hell did that come from?* She hasn't giggled in ages. These days she never knows what next will blurt from her mouth. Her eyes laugh and quell the tension.

Jenny shifts her gaze to the grime-streaked window reflecting distorted images. She sees them as balding bobbleheads bouncing in rhythm to the vibrations on the train.

Her companion sighs. His eyes narrow and his voice softens. "I'm on my way to the University of Chicago Hospital. Getting treated for prostate cancer."

She wonders if this is a confession he's been craving to reveal. She's become used to strangers disclosing their maladies to her. The train screeches on.

"Oh, I'm so sorry."

Red Backpack blinks. "Thanks. The cancer's taking its toll. My days trading cattle futures at the Merc are finished. I'm moving to Kenosha so my sister can take care of me."

"U of C is superb. I'm sure you'll do well there." She feels his sorrow. The weight of it ignites a chain of spasms down her affected leg. Rat-a-tat-tat. Jenny's Oxford rattles on the base of the Amigo. *Get a grip, Jen.*

Jenny strokes her Cashmink scarf and her mind fills with a picture of Matt crushed beneath his motorcycle, lying beside her. Matt's hollowed eye sockets haunt her.

The train whistles. A warm current swishes between Jenny and her companion. Matt is suddenly upon them. He appears smiling, wearing his lab coat and sneakers, with a stethoscope slung around his neck. She watches Matt reach out to cup Red Backpack's hand with tender reassurance.

Jenny massages the right side of her head. *Damn brain injury.* As the hallucination fades, she feels tugged toward the commuter by an invisible cord.

She inches her scooter into the Musk, touches his sleeve and whispers, "I understand more than you know."

"Of course." His slender fingers yank a water bottle out from his bulging pack; he tosses his head back and takes a swig as if he's downing a shot of scotch to kill the pain. The overhead speakers boom, "Ogilvie Station. Downtown Chicago next." Darkness envelops them as they tunnel into their destination.

Commuters shoot from their seats, sloshing past her in galoshes, boots, and loafers. She ducks her head away from their colossal backpacks and averts her eyes, to notice that the black high-tops remain planted along the red pack on the floor beside her.

When the pathway toward the interior doors empties, she angles her Amigo to exit. With sudden urgency, Red Backpack leaps from his seat to follow her.

One black strap of his pack is off his shoulder. His face has relaxed, eyes cleared.

After they alight the train, he taps her scooter. "Meeting you was the highlight of my week. You're such an inspiration, overcoming your stroke and all."

Her eyes light iridescent. "Thanks, but don't call me 'inspirational.' Think of me as 'Biker Gal!'"

He beams, flips thumbs up. "You got it, Motorcycle Momma."

She giggles (again).

Jenny can almost taste the lingering Musk cologne that mixes with the locomotive fumes as she hears him shout, "Later."

She tightens her scarf, dons the matching hat, cranks her speed up from "turtle" to "rabbit" and roars her Harley into the forest of thermal wear.

JUDY PANKO REIS

Judy has published numerous papers and book chapters addressing healthcare disparities affecting people with disabilities. Her essay, "Under the Volcano," was published in *Shambhala Sun* magazine in 2015. Her 2019 poem, "Chicago's Heaven Lost," was published in National Louis University's LLI literary magazine, *The Review*, and awarded first prize for poetry.

A New Life

by Susan Van Dusen

From the time I could sit on the back of his motor scooter, Papaji, my father, had bumped through overgrown paths in the jungles of India to visit priests to ask just one question, "Will my daughter Leelah live in America?"

That was his dream, and it became my dream, too. "You will not have 10 children and squat at a stove, cooking and cleaning every day," he insisted. "You will go to America and be something great."

As a teenager, every time a gentleman walked into my father's watch store, he would ask, "Sir, do you have perhaps a young son studying in America? I have a beautiful daughter who would be a good wife if you are interested."

And so it was that one day a man told my father that his son was returning to India to choose a wife. Uproar reigned in our little house. My mother bought new dishes and recovered our floor pillows. The young man's family came, sat around my father's huge bed, and talked and ate for hours. I was nervous serving water and refreshments. Any small mishap could cause the family to look upon me with disfavor. I had never met Satish before. Later we took a quick walk in the garden. He told me, "What you see is what I am, nothing more, nothing less." He was pleasant to look at—slicked-back brown hair, a straight, serious mouth, thick black spectacles. But would he be my prince?

How could I know?

Satish did not sweep me off my feet. He did not ask me about my favorite movies or books, or tell me I was pretty. Instead, he peered at me and, with a nod, said, "I think you will make a good wife. Do you think I will make a good husband for you?"

"Yes," I said, staring shyly at the ground. But to myself I said, *At least we will finally be in America!*

153

After two days my family heard nothing.

"He is shopping for brides elsewhere," my Auntie said. She assured me, however, that I would be his choice. "He is in a hurry," she said. "He needs to be married and packed for America in two weeks to begin a new job in electrical engineering. You are young, pliable. Yes," she nodded with conviction, "you will be his bride."

On the third day he proposed. We had little chance to get to know each other. "Plenty of time for that later," Auntie laughed.

I canceled my studies. We frantically packed; hundreds of people came to wish us well at a tumultuous wedding and departure planned in just 10 days. Auntie wouldn't even let me pack my beloved sitar.

"Frivolous girl," she laughed. "There will be little time for such music in America."

"But Auntie, my sitar is part of my heart," I pleaded.

"Girl," she shook my shoulders, "your heart is now Satish's. Get used to it."

The matter was closed.

Finally, there we were, Satish and I, husband and wife, sitting together on an airplane, miles up in the sky.

"Look out the window, Satish. I can touch the sun. It is so small, I can almost put it in my pocket," I laughed. It was 1978, and I was just nineteen. Flying from Mumbai to Chicago. My eyes were glued to the window, watching the gentle blue silk ocean billowing out forever. Was it true that the streets of my new country were really paved in gold as my friends told me? Imagine, I squeezed my new husband's hand with excitement; anything can happen in America.

Satish smiled at me the way one would smile at a small child, and continued reading. If only I was as interesting as the shiny pages of his airline magazine.

Upon our arrival, we moved into an apartment in Chicago's Hyde Park. I remember clutching my little cardboard suitcase, entering our tall, yellow-brick high-rise with an elevator, just a few blocks from Lake Michigan. With my head pulled back, I could scarcely see the 21st floor. How lucky these people were to be living in the sky, waking up in the morning surrounded by clouds.

Satish unlocked our door and guided me through the apartment. By that time, I was so exhausted from the trip and the realization that I had given up all that I had known—my beloved Papaji, my extended family, my lovely room with peach-colored walls, my education—for a completely empty apartment. Not a pot nor a spoon, no bedding, no soap. I was overwhelmed. A wife expects to enter a home with everything she needs in place. Here, we had nothing. What could an Indian woman say to her new husband? We were expected to respect and serve our new mate, not whine like a disappointed child.

"There was no time," he explained with a guilty shrug. "But I promise, I will make it up to you tomorrow. You will see."

I took a deep breath, and smiled shyly at Satish. "This is, indeed, a palace," I murmured.

Night had fallen. We stood together in the darkness. The moon was a blur behind ragged gray clouds. Just like my life.

"Come." Satish led me to our bedroom. "We will have an adventure…," and we slept upon our coats, wearing layers of clothes to keep out the fall chill.

I awoke feeling stiff. Our mattresses in India were not so soft, but they were far more comfortable than our bedroom's black, speckled linoleum floor. We had a morning tea in a small restaurant near our building. Pah! I almost spit it out on the sticky tabletop. I told Satish that it tasted like dirty well water. He laughed and promised to buy me pots and milk and spices that very day so I could make a proper tea.

"I am so sorry," he apologized again. We both understood that his "adventure" was like a leaking balloon. He announced, "We will go to a store such as you have never seen, and buy everything you will need to make a good home."

True to his word, we filled two shopping carts, and I could have continued forever, but Satish cautioned that we couldn't carry more home. After dragging our bags from a taxicab, up the elevator and down the hall to number 704, Satish and I fell into our apartment giddy with delight.

Is this the way it's going to be? I laughed to myself. A life of shiny new brass and metal pots in the cabinets, the little circular spice holder with indentations for our condiments and sacks of yellow lentils and brown rice? There was even a white porcelain four-burner stove that came up over my waist. Satish showed me we could simply start it by turning one knob. To cook standing up was such a luxury, I forgot I did not yet know how to prepare a single American dish.

I am an Indian wife. I have my own apartment, a treasure trove full of wonderful things to show off to any mother-in-law who would inspect my kitchen.

Then it struck me again. No mother-in-law would be inspecting my kitchen any time soon. No friends would be sitting on my colorful floor pillows. I would not be able to finish my education until I learned enough English. That could take years, I sobbed gently. I felt hopeless and alone, even though I had Satish.

Soon after, a notice with my name on it said there was something for me at the post office. I went while Satish was at work. It was a very well-wrapped box some five feet long. My heart soared. I began to laugh and cry at the same moment. Papaji had sent my sitar. I hugged it as I would a baby, then decided to hide it under our big bed. I was not so sure Satish would be pleased at a surprise like this.

One evening, some weeks after our arrival, there was a knock on the door. An Indian couple who lived above us had noticed Satish and me around the building. In those days it was rare to see people from the homeland living nearby.

"Have you eaten yet?" asked Neelu, a plump woman with a long, dark braid down her back and a ready smile. We had not. Within minutes, we were upstairs in Neelu's apartment with her husband, Ravi, and their infant daughter, Raina, sitting on gossamer-filled floor pillows, eating a delicious meal with our fingers. Both spoke our native language of Gujarati. Neelu was my age, homebound with an infant and pregnant with a second. We connected immediately, and I had my first friend in America.

"What do you want to be?" I asked as Neelu and I cooked dinner in her kitchen a few months later. She looked at me the way one regards a crazy person.

"I want to be a mother; care for my children; keep a clean house. It is our way," she said.

"Wouldn't you like to have a profession? Be a dentist or a nurse?" I asked.

"This is all I require," Neelu said. "Ravi will take care of the rest. To wish for anything more will lead to an imbalance of our lives. Our gods say the woman is the caretaker; the man is the provider. That is the way to a good and peaceful life."

I lowered my head and stirred our stew. I did not want to tell her that I had a different plan.

Sometimes, when Satish was away at work, I would gaze in the big mirror above the dresser across from our bed. Who is that olive-skinned beauty? The woman with long, shiny black hair framing her face, wearing a purple turtleneck sweater over brown slacks that clung like a skin to her curvy hips? Satish liked me being an American housewife, wearing American clothes. I did, too.

I would sit on our bed and imagine myself as so many different things. A doctor, a dental assistant, a teacher. Other times, if I was feeling sad and especially alone, I would take my sitar from under our bed and play ragas on my beautiful instrument. The long, Indian sitar had a sweetness, a fullness, that could not be found in a guitar. The bass had a rumbly, earthy sound; the soprano, played by fingers swiftly going up and down the scale, breathed life back to me from my Indian home.

I would sigh, then put on my gray wool coat and brave the cutting lake wind to walk to the market for a gallon of milk and two cans of chickpeas. I wanted to be more than a woman who kept house for her husband. In fact, I went to the local church and learned English as diligently as I could. It was so difficult. Satish pushed me to study even harder. He was so disappointed that I could not yet take over a store.

"A store?" I asked.

"Leelah," he explained, as we stood like soldiers by the edge of our bed, "you must continue going to English class and learn how to speak well. We will save our money, then we will purchase a candy store or a little grocery that you will run while I keep my job. With our savings, we will buy an apartment building or two. You will see, that is the way to succeed in America."

The arrogance of that man. He had decided that I would willingly pass my time selling lentils to strangers. My fingers cut into my palms; my head grew hot.

I remembered the beginning of our relationship when he said, "What you see is who I am. No more, no less." I was discovering that I wanted more, and somehow I would find it.

One rainy day, Neelu and Raina came over. I was sitting on the living room floor, playing the sitar.

"Leelah, I did not know that you played so beautifully." She and her daughter were enraptured, as tunes from our youth—sometimes melancholy, sometimes joyous—softly rose from the sitar. Raina fell asleep, but Neelu begged me to continue. Tears fell from her eyes.

"Leelah, you have a gift," she said. "You should play for others who would love to hear the songs of home." Darkness came. Rain lashed at the window. Neelu carried Raina upstairs to cook dinner. I continued playing, feeling free and at peace. Satish came home from work and turned on the living room light.

"What is this?" He demanded, sniffing the air. "Where is dinner?"

I did not hear him. It was as though I was on a boat floating far off on a placid lake on a summer day.

"Leelah," he yelled, "what is going on with you? Stop playing that thing,"

I looked up at him, surprised to be so rudely brought back into our world.

"Why are you playing that when it's time for dinner? I have found a small grocery store that I wanted to show you after dinner. We can buy it for a good price."

"You did this without telling me?" Anger erupted inside of me.

"I did it for us. You will run it during the day while I work. Then we'll take those savings and buy an apartment building. That is how we will make our fortune in America."

He said it so matter-of-fact. I remembered hearing this earlier, but it was his dream before. Now it was real. Finally, I spoke my truth.

"I will not work in your store," I said, quietly. "I will improve my English, then choose a profession. You cannot make decisions for my life, Husband."

He stared at me as though I was a mad goat.

"Spoiled woman," he hissed. "You are my wife. You do what I say. That is how it is done in India."

"But, Satish, we are in America now. We can do what we wish here."

Neck muscles throbbing, teeth grinding, fists clenched, red-faced, he marched toward me. I was afraid to move. As he reached down to grab me by the hair, I heard a crack. He had stomped on the bowl of my sitar and smashed it to bits.

Neither of us said a word. I was shocked. My heart had been crushed. Satish fell to the floor beside me.

"I'm sorry. I'm so sorry. I'm so very sorry, Leelah," he mumbled.

I rose, gathered up the pieces of my sitar, lay them in the bedroom closet, closed the door, and ran up to Neelu's. I wept for the loss of my ties to India, for the loss of my father, and for the loss of my dreams. I would not be a shop-keeper selling chickpeas. I would be more than that.

Neelu couldn't help. "This is the way it is," she said simply. "The men make the decisions; the women follow them."

I was beyond consolation.

I returned to our apartment and prepared for bed. Satish was already in our big bed. I huddled on my old sleeping mat by the side of our bed.

"Come here," Satish said.

I did not move. He wanted to make love, to apologize. I could not bear the thought of his hands on my body.

I did not speak to him the next day or the next. Instead, I went to my English classes, then looked up the addresses of music schools and music stores that might sell sitars.

I gathered up my grocery money and took a Yellow cab to Chicago's Uptown area, where I entered a dark hole of a shop. The Indian store owner listened to me tune and play an ancient sitar that was hidden in a dusty corner. Occasionally he kept time with his arthritic fingers. The instrument sang in my hands as my fingers glided up and down the strings. My heart began to heal.

"You have a gift," the man said. But when he told me how much it would cost, I began to cry, knowing that I didn't have the money to pay for such a thing.

"I'll make you a deal," he said. "This instrument has been here for a long time. Very few people are interested in learning to play one. But, we frequently have concerts here. People come to hear students and teachers play. If you perform with them, you can take your share of the ticket money and pay me back." He sighed. "It will take a long time. Sometimes I make strange decisions." He seemed to be talking to himself. "But in this case, I think the gods will bless my choice."

Back home, I invited Neelu to hear the new sitar. "We belong to an Indian social group," she said. "I'm certain they would pay to hear ragas from the old country."

Against my better instincts, I showed it to Satish. He did not ask where I got it, and he listened to my thoughts of becoming a professional sitar player. I also promised him that if my idea didn't work within two years, we could buy a little store. To my surprise, he agreed, and we began speaking again, really talking, about more than the weather.

A week later, the store owner called. His students and teachers were performing and he wanted me to play, too. I agreed. Without any argument, a shamefaced Satish helped me fit the large instrument into our sedan. The night of the concert, more than a hundred people squashed into a small basement, like betel nuts in a paper bag. Would I fail? Would they laugh at me? I began to play a simple raga that I had learned as a child. The rhythm picked up and suddenly I felt as though my fingers were flying through the air from Mumbai to America. It seemed like every instrument in the world was singing through me. When I stopped playing, there was a brief silence. Then the crowd stood, shouting and clapping for more. I felt like a queen.

On the way home, my husband parked the car in front of our apartment and sat facing ahead. I saw from the streetlamp that tears were falling from his eyes.

"Satish, what is wrong?" I asked.

"Leelah, I am so sorry I broke your sitar, but I was so frustrated. I was always pushing to become successful in America. I forgot what success is." He turned to me and took my hand.

"Tonight I saw you for the first time. Your music made you happy, joyous. That is who I want for my wife. Tomorrow I will tell the store owner we are not interested. Somehow, we will make our own way in America together."

My eyes were misty, too. There are many ways to gain riches in America. Not all roads are paved with gold.

SUSAN VAN DUSEN

Susan is an award-winning writer of editorials and magazine articles. She is the author of three children's books on the history of Skokie, and *The Synagogue: A Home for the Jewish People*. She has launched a series of cozy mysteries about crimes solved by the mayor's wife and a Rabbi through the wisdom of Jewish tradition.

Out of Cambodia

by Joyce Burns Zeiss

very stalk of rice Lim Thong slices is a Khmer Rouge guard. The energy to hate still lies within him. Bright and broiling, the January sun beats down on his aching body, a walking skeleton covered only by a long-sleeved black shirt and tattered shorts. The muddy water sloshes beneath his feet and sharp sickles whoosh in the air as he and the other slave laborers cut down the ripened stalks.

Lim peers up from the rice paddy. The Khmer guards have disappeared. Every day for four long years, Lim and his family have been forced to work in these fields in Cambodia. Every day the young guards in their black uniforms and checkered kramas, AK-47s slung on their shoulders, hover over the workers; anyone daring to stop and rest is beaten or shot.

Since 5 o'clock in the morning, Lim's been at work with only a small bowl of watery rice in his stomach. He resists the urge to sneak some of the rice into his pocket: workers have been executed for stealing. With luck, he might catch a rat, or a bug. The coconut and mango trees mock him with their abundance of forbidden fruit.

Medicine does not exist. When Ty, his youngest, came down with a raging fever, all Lim could do was pray to Buddha. The sight of his wife, Suy Chuon, cradling Ty in her arms as he hung near death made Lim want to scream until even the moon could hear him. He tries not to think about their life in Phnom Penh—before the city was evacuated, before they were forced to leave everything, before the three-day march into the countryside—because thinking brings memories and memories bring pain.

Lim whispers to the stooped figure next to him. "Where are the guards?"

"The Vietnamese have invaded. The Khmer Rouge are on the run."

"Are you sure?" Lim puts down his scythe and scans the yellow-green field.

"I heard the guards talking." The man wipes his brow.

Lim continues to cut the stalks, but his hand shakes. His heart teeters on the edge of hope and then withdraws.

161

That night his family packs their few belongings; a bowl, a small cooking pot, and a thin blanket, and begins the long walk to Thailand, reportedly a safe refuge. Suy Chuon's face is pinched with fear. Peng, his oldest son at 18, carries seven-year-old Ty, his youngest. Lim had eked enough out of his earnings to send Peng to Chinese school with the hope of a better life. Kang, 16, with his quick laugh and soft heart, helped Lim in his noodle shop. The girls—serious Muoy, 14; outspoken Ny, 12; and shy Ah, 10—hold hands as they prepare to leave.

They meet with a group of other frightened families in the twilight of evening and together they flee the emerald paddies and the stilted grass huts where so many died.

When the first rays of light filter through the forest, they rest; they must hide from the retreating Khmer Rouge—and the advancing Vietnamese. At night, Lim leads his family down the rutted road.

This is not the first time he's fled for his life. As a boy of 15, he saw his parents die when the Japanese bombed Shanghai. He had run to Vietnam and then to Cambodia, where he married and started a family. War has followed him like a stalking leopard.

When the escaping families reach the border between Cambodia and Thailand, the Thai soldiers demand bribes. Lim clenches his gold-filled cigarette between his teeth and gives the guards a blank stare. Suy Chuon hides behind him, a gold bracelet sewn in the hem of her blouse.

"We have nothing to give you," Lim says. *Please, let us pass*, he prays.

The guards search them and take their cooking pot, bowl, and blanket. Lim's heart quivers. *Don't take the cigarette*, he prays. The soldiers motion them on. They demand a bribe of the next group and drag one of the men off the road and into the forest. Lim hears a pop. The soldiers return, but not the man. Lim's first instinct is to run, but petrified the soldiers will turn their guns on his family, he motions the children to simply walk faster.

After five days they arrive at the Thai refugee camp, where they are allotted a small area in a huge plastic-sheet tent teeming with other families. They lay a large cloth on the muddy ground to stake out their territory. Food and water are scarce. No hospital.

All night long cries echo across the camp as Thai soldiers rape and rob the refugees. A young girl is dragged from their tent, her screams ripping the dark fabric of the night. Lim lies down, but stays awake, watching, guarding his family.

The next day Ny and Muoy slip out of their barbed wire prison and beg for food from a kind woman at the local market. They manage to sneak back in the camp, unnoticed, by attaching themselves to another refugee family.

Every day more and more emaciated refugees spill into the camp. Every day, more and more refugees die from hunger and disease.

In August buses line up outside the gates and the Lims are among the many ordered to leave.

"Where are we going?" Suy Chuon cries.

"To another camp," Lim replies, repeating a rumor he's heard circulating through their tent. "Too many of us here."

The buses, loaded with apprehensive men, women, and children, drive all day to the border area between Thailand and Cambodia and abandon them in the forest.

Lim gathers his family around. They have only a few handfuls of rice left.

"What will we do when the food runs out?" Suy Chuon asks, clutching Ty.

A day later when the food is gone, Peng forages for berries and plants in the forest with Kang, Muoy, and Ny. Lim feels himself getting weaker and weaker. Ty sits on his mother's lap and closes his eyes. Ah lies in the shade of a tree and whimpers.

"We'll have to go down the mountain to that village we passed. Try to buy some rice." Lim tries to sound hopeful.

Suy Chuon shakes her head. "Too dangerous."

"We'll be careful," Peng says.

The next morning Lim, Peng, and Kang leave. The sun is searing overhead by the time they reach the outskirts of the village. With the grains of gold from Lim's cigarette, they buy one large bag of rice and three bowls of soup at the local market. After devouring the soup, Peng shoulders the heavy bag. Lim pictures the excitement on his family's faces when they see the rice he and his sons have brought.

"It won't be long now." Lim, strengthened by a full stomach, is hopeful again. A black hawk circles overhead and caws. Peng and Kang take turns carrying the rice as they struggle back up the mountain, their bodies soaked with sweat. Kang leads. Peng follows with the bag slung across his chest. Lim is last. The sun slips nearer to the horizon as the day wanes. They are almost up the mountain. Suddenly the ground explodes. A rain of earth, metal and rice fills the air. Kang dissolves into a spray of blood. Peng falls. The smell of burnt flesh and gasoline sears Lim's lungs. Fragments of metal shrapnel pierce his hands. He winces.

Kang, his leg a bloody stump, moans. Peng lies prone on the ground, saved by the bag of rice, now destroyed.

Lim calls to Kang. He wants to go to him, to press leaves on his leg to stop the bleeding, but he's afraid of another landmine. Kang's moaning ceases and his lifeless body lies in a pool of blood. This wasn't supposed to happen. Lim says a brief prayer. *Goodbye, my son.* He stares at Peng, fearful that he, too, might die.

Another half mile and they would have been back in the forest with their family. Has anyone heard the explosion? Lim wets his lips and tries to call for help, but his parched mouth produces only a dry croak. Above, the black hawk circles. What will happen to his family if they don't return?

"Peng, can you hear me?" Lim leans down and feels Peng's pulse, strong and steady.

Peng cracks his eyes open and gasps, "What happened?"

He groans and pulls himself to a sitting position and reaches for his bloodied legs. When he sees Kang's body, his eyes well up with tears. Lim touches his shoulder.

"Father," a voice calls. Muoy appears. "We heard the explosion." Her face fills with fear.

Lim points to Kang and Peng in silence. Muoy starts to weep.

"Go back. Leave us before you get hurt."

Muoy stays. "I will die with you."

"Can you move?" she asks Peng.

Peng nods and pulls himself along the path, crawling. Together Lim and Muoy help Peng inch back through the forest. Muoy steps gingerly, throwing rocks ahead to try to detonate any mines. Lim coughs and gasps for air in the stifling heat. With each step, he prays to Buddha.

Ny glimpses them first as they emerge through the trees. She cries when she sees Peng's wounds and her father's face. "Where's Kang?"

"Killed by a mine," Lim answers softly. Suy Chuon starts to wail, and soon they all sob, huddled around Lim and Peng.

Suy Chuon washes Peng's wounds. Ny goes over to the stream to scrub the blood from his pants. Tears run down her face as she dips the cloth in the cold water. Lim can't look at his family. No rice. Kang dead. Soon they will die too.

Ty wails all night from hunger. Suy Chuon gives him a piece of tree bark to chew on. Peng lies sprawled on the forest floor, his face wrenched with pain. The girls, Muoy, Ah, and Ny, huddle together like a pile of puppies, whimpering in their sleep. Lim leans against a towering phdiek tree, its evergreen branches providing scant shelter, and stares into the darkness.

The next morning the hum of an engine rings through the trees. Lim stands up and stumbles to the road, where a Red Cross truck squeals to a halt. Two men climb out. A camera hangs around the neck of the first one, a tall, freckled man with the reddest beard and the bluest eyes Lim's ever seen. The driver, a head shorter, his eyes as black as his hair, looks Cambodian. Lim shades his eyes from the sun and stares in disbelief. He must be delirious from hunger.

The Cambodian speaks to him. The Red Cross has come to rescue them and all the other refugees abandoned in the forest with them. Through the translator, the man with the camera tells him he is from a newspaper in the United States called *The New York Times*. He will take their pictures and promises the world will hear their story. Then the two men haul out large bags of rice as more refugees come running from the forest.

The next day buses come to carry Lim's family and the other refugees to Bangkok. He and Peng travel to the hospital, where a doctor treats their wounds. Lim can't stop coughing. He takes off his shirt and the doctor moves his stethoscope around on his chest, listening. Then a picture is taken of his lungs. The doctor studies the X-ray and shakes his head. The nurse brings a cup in for him to spit in. He takes a deep breath, inhales, then exhales. Then inhales again and coughs hard. A mass of green phlegm lands in the cup. The doctor tells him to return in a day. When he does, the doctor's face is somber. Tuberculosis. Lim chokes a sob and his face withers. Is he going to die? No, the doctor assures him. They have medicine to treat him.

When Peng is well enough to travel, Lim's family will go to the United States without him. He will follow when he is not contagious. They refuse to leave him alone. One of the family will stay with him. Peng volunteers, but Lim shakes his head. Suy Chuon and the children need him. With Kang gone, Muoy is the next oldest.

"I'll stay." Muoy takes her father's hand.

"Go, go," he pleads.

She looks up at him, with love and loyalty, and refuses.

"Will we be forced to work in the rice fields in our new land?" Suy Chuon asks. Her small shoulders sag with weariness and fear. "I don't want to go without you."

He pulls her close, while the children cry and hug him.

Tears pool in Ny's dark brown eyes. "We need our father."

"I'll come soon, I promise." Lim pastes a smile on his face.

A week later his family leaves for the Bangkok airport, turning to wave. He and Muoy wave back. The family boards a big yellow bus that shrinks into a tiny speck as it disappears down the road. The pain inside him explodes like a grenade.

— JOYCE BURNS ZEISS ——————————————

Joyce is a retired teacher whose experiences resettling a Cambodian refugee family in 1979 and her trips to work in African refugee camps fueled her interest in the plight of the refugee. Her novel, *Out of the Dragon's Mouth*, is based on the true-life experiences of a Vietnamese boat person.

Jamie

by Melissa Ann Weidner

If there is one thing I dislike more than Chicago morning traffic, it's Chicago morning traffic in a snowstorm. With each sliding stop and tire-spinning start, my emotions churn.

What if Donald doesn't want the baby? What about Caroline? Could I still have the baby if Donald doesn't want it? Think positive, Paige. He'll be thrilled—or not.

I pull into the medical office parking garage and make my way to my ninth-floor desk. Being a receptionist for the urology department wasn't the X-ray technician job I wanted and had trained for, but after searching for months, this was the only decent job I was offered. At least the job comes with insurance, which will cover the childbirth.

Briefly, I place my hand on my belly. *I wonder if you will be a boy or a girl. Perhaps I'll name you Jamie.* My favorite baby doll growing up was named Jamie. And it happens to be unisex. In my mind's eye I see a yellow-themed nursery.

How will I tell Donald? My memory fades back to the first time we met at that café; the first day I met them both—Donald and Caroline.

My breath shortened as I entered the seventh-floor gynecology office for my X-ray technician interview. I took a few deep breaths to calm myself and prayed the anxiety—and sweat—didn't show through my lavender power suit.

The chipper receptionist—Caroline—put me at ease, with her kind eyes and innocent, child-like demeanor. We chatted casually after she checked me in for the interview. I asked her about the job and office environment.

"Well, between us girls," she told me, "this office is run by a mostly male staff. Odd, isn't it? An OB/Gyne department run by men! As if they innately understood anything about females!"

We had a good laugh. I thanked her and took a seat in the waiting area. A couple minutes later, my world changed.

Donald entered the office. His raven hair was slicked back and he wore a suave blue suit that made him appear taller than he was. He flashed Caroline a killer smile and told her he was there for his interview.

I combed my fingers through my short frizzy hair, aware of how mousy and dull it was compared to Caroline's. She had long, bleach-blond hair with roots as dark as demons' eyes.

She must be as dense as a doornail.

I was taken aback by my willingness to give in to the misogynistic stereotype—especially considering the wonderful conversation I'd had with her just prior, where she had presented herself as sweet, perhaps a tad immature—but not dense.

Caroline wished him luck.

"Thanks, sweet Caroline." He had a soothing voice and the kind of smile that made you trust him.

"Anything for you, Donny," she replied.

Maybe I should dye my hair blond.

I disregarded the thought just as he caught me staring. He studied me for a few seconds.

"Excuse me, but I believe you're in the wrong place—the Miss Universe pageant is elsewhere," he said, taking a seat next to me.

Heat burned along my chest and spread up my neck to my ears.

"I'm definitely not interested in pageants," I replied.

"Well, you don't seem like a patient, either," he said. "Are you here for the job interview?"

My mouth went dry.

"I'm Donald," he said as he extended his hand. His ears might've been a bit too big for his head, but his dazzling blue eyes made up for it. "What's your name, pretty lady?"

"My name's Paige," I said, accepting his handshake. I hoped my sweaty palm didn't disgust him.

Play it cool, Paige.

"So, you here for the interview?" he asked again.

"Sorry. Yes, the X-ray tech job," I replied.

He moistened his lips and leaned in close. "I have a confession, Paige. My interview's also for the X-ray tech position." He pulled out a card from his suit pocket. "Let's exchange phone numbers and whoever gets a job offer first can call to let the other down gently. Or if you just want to chat."

I wanted to do more than chat with him. I pulled out my own card to exchange. How I wished I could feel his hands all over my body and feel his lips pressed against mine. My fantasies were cut short when I was called in for my interview.

"Good luck, Miss Universe," he said.

After my interview I looked around for him. He was nowhere to be seen, so I chatted with Caroline. She asked me how it went.

"It went okay. I was interviewed by a man, of course."

"Of course," she said and handed me her card. "My friend two floors up mentioned a receptionist opening, in case you don't get the job."

From the window view, the world looked like a snow globe. I thanked Caroline and decided to wait out the storm at a nearby cafe.

Donald's card fell out of my coat pocket as I sipped a hot cocoa. My cellphone rang. I glanced at the number on the phone and back at the number on the card. *Could it really be him?*

"I thought today was going to be just another drab day," said Donald when I answered. "And then I met you, Miss Universe. Today is the first day of the rest of my life."

"Not only are you handsome, but charming too," I replied.

"You still in the area?" he asked.

Minutes later, Donald gazed at me from across the cafe. He looked confident and sexy as hell, even from afar. I stood up and took a deep breath while I smoothed my pantsuit. He approached me and before I could say anything, he placed his finger against my lips. He then replaced his finger with his lips.

We've been dating ever since. We still meet at the same cafe on our lunch break. The cafe is relatively quiet today. As lunch break approaches, I grow apprehensive.

Recently, I found out he's been sleeping with Caroline.

I haven't said much to him since I found out. I need to know he wants this baby and I need to know he will stop sleeping with Caroline. A quick lunch break isn't the right time to throw out the pregnancy news, but I can at least start the Caroline conversation. We will be attending a farewell party for one of our co-workers at a local tavern after work. I will tell him about the pregnancy right after.

Before Donald takes his first bite of sandwich I tell him I have something important to discuss. I try to start the difficult discussion, but I stumble over my words and blush.

Be tough, Paige!

My voice is louder than I intend it to be. "Donald, I know you're sleeping with Caroline. It's time you made a decision—Caroline or me."

He puts down his sandwich and looks at me as though I've wounded him. "Where's this coming from, baby? You know I'm crazy about you. I thought we've been happy with the way things have been."

I have a desire to slap him, but opt to point an accusatory finger in his face instead. "*You've* been happy with the way things have been. *I* haven't exactly been aware of how things have been up until now. You better make a decision and you better make it fast. Me or her. End of story."

Instantly, I regret yelling at him.

He grasps my shaky hand. "Okay! Settle down, baby. Of course I choose you. I'll talk to Caroline and let her down gently."

He does love me.

In my toughest voice I press him. He tells me he will break the news to her tonight at the party. I thank him. Filled with renewed hope, I almost blurt out the pregnancy news, but I hold my tongue for later. Our lunch break is drawing to a close.

In truth, I like Caroline. We've gotten closer over these past few months. She's actually the one who recommended the urology receptionist job. If we weren't sleeping with the same man, we could even be best friends. I remind Donald to let her down gently.

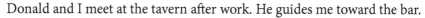

Donald and I meet at the tavern after work. He guides me toward the bar.

"Two whiskey doubles!" he shouts at the bartender. He turns to me as if I am an afterthought, "Oh, crap. Where are my manners, baby? Would you care for one as well?"

I shake my head and order a glass of water. I'm bothered by his increased drinking, and lately, his mood sours with each drink. He downs his first whiskey double before I finish a sip of my water. A moment later, he looks intently toward the tavern entrance. I turn to see what he's staring at.

Caroline is wearing a form-fitting red lace dress with red lace stilettos. I look down at my own sober navy pantsuit and gray flats. I could never pull off wearing those heels—or walk in them, for that matter.

Donald downs his second glass of whiskey. "Alright. Caroline's here. I'm going to talk to her."

"Good luck, baby," I say.

I rub my belly. It's just about time to break the news. *Why am I feeling so afraid?*

Donald takes Caroline by the hand and leads her out of the room and down a staircase.

Keeping my distance, I follow them down the winding staircase. It leads to a basement with empty unlit banquet rooms that appear to be under construction. I catch a glimpse of Donald leading Caroline through an entryway and into one of the small banquet rooms. I take cover behind a post close enough to hear their conversation and poke my head out just enough to see them in the dim light.

"I'm so glad you pulled me away from the party. I've something important to discuss," she says.

"I've something important to discuss too," he replies. "I dropped Paige for you, baby."

What the hell?

Caroline is not pleased. In fact, she looks angry. Ignoring her reaction, he pulls her toward him and tries to kiss her.

She pulls away.

He tries again. Caroline pushes him away again, and shouts, "I'm pregnant!"

That stops him. Clenching his fists he turns away. "You can get an abortion—I'll pay for it."

Caroline places her hands on her hips. "That's how you respond?"

"You want to keep it?" he questions. "No. No. No!"

"Yes. Yes. Yes!" Caroline retorts.

"This isn't a request or discussion," he says in a menacing tone.

Scared and not knowing what to do, I freeze up, but I continue to watch.

Caroline slaps him. "You can't tell me what to do. I wish I could abort you!"

Donald's shoulders shake. He hunches his back and curls his fists tighter. He punches Caroline's belly so hard it knocks the wind out of her. She collapses to the ground.

A sickness sinks into the core of my being. The hands that I had loved to feel all over my body were the same hands that just battered poor Caroline. *Who punches a woman—especially a pregnant woman? What will he do to me when I tell him about Jamie? What should I do?*

I finger my cellphone and the pepper spray in my purse, terrified of what he might do next. I silence my phone and text 911.

Donald hovers over Caroline's crumpled body. "If you breathe a word of this to Paige—or anyone else—so help me, I'll fucking kill you."

Caroline struggles to get up on all fours. He readies his foot to push her down, and I raise the pepper spray.

I don't know where this sudden strength comes from, but I leap into action. I charge him, prepared to kick him in the back.

He hears me coming and spins around. I let him have it with the pepper spray. I spray him and spray him. He flails his arms and I duck to avoid them. I spray him again. His eyes swell shut and he yelps as he falls to the ground, crying like a helpless child.

I put my foot on his chest and threaten him with more pepper spray. "Don't move. Don't even think about it," I warn him, holding the spray inches from his face.

Donald whimpers and acts like he's not listening. I know he can hear me, though, the little prick.

"By the way, *baby*, here's the news I was going to share with you. I'm pregnant too. And you can bet your ass I'm keeping the baby. I'm not keeping you."

"Me too," Caroline chimes in.

"Are you alright?" I ask her, keeping my eyes on Donald. He is a blind, crying, pathetic mess. *What did I ever see in this creep?*

Caroline rises to her feet. "I think so, but I'm worried about the baby," she replies, examining herself for injuries.

Quicker than I thought possible, the police arrive.

Several days later, I invite Caroline to my apartment. We sip hot cocoa and talk about our shared traumatic experience. She tells me how scared and alone she felt right up until my grand entrance. She is surprised how tough we both were—how tough we both *are.*

I confess that I, too, was surprised. "We really are a couple of tough cookies."

"We are a couple of tough cookies who don't need a man!" Caroline declares.

She surprises me again when she gives me a heartfelt hug and says, "This entire situation really could've pinned us as enemies, and I'm so happy it actually brought us closer together, instead. Now we are two best preggo friends!"

"If our babies turn out to be girls," I say, smiling, "I hope they'll turn out like us. And if we have boys, I hope we maintain our strength to ensure they'll never be like Donald."

Caroline takes a sip of her cocoa and says, "He was the devil, wasn't he?"

— MELISSA ANN WEIDNER —————

Melissa is a medically disabled writer on a mission to help others. She published her first short story in the 2019 OCWW book, *A Reason to Be Here,* and is currently working on a book about mental and physical health stigmas. She has served OCWW in many capacities since joining in 2015.

LIFE'S LESSONS

Short stories from long lives

Harry Loved Zola

by Thomas Sundell

Harry should have known by the smell of the perfume, but he was looking at his cell phone and not paying attention. It isn't until stepping into the elevator, the closing doors cutting off his cell's reception, that the too-familiar cloying smell catches his attention. Looking up, he stares into the eyes of his ex-mother-in-law, Carlotta, a grimace of pure contempt on her face.

He looks away, his face mirrored in the elevator door with a nearly identical grimace. Alone in the elevator with this woman whose years of acid complaints about him wore away the happiness he and her daughter enjoyed. Since the divorce he avoids thinking of Zola.

He steps to the opposite corner from her and her constant stench of overripe perfume. God, she must pour the stuff over herself.

The elevator's descent is slower than usual, then it lurches, shudders, stops. They are between floors. The lights flicker and go out; the fan ends its whirring. Damn, what's happening? He presses the emergency button. Nothing. Tries the intercom, nothing. Well, crap.

With an inarticulate bark of rage, Carlotta shoves by him, trying button and intercom as well, obviously not trusting that he's done it properly. The results are the same; nothing.

Though he knows it's futile, he tries calling out on his cell phone, hoping that the cut-off was only a glitch. No signal.

That their lawyers' offices are in the same building is the only reason they must now be occupying this small space together. He here to amend his will. She…who knows? Suing someone? Making someone else's life miserable.

An old building with cheap lawyers—and a decrepit elevator.

In the darkness he can feel Carlotta's presence like a seething malevolence. Carlotta, who forced her Zola to divorce him and to press charges for wife-beating.

It's true he hit Zola. Twice. Slapped her, actually.

He regrets it. Would like to be able to take it back. Would like that his wife never had an affair with Makarios, who owns the convenience store on the first floor of their former apartment building. But life doesn't work in reverse.

Stupid really, to have married a girl twenty-two years younger. To have a mother-in-law his age. A mother-in-law who opposed the whole thing from before the wedding bells.

Carlotta is trying her cell phone. Says, "Shit," with no better luck than he'd had.

"No signal," he says to her.

In the light of her phone, he sees her glare. She barks, "Is the shaft lined with lead?"

He shrugs, saying, "Someone will notice that the elevator isn't functioning." She snorts, but adds, "Can't be soon enough."

Surprised that they're talking, given how much he dislikes Carlotta. She calling Zola frequently, badgering her about his supposed faults. Maybe talking is too strong—exchanging words.

This could be a long wait. He sighs, sits down in his corner.

A rumble tells him the neighboring elevator is still working. Why didn't he take that elevator? He stepped in about six o'clock. Most of the offices ended their day at five or five-thirty. People vacating quickly on a Friday, ready for the weekend.

Time seems suspended. He tries breathing shallowly. Is it possible to get used to the perfume?

At least fifteen minutes pass, Carlotta asks, "Aren't you going to do anything?"

He stands, raps on the elevator door.

"Hello? Hello?!" he calls. Raps harder. Uses the flat of his hand, then pounds with his fist.

Nothing.

The neighboring elevator goes by again. Carlotta pushes him aside, using the heel of her shoe to hit the elevator door. Hard enough that the heel breaks off. Stiletto heels. Without them, Carlotta is a good two inches shorter.

Zola is short, too. A sweet girl, truly, he thinks. Though maybe as she ages she'll turn into a Carlotta. The thought causes a shudder in Harry.

He's sitting again. Carlotta is cursing. Inventive invective, though he's heard some of the phrases before, applied to him.

The deviling thought of Zola with Makarios. Harry knows he's no Makarios, six foot two, dark curly hair with some gray at the temple, chiseled features and a ready smile.

Whereas Harry is fifty-three, not fat but maybe starting to plump, balding. He considers himself a mensch. Not perfect, but well-meaning. Kind most of the time.

Married to Zola for four years. Though the last nine months shouldn't count given the divorce and court proceedings. Now completed, eight weeks past. He doesn't want to think about these past months despite the presence of his ex-mother-in-law and her overwhelming aroma.

Time grinds its way along, inch by inch. He'd try the breathing exercises his qigong instructor recommends for calm, but it would mean taking in drafts of the perfume. He tries dozing instead.

He's kicked awake by Carlotta's stockinged feet.

"You're snoring," she accuses. "God, you're repulsive."

"Your daughter didn't think so."

"She thought you had money."

He does, actually. Harry clears between $75,000 and $100,000 a year from HMJ Productions. Has three employees. Has a fair amount invested. Not money enough for Zola or, more likely, Carlotta. He remembers well the day he auditioned Zola for a small part in a commercial he was shooting for the local coffee shop chain, though he ended up using a real barista rather than Zola.

Still, there was something about Zola that appealed to him. An innocent manner coupled with a natural sexuality. Not the brightest, but a cheerful girl.

Not so cheerful anymore.

"So is Zola going to marry George Makarios?" he asks.

Carlotta sniffs, which he takes as her way of saying it's none of his business.

Silence stretches between them. Harry feels drowsy again, the elevator becoming warm with the fan shut down. Rouses himself after a time with the thought that maybe there's not enough oxygen in the elevator. To die here with Carlotta would be like a joke, one of the gods laughing.

He touches his phone to see the time, 9:17 at night, three hours or so trapped in here.

From the wheeze of Carlotta's breath he can tell she's asleep now, too.

He settles back down, closes his eyes, though it's dark enough that it hardly matters. Composes himself to sleep.

When he wakes next it's with Carlotta pacing a few steps back and forth on her side of the elevator box. He touches his phone again for the time, just after midnight.

At the brief light from the phone Carlotta exclaims, "This is impossible."

He sighs, "I'm guessing we'll have to wait for morning."

"I can't."

"Not a lot of choice." Not wanting to think of what's urgent for her. He has an empty apartment, no one waiting on him. Tomorrow's different, two meetings scheduled at the office, the first one at nine-thirty, one of his more demanding clients.

He heaves himself to his feet, using his phone as a flashlight, tries the emergency buzzer and the intercom again. Still nothing. Tries to call out on his phone even knowing it's fruitless. Tries 911. Nothing.

Carlotta starts pounding on the elevator door. Strenuously for as much as ten minutes, then subsiding to a steady rap, rap, rap for another ten before desisting.

"When this is over, I'm suing someone," she says. "The building management, the elevator company, the security guard firm, someone. All of them."

"Well, you're in the right building for that," replies Harry. Harry can't imagine the litigation being worthwhile. Just more aggravation.

Silence again, save for their respective breathing. Then Carlotta says, "Zola marrying you made no sense."

He considers, says, "In retrospect, I guess I agree. I never did understand what she saw in me." He adds, "Though you said it was just for the money."

Carlotta doesn't reply at first.

"Not money as such," she says grudgingly. "She thought you'd make her a star. She believed in you. Foolish girl."

"I loved her." Harry unwilling to think that's all Zola wanted.

"Oh, please. You wanted in her panties."

Turning away, Harry doesn't choose to reply.

Minutes are in slow motion; time floating in the still air.

After a while, he says, "I wanted to take care of her."

Carlotta snorts derisively.

Later, Carlotta is up and doing her short pacing. Back and forth, back and forth to the shuffling sound of her feet. "You hit my daughter," she says.

"Yes," he admits. He's never described the actual circumstances, nor has Zola to the best of his knowledge. He'd slapped her hard enough to bruise her, leaving marks on her face.

"Because she slept with George Makarios," says Carlotta. "My ex slept with any number of women."

Harry doesn't need to wonder why. "Actually," he says, "I don't think they slept."

"You know what I mean."

He closes his eyes, the image still vivid, that moment of discovery. "I walked in on them. She was on her knees and he was coming in her mouth."

Carlotta stops pacing. "Why didn't you hit him?"

"I didn't love him," he answers.

Nothing more is said. She paces. He sits.

Near three in the morning, she says, "Damn it. I have to pee."

Harry does, too. Ever more conscious of the pressure. And he is hungry, not having gotten to supper. "Use your corner."

"Not in front of you."

"It's dark, you're not even a blur."

"Turn around," she orders.

He complies. Shortly hears her shifting her clothing, then the sound of splashing. Thinks to himself, thank goodness her perfume is strong. Then, hopes the puddle stays on her side.

Not more than an hour later, he says, "I think it's my turn."

"What?"

"To piss."

She grunts.

"Probably best if I use the same corner."

Her sigh is expressive of her disdainful patience. He finds his way, unzips, and adds to the wet.

Afterward, they are both diagonally across from their improvised privy, shoulder to shoulder, leaning against the elevator wall. Hard to believe they're in this situation, he thinks.

His stomach growls loudly.

More minutes go by. His stomach growls again, louder.

"I have a small bag of trail mix," she says. "Are you allergic to peanuts?"

"No, peanuts are quite acceptable." Is this a truce, wonders Harry?

He hears her rummaging in her purse, an oversize bag. Apparently she finds the trail mix after a bit, for he hears the bag being torn open, with much of it spilling in her purse, some on the floor.

"Where's your hand?" she asks.

He touches her hand with his cupped to receive pieces of trail mix. Four or five pieces fall onto his palm.

"I spilled most of it," she says.

"Thank you." He puts the pieces one at a time in his mouth, chewing slowly to get the maximum effect. Five pieces, as it turns out; a peanut, a raisin, and three smalls clumps of mostly toasted oats.

His stomach still growls.

She yawns loudly. "Excuse me." Yawns again. "I can't remember the last time I was up all night."

Harry can. His wedding night. A bachelor until 49, then Zola.

"We'll survive this." He's thinking not only of the elevator.

"I suppose so," she agrees.

After five in the morning, she says, "No, she's not marrying Makarios."

"Oh?" Thinking, isn't he rich enough for her, owns five stores? Then an instant of elation that Zola's not committed elsewhere.

"I just want her to be happy."

He blurts, "I thought we were happy. I was anyway."

Carlotta sighs, "She was too that first year."

Nothing more gets said. Though Harry feels an uncertain sense of possibility. Zola was happy.

But it's too late, right?

At six a.m., the light and fan come on. Moments later the elevator moves, descends normally. At the first floor, the doors open. Blinking from the sudden light, they step out. Carlotta, holding her shoes and purse, moves quickly, escaping toward the building's doors. He follows more slowly, glad to be free. Neither wants to explain the pissed-upon elevator.

Outside, in the sunlight, Harry stretches, runs a hand over his whiskered face, thinking he's going to get breakfast next. Then he chuckles, thinking of

Carlotta. Will she tell Zola of their night together? Wistful, he hopes Carlotta does tell Zola. Reminds his wife—his ex-wife—of his existence. No longer wanting to block his thoughts of Zola.

THOMAS SUNDELL

Thomas is the author of *A Bloodline of Kings* (Crow Woods Publishing), translated and published in Greece as *Philip of Macedon* (Minoas SA), and nineteen other novels. He writes mornings and sketches most afternoons. His novels, short stories, and fiction can be found at sundellwritings.word-press.com, with postings each Wednesday.

Grand Gestures

by Susan Bearman

"Congratulations again!" Our attentive waiter smiles at the happy couple. "Are we ready for the check?"

The four of us are two-and-a-half hours into a festive dinner. My beautiful sister is now officially engaged to her long-awaited prince, Calvin, and we have just been given the play-by-play of the proposal "event"—complete with iPhone slow-motion replay. Let's just say it involved a Jumbotron and a major Chicago sports team.

Katie is not ready for the night to end.

"What's the most romantic thing you've ever done?" she asks my husband.

"I'm not super romantic," Teddy blushes, looking down at the table and then at me. "Jules knows that."

"That's not true," I disagree, and give him a little wink. Twenty years in, that blush still slays me. Teddy is a good man. Stable. Thoughtful. A bit prosaic, perhaps, but I'm not a fan of drama.

"Tell me," Katie insists, though I'm not sure she's listening, transfixed as she is by her heart-shaped diamond. She's bubbly—both from engagement euphoria and (too much) champagne. Katie has always been a romance addict, but really, at 40, she could tone it down a bit; I'm already getting flashes of bridezilla. And Calvin will go along. Just *look* at him. He worships her. Ridiculous. They're acting like teenagers.

"That's personal, between Ted and me," I say, remembering that long-ago morning, just the two of us cocooned in the fog surrounding the Garden of the Phoenix footbridge in Jackson Park. Teddy was blushing then, too, shy, but his brilliant smile broke through right along with the sun when I said, "Yes."

Katie sighs impatiently and pouts—pouts! It brings me back to the present, and suddenly I'm feeling a tad mischievous. "But I will tell you the *second* most romantic thing that's ever happened to me." Katie leans in, both hands around her champagne glass, her ring and the crystal snatching candlelight

185

and shooting sparks across the table. The guys lean back. Calvin signals for more champagne. He likes bubbly—in his wine *and* his fiancée.

"What did you *do*?" Katie giggles at Teddy and his eyes try to bore a hole through the table. I hope it doesn't work. The candle would probably fall through and set the linens afire. That would cause a scene and Teddy hates the spotlight.

"So, there was this guy…," I begin.

"It wasn't *Teddy*?" Katie gasps, and Teddy's eyes jerk up toward me. Now they are both paying attention.

"I already hate this story," Teddy grumbles, eyes going back to drilling duty. We've never spent a lot of time focusing on exes. What's the point?

This particular story is about a grand gesture from an old flame. We had only been seeing each other a short time when he had to go abroad on business for nearly a month. While there were cellphones back then (I'm not a dinosaur), international calling was expensive, and I didn't expect to hear from him while he was gone. I did want to see him again, and we had sex a couple of nights before he left. Not exactly Fourth-of-July fireworks, but he was pretty cute and quite tall. I liked that. Plus, he wore suits.

He promised to call when he returned. "Don't forget me," he said, and dipped me for a goodbye kiss. I was terrified he would drop me and could barely summon up a decent pucker, let alone a soul-stirring send-off.

But that's not how I'm telling the story now. For now, he's Prince Charming and I'm, well, Cinderella. My sister's princess fetish has been around since she tried on her very first plastic tiara in the dress-up corner at preschool, so I'm laying it on pretty thick for her. And this story *is* romantic…mostly.

The day Peter left (I call him Peter; I do not remember his name), my assistant, May, poked her head into my office. "You got a flower," she said.

"A flower? Singular?" She nodded. "Bring it in. I think I have a vase here somewhere."

"The delivery guy wants you to come get it yourself." Ugh. I was busy. I did not have time for nonsense.

I walked around my desk to May's, just outside my office door. A uniformed cherub (he must have been at least a teenager, but, honestly, he looked 10) was standing there holding a tall, clear cylindrical vase with a single, stunning, variegated tulip. The boy and the vase both held that flower with reverence. It was like nothing I'd ever seen—the offspring of a cancan dancer who had mated with a gay pride flag and given birth to a flouncy, fiery flower of fuchsia, crimson, cadmium, and indigo, licked here and there with lines of lime. It was the size of a human heart. I couldn't take my eyes off of it.

Delivery boy was reciting a history of this pastiche from memory—where it was cultivated, its scientific name, blah, blah, blah. All I really heard was "The Netherlands" and "Rainbow Parrot Tulip." Uninspired, I thought, and my mind set out to rename it: the *Petticoat Tulip* or, perhaps, the *Burlesque Tulip*. Better yet, the *Rosse Buurt Tulip*—for it was surely conceived in Amsterdam's Red Light District.

I only started really listening when the boy stopped lecturing and read Peter's personal note. Gabriel—his name was embroidered on the striped uniform shirt that made him look like a fugitive from a junior barbershop quartet—would become my personal angelic messenger. (I recall the exact words of Peter's note, not because I have a stellar memory, but because I reread it a couple of million times in the days, weeks, even years that followed. It may or may not still be buried in the bottom of my Lane cedar keepsake box. I couldn't say.)

> By the time you get this, I should be at Luchthaven Schiphol, the Amsterdam Airport, where I have a six-hour layover. It's only my first stop and I miss you already. Vergeet me niet— don't forget me.
>
> PJB

He signed his initials; "Peter" is still just an educated guess. The note I remember; the man—not so much. I don't mention this in my current retelling.

The next day, another stem arrived: a divinely fragrant sprig of lavender from the fields around Mont Ventoux in the Luberon ranges of Provence. Or so sang messenger Gabriel. Peter's note was much the same as his first, and again ended with "*Ne m'oublie pas*—don't forget me."

By this point in my tale, Katie's chin rests on her folded hands, propped up by her elbows on the table. She's staring wistfully into the candle flame. I think I hear a sigh as I rev up for the rest of the story.

Each day, Gabriel arrived with a new flower from wherever in the world Peter was at that moment: a bird-of-paradise from South Africa, an Allium

Barbey from Israel, an Orchid Bauhinia from Hong Kong. As the bouquet grew, Gabriel brought an ever-larger vessel to accommodate it. He was a genius at arranging, and stealthily replaced faded blooms with fresh ones. By week three, a growing crowd gathered each day after lunch to hear Gabriel's botanical epistolary. They praised him and he shined in their light.

By the end, the arrangement stood several feet high and just as wide. It would have belonged on an altar in a cathedral, were it not for the staggering, distinctly secular scents and clashing confetti colors. It overwhelmed my office.

"What happened when Peter got back?" Katie asks.

"I thanked him profusely," I say.

"And?"

"And…that's the end."

"That's not an ending. That's a beginning. What happened to Peter?" Katie pouts again, but I'm over it.

Calvin and Teddy fight over the check; Calvin's not fighting hard.

"Our treat," Teddy says. He doesn't say anything in the Lyft home, but he's a quiet man.

Once home, he is less quiet. In fact, I get the impression that he's being a little bangy with doors and drawers.

"Something wrong?" I ask.

"Calvin's a nice guy," he says flatly. "That was some proposal."

"Quite the gesture," I agree, taking off my earrings. I smile as I hang them on the rack in our bedroom. Teddy brought this pair—marcasite—from Montreal. All the glitter for not much of an investment. He never knows what else to get me, so he buys interesting, inexpensive earrings. I have hundreds and love them all.

The closet door slams shut and I jump. "Why did you even marry me?" asks Teddy. He's almost yelling, his palm splayed flat on the back of the closet door.

"What are you talking about?"

"Why aren't you with *Peter*? Mr. Romantic?"

"Oh, God, Teddy, that was two eons ago. I barely remember him."

"You remembered him well enough tonight."

"I don't, actually," I say. "I remember his grand gesture, that's all. The fairy tale was for Katie." I give his chin a brief caress as I slip by him. "I'm going to make some tea."

I flick on the gas fireplace in the den and settle into the sofa, tucking my feet up under me. Teddy converted the fireplace to gas for me shortly after we bought the house. This is my favorite spot in the world. Teddy comes down in his loungewear: flannel drawstring pants and his tatty Michigan sweatshirt. He looks cute. My bear.

"Sit," I say, patting the sofa beside me. "Would you like some tea?"

"No tea," he plops down and crosses his feet on the trunk that serves as our ottoman/coffee table. He's still brooding.

"Let me tell you the rest of the story," I say.

"No," he shakes his head. "That will do me in."

"Trust me." I rub his knee.

"You were pretty dismissive of the guy," Teddy says, accusing. "What he did was really nice. Amazing. Epic, even. Like other guys will hate him forever for that. *I* hate him. How could you not love him?"

Teddy blows a deep breath up toward his forehead, disturbing his hair. He has good hair. A little gray now, but still all there. "Fine. Tell me the rest of the story."

I do. The day Peter got back, he called me sometime early afternoon. I had an evening meeting, and he was wiped out from his trip, so we agreed to meet the next day for dinner.

"I'm going to try to stay awake until at least 8:30," Peter said. "But I'll probably crash soon and wake up at three in the morning."

"Call me if you do," I said. "I won't mind."

The partners were in town and had taken my department out for a dinner meeting. It sounds fun, but it wasn't. It took me a long time to wind down when I got home, and I ended up reading in bed until well after midnight.

At precisely 3:01 a.m., my phone rang.

"Hi," he breathed.

"I've missed you," I whispered, so as not to wake my then-roommate.

"Miss you, too," he sounded hoarse. Or maybe he was just whispering—in response to me, or the late hour, or jet lag.

"Thank you for the flowers," I said. "They're so beautiful."

"You got them," he murmured. "The roses?"

"Yes." I think there was a rose in there somewhere. "You must have spent a fortune, not to mention the time and effort you put into planning. Thank you, truly."

"Glad you like them," he said. "I like *you*. I *love* you."

What? "What?!"

"I love you," he groaned.

Oh, my God. We were nowhere near the "I love you" stage. Were we?

"You do know it's me—Jules—right?" I chuckled nervously.

"Of course it's you. I love you, Jules."

At this point, Teddy interrupts: "I thought this part of the story was supposed to make me feel better."

"It is," I say.

"It's not working." He purses his lips.

So anyway, I said something like, "I guess you can't sleep, huh?"

"You can help me fall asleep. Help me, Jules," he pleaded.

"What did *that* mean?" Teddy asks.

I ignore him, skipping over the phone sex details, and continue with the story.

The next night, Peter picked me up after work and we stayed downtown for dinner. He circled the block three times before he found a spot right in front of the restaurant to park his fancy red sports car. He turned down several available tables, insisting on one by the window. He seemed a bit surly, staring out at his car and only grunting at my attempts at small talk.

I stared past his car to the Heartland Bakery sign across the street—a giant neon bread loaf with a heart in the middle, which flickered nervously. I was a bit uncomfortable about his lack of eye contact and the whole "I love you" thing from the night before, as I hadn't said it back. Maybe that's why he was grumpy.

After the server took our order, Peter suddenly turned away from the window and kind of spit out: "Did you even *get* my flowers?"

"Yes, my God, Peter, yes!" I was mortified that he thought I hadn't been appreciative enough. "They're magnificent. Thank you. Thank you so much!"

He shifted in his chair. "It's just that you didn't even say anything."

"As I said last night, they're gorgeous. Thank you!"

He stared at me. "What do you mean, last night?"

"Well, it was really more like this morning," I demurred. I got it. He was embarrassed about his love confession, trying to backpedal. I let him off the hook. "You were tired when you called. Barely awake."

"Jules, I didn't call you last night."

"Okay, you didn't."

"I didn't," he insisted. "I took an Ambien and was out until noon."

Dinner arrived and we changed the subject, talking about his trip. That seemed to cheer him. We ended up back at my place and he spent the night. He hadn't done that before because he didn't like that I had a roommate.

"Still not making me feel better," Teddy says, worrying the edge of a magazine with his toes.

"Anyway, we fell asleep." I hesitate.

Teddy looks over at me when my pause stretches into a gap. "And?"

Now, I'm embarrassed. "And…at precisely 3:01 a.m., my phone rang…"

The rest of the sentence hangs there, hidden in plain sight, for an eternal instant. Teddy's eyes grow big and I know he knows. I brace myself, but am still not ready for his sudden reaction: he's laughing hysterically.

"Oh, my God, Jules! You had phone sex with a pervy stranger." He's crying/laughing, doubled over. I'm burning with shame.

"You caught on quicker than Peter did," I mutter. This only makes Teddy laugh harder. "So glad *that* makes you feel better." I try to disappear into the corner of the sofa.

"What did Flower Dude do?" Teddy asks, still chortling.

It takes me a minute, but I finally tell myself, fuck it, it was a long time ago. "When the phone rang, I jumped about a mile, horrified because I knew who it was. Or rather, realized that I *didn't* know who it was."

"Aren't you going to pick up?" Peter asked. "No one would be calling this late unless it was an emergency."

"Funny story…," I said.

Suffice it to say Peter had not seen the humor. He went from outraged to furious to vicious slut-shaming in three sentences flat. Like the note I had reread so many times, those words have played over and over in my head during these many intervening years.

"I can't believe you don't even know my voice," he said. "You're a freak, you know that? A fucking phone whore!"

This stops Teddy cold. He looks at me, genuinely puzzled. "Jesus. Then what?"

"He left."

"Oh, babe," says my Teddy, reaching for my hand. He has to come find it, because I'm still too humiliated to reach back. He holds my hand, rubbing the top of it with his thumb until I look him in the eyes. "He should have laughed," he says.

In that moment, I realize the truth. What Peter did wasn't about me. It was about him. I smile at Teddy, because he's right. "He *should* have laughed," I say with a wink. "Who knows, I might be 'Mrs. Flower Dude' now…if only he had laughed."

Teddy puts his arm around me and squeezes my shoulder, and I know he gets it, too. We snuggle quietly, staring into the firelight.

"You know what this means," he says after a minute.

"Hmm."

"It means that you used to have terrible taste in men. While *I*, on the other hand, have always had excellent taste in women."

It's not true, of course. But it is a grand gesture.

SUSAN BEARMAN

Susan writes across genres. She is an editor, creative writing coach and teacher, and author of *The Animal Store Alphabet Book*. Susan is also a reluctant pet store owner, creator of WordPress websites, mama of four, and stepmama of two. She lives with her husband in Evanston, IL.

The Marriage Bed

by Adrianne Hayward

YEAR 6

Cecily hummed softly as she navigated past the last few moving boxes on her way from the hallway bathroom to the bedroom of their new home. After a long day of unpacking—and fresh from a soothing, scented bubble bath—she was tired but happy. All she wanted was to snuggle next to her husband in their big, new bed, delivered that morning.

Jerome, already in bed, offered an appreciate grin as Cecily shimmied off her fuzzy pink robe and exchanged it for a silky blue nightgown. She sat on the edge of the bed, removed her slippers, and leaned back. "Scoot over a little, Babe; make some room for me."

"There's plenty of room on the other side."

"But this is *my* side of the bed." She pushed hard against him, but he didn't budge. Despite being exhausted (or maybe because she was) Cecily bounced up, snatched the pillow from under his head and swatted him with it. "Stop being so pigheaded and selfish—move over!"

When he laughed, she bashed him harder. Jerome grabbed the pillow mid-swing and eased it and her to the floor.

"Hey, didn't we promise never to go to bed angry? Maybe we should say a prayer." Chastened, Cecily walked around to the other side of the bed and knelt. Jerome knelt opposite her, his head bowed.

Cecily silently prayed for forgiveness, feeling guilty for being angry, resentful, and petty.

Jerome reached across the bed, grasped her hand, and held it tight as they both climbed under the covers. Cecily lay quietly at first, listening to Jerome's soft snore. She soon shifted onto her back, then turned from one side to the other, struggling to get comfortable on the wrong side of the bed. By the time she fell asleep, her back was to Jerome. In the morning, he complained that she'd rolled over in her sleep and pulled all the bed covers with her.

The following Saturday, Cecily attended her cousin Gina's bridal shower. Afterward, as she helped load shower gifts into Gina's car, her cousin confided, "I'm scared, Cuz. What if I can't make this whole marriage thing work?"

"First, it's not *your* job to make the marriage work," Cecily answered. "Both of you have to commit to the effort, and that means communicating and compromising. Now, you know me, so you know I like having my way—but I also hate arguing, so I try to avoid major confrontations. Besides, Mama taught me never to ask questions unless I really want to know the answers."

"Yeah, I *do* know you, Cuz—big time passive-aggressive. Like when you squealed and raved about how much you loved the 'absolutely perfect' engagement ring Jerome surprised you with, then convinced him to replace it with a bigger, better one. But I want to talk about Henry and me."

"I'm getting to it—and, for your information, I'm *not* passive-aggressive. Anyway, when Jerome and I disagree, I always communicate my feelings about the situation and, because he's a good guy, I usually get my way. But if I can't persuade him, I offer a compromise, and if that doesn't work, I give in before the argument turns ugly."

"And that works for you?"

"Yes, it works. Just remember, trust is essential. Loving each other isn't enough. You should be friends, too, and it also helps if you can make each other laugh. Everything else gets old."

Gina nodded. "Look at you, Cuz, giving wise-old-married-lady advice."

"One more thing, Gina. When it comes to money, you two need three bank accounts: yours, mine, and ours. Life's too short to argue about money."

Cecily lay in bed savoring that delicious, still half-asleep state and the comforting illusion that all things are possible on the cusp of a new day. Even with her eyes closed, she knew Jerome was no longer in bed beside her. The soothing, staccato sound of the shower running in the hallway bathroom confirmed it.

How did I manage to marry a morning person?

Her thoughts were interrupted by a shrill report from the bedside clock. She slapped the alarm silent, then reached for the thermometer and chart resting next to it on the nightstand. She shook the thermometer and slipped its cool, tip under her tongue. As she waited for it to register, she frowned, thinking how unfair it was that they had been trying for more than a year to achieve something two teenagers could do on a damn whim in the backseat of a car.

The thermometer's reading compounded her frustration, but Cecily was determined to remain hopeful. Blinking back tears, she jumped up, recorded her basal temperature on the chart and began making the bed. When Jerome entered the room, tall, broad-shouldered, fresh-shaven and smelling of the Cool Water cologne they both loved, she smiled.

"You lucked out, Romeo," she teased. "No baby-making duties for you this morning; no second shower or risk of being late for work."

On her way out of the bedroom, Cecily brushed his cheek with a kiss before adding, "But if you're lucky, I'll throw in a freebie tonight."

Jerome laughed and made a grab for her, but she escaped to the hallway bathroom and turned on the water so he wouldn't hear her crying.

Would things have been different if I hadn't insisted on waiting until we'd saved enough to buy a house before starting a family?

Cecily was nearly dressed for work when Jerome returned to their bedroom. Now wearing a knit cap pulled over his ears and a hooded, down jacket over his gray business suit, he handed her a mug of black coffee. His incongruent outfit matched his job: IT manager at a major bank.

"Better dress warm," he said. "They're predicting more snow tonight, plus high winds."

He lifted her chin with his forefinger, quickly kissed her and headed for the door.

"Love you, Babe," she called after him.

"Back at you."

As she left the house, Cecily was hit by a cold blast from the open door of their attached garage. Jerome had left her car running, to warm it up for her. She smiled, recalling all the thoughtful things he did: a rose on the dashboard;

an éclair in the fridge and love notes on the bed pillow—especially when their schedules conflicted or before one of them left for a business trip.

Cecily reflected on how much she loved Jerome and desperately wanted them to have a baby.

That would make us a real family.

She knew how important family was to Jerome. If the snow prediction held, no doubt he'd get up extra early tomorrow morning and swing by his parents' house to clear the snow from their sidewalk and driveway. She was sure he'd be a terrific father because he loved roughhousing with his sister's two older boys and going to their Little League games. Once, she watched as he gamely tried to change his youngest nephew's diaper—she thought her heart would burst.

When she arrived at her office inside a prestigious, downtown marketing firm, Cecily texted: *Thanks 4 warming car 4 me Luv U*. She smiled when Jerome immediately hit her back: *Luv U2 Working late 2nite*.

That night, as she did whenever Jerome worked late, Cecily slipped into a light sleep (sleeping with one eye open, her mother called it) and waited to hear the garage door open. Once she heard it, she fell into a deep sleep and was dead to the world before Jerome reached their bedroom.

A year later, as they prepared for bed, Cecily reminded Jerome about their fertility clinic appointment the next day. She'd already undergone several tests herself before she convinced him to go in for testing, too.

Their tests revealed his low sperm motility and her growing mass of uterine fibroids, their size no longer stunted by the prescriptive use of birth control pills.

Cecily took the same enthusiastic and results-oriented approach to conception as she did to her work projects, but she worried that sex seemed more of a chore to Jerome. He never complained outright, but he was spending more time at work and less with her, even when they both were at home. There was no foreplay, no kissing, no teasing, no cuddling, no innovation, no…joy.

But there was hope.

The thermometer, the chart and the home pregnancy test all pointed to success. Even Jerome was excited—intermittently yelling, hugging her and bouncing around the room like a giant beach ball. Still, they agreed not to tell anyone until her doctor confirmed it. Meanwhile, their tasty secret was like chocolate melting on their tongues—every time they looked at each other, they not only smiled, they giggled.

The night before her doctor's appointment, Cecily felt sick. She eased out of bed and staggered to the hall bathroom, her stomach cramping. Then came the blood. Her doctor confirmed the worst: yes, she'd been pregnant, and yes, she'd miscarried.

Undaunted by the risks associated with what her doctor called *elderly primigravida,* Cecily's only question was, "How soon can we start trying again?"

The second miscarriage crushed her.

Cecily lay in bed, staring at the ceiling. She felt the tangible, weighty pain of loss—physically and emotionally. She drew the covers over her head, curled knees to chest, and hugged herself tight. When she could sleep, she slept fitfully. Dark moods seized her, accompanied by incessant crying jags that left her too exhausted to think or talk.

She felt as though she'd fallen into a black hole; no light escaped. Jerome tried to talk to her; he asked her how she felt, but she didn't have the energy to respond. She stared blankly when he told her that he'd arranged her an extended sick leave from work, and that she'd been in bed for three weeks.

Every day, Jerome encouraged her to eat, but she had no appetite. Days passed, and when she still refused to eat, Jerome spoon-fed her. When she cried, he hugged, rocked and consoled her. Day after day, he begged her to seek counseling. Finally, he lost his patience.

"Fine with me if you want to live your life as a zombie!" He slammed the door behind him.

His departure added fear to her mounting anxieties. She'd already lost track of time, ensconced in the darkened bedroom, but she guessed she'd been alone for two or three days now.

What if he never comes back?

When Jerome returned, he brought her a bowl of soup. He urged her to eat, but insisted she feed herself. He also insisted she see a therapist.

Cecily weighed the prospect of being alone and doubted she'd survive the added pain of losing Jerome, too. Compelled by fear, she agreed to a series of intensive, three-times-a-week sessions with a brilliant therapist who helped her rescue herself from debilitating depression.

Jerome was supportive throughout, but their relationship was strained, and their sex life was practically non-existent.

Has he found someone else?

Ironically, Jerome said no when she suggested marriage counseling.

For days, Cecily had mentally rehearsed clever ways to address their flailing love life. She intended to discuss it tonight, before they went to bed. But instead of talking sex, she asked, "Have you ever thought about adoption?"

"No."

His face was expressionless but, to Cecily, the way he tightened his pajama drawstrings seemed to underscore his terse response.

"Why not?" Cecily tried to make eye contact, but he averted his gaze.

After a long pause, he added, "Why would I want to raise somebody else's kid? Besides, I'm not even sure I want to stay married."

Thunderstruck, she gritted her teeth and said nothing as Jerome headed for the hall bathroom to brush his teeth. An instant later, she jumped up, slammed and locked the bedroom door.

Mama told me about asking questions.

YEAR 12

Cecily woke with a start, jumped out of bed and, disoriented, panted softly as she spun slowly, her eyes darting, searching every corner of the bedroom.

Jerome rushed to Cecily's side, caught her by the shoulders, then protectively embraced her. "What's wrong, Babe?" When she didn't answer, he cradled her face in his hands to focus her attention. This time, his voice quivered, "Babe, what's wrong?"

Cecily took a long, deep breath and returned his gaze.

"It was just a dream," she stammered, "but it was so real. I dreamed we had a beautiful baby girl and I panicked when I woke up and found her missing. I'm sorry to upset you."

"I'm not surprised you dreamed about a baby. The christening's tomorrow, and that's all you've been talking about since Gina and Henry asked you to be godmother."

"Yeah, you're probably right." Each of Gina's three pregnancies was like a gut punch to Cecily, but she hid her jealousy well. This time around, she was determined to be gracious and grateful, honored to be part of their young lives. She forced a smile.

"This is Gina's first baby girl, and I can't wait to spoil her."

"Tell you what, Babe. It's Saturday, so why don't you go back to bed? I'm going to go for a run and, on the way back, I'll pick up breakfast. Deal?"

"Deal," she said, and dutifully climbed under the covers and closed her eyes. Sleep eluded her, however, as she pondered her dream. She thought she'd moved past all that long ago and accepted their fate as a childless couple.

At least they were still a couple. She sometimes wondered whether Jerome stayed with her out of obligation. She dismissed the thought, feeling sure of his devotion to family.

A wife is family; I am his family.

Sleep claimed her, and she awoke to the smell of the hazelnut coffee and apple cinnamon pancakes Jerome carried in on a wooden breakfast tray.

"Breakfast in bed," she declared to her grinning spouse. "I love it when you pamper me."

She glanced at the clock and realized she'd been asleep about two hours.

"That was a long run, not that I didn't enjoy the extra rest," she said as she sat up and rearranged the bedding. She gave him a thank-you kiss as he set the tray before her. "Where's your wedding band?"

"Oh, uh. I didn't want to risk losing it while I ran; my fingers aren't as fat now that I'm losing weight. May have to get it re-sized."

She wanted to believe him, but she couldn't.

Does he really think I'm that stupid?

Watching Jerome undress to take a shower after his run, Cecily considered the contrast: Jerome had taken up running and was slimming down nicely, while she was pigging out on deep-dish apple pancakes and, thanks to her fibroids, looking four months pregnant.

Ever since he told her he wasn't sure he wanted to stay married, she'd suspected he was cheating. Back then, she'd banished him to the spare bedroom for months, ignoring his daily apologies until he reminded her how he stood by her during her battle with depression. She told him he was comparing apples to oranges. What really got to her was being reminded of how diminished she felt back then, and how afraid she was of being alone.

So, she forgave him. She also warned him that she wouldn't tolerate any disrespect.

YEAR 18

Cecily fell asleep waiting, in vain, for the sound of the garage door opening. She awoke to the sound of her alarm, an empty bed and absolute silence.

Jerome hadn't come home last night. Furious, she kicked off her tangled bed covers and stomped through her morning routine.

If there was an accident, someone would have called me; if there was a family or work emergency, Jerome would have called me.

She called his cell phone, cursing him when it went directly to voicemail. At lunchtime, she sent a text. Before leaving work, she called his office and left a message on his desk phone. Then she grabbed Jerome's framed photo from her desk and shoved it, smiling face-first, into the trash can.

Cecily never wanted to be one of those women who checked up on their husbands at work, but she phoned Jerome's office again, armed with a freshly concocted lie. This time, instead of keying in his extension, she waited for one of his co-workers to pick up.

When the ringing stopped, a woman answered with a sing-song recital of the company greeting.

"Hi, this is Cecily Anderson, Jerome's wife. I've been out of town on a business trip and my flight's been delayed," she lied. "Jerome needs to know he doesn't have to pick me up from the airport—I'll just catch a cab home whenever I get in—but I haven't been able to reach him, and I don't remember what shift he's working this week. Can you help?"

"Hi, Mrs. A, this is Kelly—we met at the Christmas party last year. I saw Mr. A around here a few minutes ago. I'll go find him for you."

A moment later, Jerome picked up the phone.

As soon as she heard his voice, Cecily hung up.

She wanted to scream. Instead, she paced. Now that she knew he was alive and well, she was livid.

"What makes him think I'll put up with this? This is total BS," she shouted to the walls. She fisted her hands and bit her lip, fighting back tears and an urge to scream. Then, it occurred to her to check his closet. It wasn't empty, but his favorite suits and ties were missing. So were his running shoes and Air Jordans. Her eyes welled and her hands clamped the sides of her head. She screamed.

Cecily curled up on the bed and grappled with her thoughts, hoping to fall asleep—knowing the garage door wouldn't be opening.

Did I actually marry a man so cowardly that he left me without saying a word?

What had she done? Why hadn't she seen the signs? But of course, she had—she never questioned his work schedule; she accepted his annual buddy trips. She'd deceived herself.

When, what and how would she tell her parents, friends, church family and co-workers about Jerome's absence?

How can I face Gina after lecturing her about marriage?

The next morning found Cecily bleary-eyed and conflicted; her dreams haunted equally by sweet memories and homicidal fantasies. She marveled at how she could both hate and love someone at the same time. That night, she slept wearing Jerome's bathrobe, comforted by his smell and trace scents of Cool Water.

Every day seemed to reveal more betrayals. When she discovered his wedding band, tucked in the sock drawer, she grabbed it and hurled it across the room, cracking the alarm clock's face.

Incensed, she hauled all of Jerome's precious electronics out to the garage, dropped them on the floor and threw his clothes on top.

The mail brought delinquent household bills for her to pay. She ignored Jerome's personal accounts, but when his AmEx bill arrived, she took the unprecedented step of opening his mail. Her mouth dropped open when she saw the Target Store charges for diapers.

Diapers!

The next morning, Cecily called for an appointment with a high-profile divorce attorney she'd read about in *Chicago Magazine*. That night, she slept in her own night clothes and reclaimed *her* side of the bed.

ADRIANNE HAYWARD

Adrianne began her professional career as a newspaper reporter before moving into corporate communications, including employee and benefits communications, public relations, and cause-related marketing. Her creative works include short stories, poetry, and humorous essays. Currently, she is working on her first novel.

Infinite Monkey Hypothesis

by Linda S. Buyer

"I can't believe that I'm defending my thesis today." Susan and her advisor, Sam, were seated in his paper-stacked office on the first floor of the University of Illinois at Chicago's Psychology Department after lunch. He was leaning back in his chair, his Wallabeed feet crossed on his desk, hands behind his head.

She was perched on the edge of her chair, nervously twisting the front strands of her shoulder-length brown hair around her forefinger. Her well-worn leather portfolio was folded open in her lap. Her pen ready. "Any last-minute notes?" Susan eyed Sam's teal plaid button-down shirt and the brown slacks she'd seen many times, worried she was overdressed in the new suit she had bought for the occasion.

"No." He tapped his bald spot. "You know the literature. You designed a clever experiment. You write well."

She smiled to mask the anxiety her clenched jaw betrayed. "You know… the Infinite Monkey Hypothesis says that given enough time and a type-writer even the monkeys in the colony you have in the basement could write *Hamlet*…"

Sam picked up his copy of Susan's thesis. "For goodness sake, of course they couldn't! Why are you so nervous? The deadline was last spring, and I thought it was ready then. Instead, you opted for probation, 'because it needed more work.' You've had all summer to polish it. It is done." He smiled warmly. "It's almost two. Time to defend."

The committee was seated around the table in the glass-walled seminar room reserved for her defense. The Director of Graduate Studies opened the meeting by asking Susan to describe her experiment. She hadn't gotten very far before Professor Phil Wilkins interrupted and asked about a table in the results section. After that, the meeting consisted of rapid-fire questions from all four faculty, each of which Susan responded to by fiddling with her hair before answering tersely. Ninety minutes later, all their questions answered, the committee asked Susan to wait outside.

Her watch indicated only fifteen minutes had passed when Phil motioned through the glass for her to return.

Too soon! They hate it!

Entering, Susan found herself holding her breath. She wanted Sam to give her a sign, but he was watching Phil stack papers.

He's ashamed of me!

Sam looked at Susan, smiled broadly, held up the signed *Certificate of Approval*, stood and extended his hand. "Congratulations!" Her jaw dropped. "You can submit your thesis. We don't want any changes. Go celebrate!"

Grinning widely, Susan almost skipped toward her office. Her elation quickly collapsed as she thought about all the times her parents had said she shouldn't make her little sister, Fay, feel bad about not being as smart as she. She'd never heard of "no changes" before. That was going to make Julie and the other graduate students feel bad. She frowned. She knew exactly how it felt to never be good enough. She didn't want to do that to anyone.

Susan's officemates and their Statistics professor, Kenneth Karlson, were waiting in the office, crowded into the small space in the center of the six desks arrayed around the walls.

Susan entered. Julie gestured toward the six bottles standing on Susan's desk, grinning. "Expecting good news, we each brought bubbly. And…?"

"They approved." Susan blushed, hugging herself, unable to suppress her grin. "I am so relieved. I didn't believe this would ever happen. Me. Barely made it through college: final GPA, exactly a C. Now this…"

"What'd I tell you?" Julie smiled. "What changes do they want?"

Susan tensed. "Um, none."

Proudly, Ken put his arm around Susan. "Told you you'd be fine. I wouldn't be dating you if you weren't smart."

Susan smiled up at him and congratulated herself; Ken really didn't seem to mind. Unlike her father who taught her to play chess, then never played with her again after she won the first time, furious a 12-year-old had beaten him.

Ken bent down and quickly pecked Susan's lips, then raised his glass. "No changes from a very tough committee," he toasted.

Susan stiffened. "It's just a magician's trick," she said. "Information-processing and Behaviorist predictions about creativity are directly opposed: restricting the search space vs. brainstorming. I just put them head-to-head. Even if neither was right, it'd still be meaningful."

Susan's committee, other faculty, and students who stopped by over the course of the next several hours all brought more congratulatory bottles.

Ken held up his nearly empty glass. "One more toast to Susan ..."

Susan leaned against Ken's arm woozily and smiled up at him. "Champagne's gone. More drinks at Riccardo's?"

Julie interrupted. "We've been drinking for hours. Let's eat there."

Susan turned somewhat unsteadily toward Ken. "Sweetie, may I use your office phone before we go?" He nodded.

"We'll catch up," Susan said. "I should call my mother."

Susan sat in Ken's office chair, leaned back, and triumphantly crossed her ankles between two towering stacks of papers on his desk. "Hi Mom," she slurred. "How're you?"

"Susan, are you drunk?" her mother asked.

"Yup!" Susan grinned at the phone. "It's over! They signed!"

"Go to bed. Tell Kenneth to take you home."

"Mom," Susan pleaded, no longer slurring and sounding much younger, "they didn't want a single change."

"Fine. Go home. Get some sleep."

"Fine! G'night!" She hung up, bowing her head for a moment, then, determined not to show her hurt, straightened, took a deep breath, and smiled too broadly at Ken.

Susan swung Riccardo's heavy door open and bowed Ken through with a flourish, almost overbalancing. She steadied herself using the door handle while she looked around the interior. The department members were seated on the far side of the room at a long, white-clothed table punctuated by open wine bottles.

"Julie," Susan said, plopping into the empty seat next to her. "So self-centered, I didn't ask. How'd your fiancé's first sermon go Sunday?"

"Congregation seemed impressed. I was really proud of him." Julie raised her left hand and smiled at her small, still unfamiliar diamond. "You should be really proud, too. Amazing your committee didn't want any changes."

"No big deal. I banged two hytpostheses… hsypothe… theories together like a monkey's nuts. Monkey's gonna jump no matter what… see?" She smiled broadly, cocked her head and shrugged, hands spread, palms up. "Shh." Forefinger upright on pursed lips, Susan leaned closer to whisper. "Rhoda's defending Thursday. She'll feel bad." She pulled back and continued normally. "Cool the congregation was impressed!"

Julie smiled gently. "It's harder to design research to ensure meaningful results than you think. Lots of people don't; they can't."

"You said this morning you don't know what to do about a wedding dress. I have one I bought in an antique store when I was 18. It's an Art Nouveau style, ivory satin with a long train. I'm pretty sure it would fit you. If it does, you're welcome to wear it. Doesn't look like I'm ever going to." She smiled ruefully. "Ken's not interested in getting married a third time."

Susan made herself comfortable on her couch, stuffing a throw pillow between her back and its boxy arm and propping her journal against her upraised knees. Taking a deep breath, she began her entry, reviewing the facts for the millionth time in the last six weeks: ninety minutes, committee signed off, no changes. "If I can do it, a monkey could." Susan thought about how many times she'd said just that since she defended and put down her pen. The brief thrill of defending successfully was long gone. It no longer felt like anything.

Wondering if this happened to everyone, she easily conjured up contradictory examples: middle-aged men defined by a high school touchdown that won the game, Ken's pride that his 1974 *Psychological Review* article was accepted without revisions, Harvard grads who always let you know where they went to school.

Why don't I feel anything? Don't think about it.

She continued writing. Dinner at Riccardo's. Ken's proud of me.

I earned my first monkey pellet. So what?

Susan froze. *What the hell is wrong with me? I put together the toughest committee I could. No changes: undeniably good.*

Why don't all graduate students understand that comparing competing hypotheses is pretty well guaranteed to produce significant results? It's obvious!

What if Julie's right and it's not obvious?

She panicked. *I'm becoming mom. Never happy. I've tried so hard not to be her. What if I can't help it?*

What can I do?

What is there to do? Go back to the guy Stanley and I saw for couple's counseling in college? No! Too expensive. Ignore the whole thing? Yes!

No... something's really wrong. I have to do something! University Counseling Center?

Susan seated herself where she couldn't see "Don't Stop Until You're Proud!," one of several motivational posters unconvincingly duct-taped to the bare concrete block walls.

This is a mistake.

A short, slight man with a rolling limp and a bad toupee entered the waiting room and squinted at the clipboard in his hand. "Susan?"

"Here."

"Walk this way." He turned and rocked down the hall toward his office. She grabbed her bookbag and grinned at his back while she momentarily considered imitating him.

He sat behind his industrial gray metal desk and gestured toward the guest chair opposite. He smiled. "I'm Dr. Bob Angevin. Tell me why you're here today."

Susan, her purple bookbag thumping heavily on the floor, sat cross-legged. "I just defended my thesis. I'm really messed up."

"Did a problem at your defense lead you to think that?"

"Unh-uh. This sounds nuts, but, I'm not happy about it, and I should be." She tried to smile, but could only make the right half of her mouth curl upward.

"Tell me …"

"My committee didn't want any changes, and I keep telling people if I could do it, a monkey could." Her face crumpled. "Why can't I be proud of myself?"

Dr. Angevin smiled gently. "A question we can explore together. Would you like that?"

She nodded.

"Let's start with a little history. Tell me about yourself."

Susan eyed the bookshelves behind him, speaking in a soft monotone. "I have one sister, Fay. She's ten months younger than me. My parents divorced when I was around eighteen. My dad and I both moved out when I was sixteen, him first. Me, to start college. He remarried after the divorce. I wasn't invited. I was twenty-one when my half-sister was born. My dad moved to my stepmother's hometown in northern England when Fay was four. I haven't seen him since. She's eight now. My mother and Fay still live in Evanston, where I grew up. I see them a few times a year."

Dr. Angevin made some notes, then looked up. "I have lots of questions about all that, but they can wait. That was primarily about other people." He smiled warmly. "I'd like to hear more about you."

"Nothing to say really. We moved here from New Jersey on June 29th, 1964. My eighth birthday. I did third and fifth grades in Chicago." She started fidgeting with the Victorian fob bracelet she inherited from her great-grandmother and wore most days. "I skipped fourth."

Susan looked at Dr. Angevin and smiled, her cheeks pushing her large almond eyes to slits. "I thought my parents had been called in because I flunked the third-grade IQ test."

Dr. Angevin leaned forward, putting his elbows on his desk, and rested his chin on his hands. "I'm confused. You thought you flunked?"

Puzzling over his odd gaze, Susan realized his left eye was glass. *Reassuring.*

"Yeah." She twisted her hair around her forefinger. "Mine were the only parents in the whole school that were called in. I was sure I'd messed up."

"But, you skipped fourth grade? How did you understand that?"

Susan wondered why he was harping on her thinking she'd flunked the IQ test. Did he disapprove? He didn't *seem* angry, but you never knew until it was too late.

She shrugged, trying to explain herself. "No one ever said I did well, so I thought I was being skipped because New Jersey's curriculum was ahead of Chicago's."

She paused to see if he was going to argue. That's what her high school shrink had done. He even gave her an IQ test, and then wouldn't tell her the score. She was convinced that meant her score had been average and he just didn't want to admit to being wrong.

When Dr. Angevin simply looked at her after making a note, she continued with a grin, "I was a straight-A student through eighth grade, then started getting really bad grades freshman year."

"Did something happen between the end of junior high and the beginning of high school?"

"No. Except I spent the summer with my mom's sister in Seattle. She had two little kids. I was sent because I was trouble, and she needed free babysitting."

"What did you do that made you 'trouble'?"

Susan stared at him in astonishment. She'd never asked herself that question. "I don't know," Susan said slowly. "My mom said so."

"Why do you think she said that?"

She shrugged.

"Why do you think you started flunking?"

"Don't know; being perfect wasn't working so I tried the opposite? Fay would come home with Bs and Cs and they'd jump up and down. I'd have all As and they'd ignore *my* report card. Mom said it was so Fay wouldn't feel bad about not being as smart as me."

"How did you feel about that?"

"It was true." She shrugged again. "What's there to feel about it?"

She crossed her arms, hands clutching her shoulders, her chin tucked in the nest they made. "Their response to my flunking out was, I could either see my mom's shrink or be sent to boarding school. I chose boarding school. They made me see her shrink instead."

She looked up and frowned. "He was an asshole. He was always explaining my mother's side to me. Told me things she told him in confidence. I didn't trust him as far as I could throw him." She fell silent, wondering if Dr. Angevin would defend a fellow clinician.

After pausing to see if she'd continue, he said, "Not trusting your therapist must have been difficult."

She shook her head and grinned. "I just never told him anything I didn't want my mother to know."

She paused, eying Dr. Angevin uncertainly, then continued. "I got pregnant when I was 14, between freshman and sophomore years. Tried to commit suicide." She smiled. "Another failure."

He smiled gently. "I'm glad you 'failed' at that. A good failure. How were you feeling when you tried to kill yourself?"

"Scared. Couldn't tell them I was pregnant. They would've killed me. Sad. My dad and I had a big fight over dinner about Vietnam and the draft. He said *my* opinion didn't matter!" She bit her lower lip in an effort to maintain her composure. "I thought they'd be sorry."

"You wanted your parents to be sorry?"

"Yes. No. I don't know. Maybe." She averted her eyes.

"What did you do?"

"Waited until everyone was asleep and took all their prescriptions. Don't even know what. Just took them all."

"Then what?"

"I was still awake about an hour later." She chuckled. "I thought they'd be really mad at me for taking all their pills if I didn't die. I called my shrink. Even though I was whispering, my mother heard me. She came in just as I passed out. I woke up in the hospital."

"How did you feel then?"

"Scared they'd be mad. When they found out I was pregnant, everyone thought *that* was why I took the pills, even my shrink, so I never had to explain about the fight. My parents just wanted to know who the father was so they could get his parents to share the costs. They didn't care how *I* felt about an abortion. Just told me I was having one." She fidgeted her bracelet, eyeing the floor.

"How did you feel about that?"

"I wouldn't tell them who the father was. I never even told *him*." She cocked her head, smiling seductively. "I barely knew him. Just a neighbor's older brother."

"I'm sorry, we have to stop. Can we make this time your regular appointment?"

"You think I can feel better about my defense? Then yes."

"I do." He smiled, and stood up. "You're here. That's an important first step. You're a smart young woman."

Susan rose, slinging her loaded bookbag over her shoulder. For a moment, she hesitated, looking like she wanted to object. Instead, smiling tenuously, she squared her shoulders and left without closing the door.

— LINDA S. BUYER

Linda retired from teaching psychology in 2016 and started writing short stories. When she's not writing, she's an avid photographer and Director of Special Projects for Schakowsky for Congress. Her short story, "My Turn," was published by Crow Woods Publishing early in 2020.

Late Run in December

by Sheila Elliott

Henry guided his bus down Henderson Avenue. *Quiet night,* he thought, as three pedestrians scurried across the street, indifferent to still-glittering holiday lights. He raised his foot gently from the accelerator but the muscles around his eyes were clenched in an intent stare. That was when he saw her. Sighing audibly, he slumped in his driver's chair, set his forearms across the wheel, and braided his fingers in a prayer-like clasp.

By the time his bus was beside the curb, she was curbside, waiting, a tiny woman dressed in a shapeless coat, its sleeves nearly concealing gloved hands. It was buttoned tightly at the neck, her chin clinched in the folds of its wool collar. An emerald-colored ribbon had been threaded through the loose weave of an acrylic hat and gray hairs strayed across her forehead and brushed her ears. When the door opened, she raised her face, as she did every evening.

He flexed his left leg, the one injured in a high school game, plumes of white smoke wafting from the mouth of a cowboy on a cigarette billboard. He shifted anxiously in the leatherette driver's seat, readjusted his driving position, eyes intent on what was ahead. Suddenly he noticed the forefinger of his right hand resting on one of his uniform's embossed buttons, so he pulled back abruptly. Now both hands gripped the wheel. *Better,* he thought. When he started this job, seven years before, he'd been a big guy, but time had pared him down. His jackets fit loosely now, but he hated that habit. It ruined the uniform.

The soles of her athletic shoes slapped vinyl treads as she climbed into the bus. Only after their beats stopped did he close the door, accelerate, and then toss a sidelong glance at her.

Same as any other night. One of her pale hands struggled with the coin-purse snap, the other gripped a balance bar. Wobbling tentatively, she searched for bus fare, a vinyl bag resting near her shoes. Two city blocks passed before coins jangled in the fare box and she turned away. After several moments, Henry checked an overhead mirror and saw her seated one row behind him, same as always.

213

"I pay my way," she said, the words ringing clearly in the empty spaces around her.

After another long moment, Henry answered in a toneless voice. "No one rides for free."

In the past few months he'd learned that dodging eye contact with her was easy, but muffling his ears was not. Her voice nourished images hard to ignore and he heard stuff he didn't want to know. But that was what he was up against with her—the talking. Even tonight, even on Christmas Eve. He should stop listening, he knew. He wasn't sure why that was so difficult.

For several minutes, to the sound of the tires, the bus navigated empty streets lined with half-lit businesses. Suddenly she blurted, loudly and with force, "It's the eve of Our Lord's birth." Henry remained quiet. He checked his other passengers. In the back was a woman with a small boy and, not far from them, someone slumped over, the rim of a hat draping their face. No one else. No one seemed bothered by her outburst.

Good, Henry thought, pulling out his watch: Two hours until shift's end—not soon enough. But as soon as that thought jelled, a jet of familiar guilt rose inside. He looked to the street ahead for joy or comfort, but found none.

It was Christmas Eve, Henry thought. What about tomorrow? His sister invited him over every year, but he'd never gone. It wasn't her or anything. She was four years younger and they'd always gotten on okay. Estelle had a nice place and told funny stories about her kids' day-care, or whatever. He wasn't sure why he never went. Envy didn't cover it. It was hard to explain.

He'd worked the late route for three years now and wondered if it was time to go for a better time slot, but Henry didn't make quick decisions. Nowadays, change made him nervous. It didn't before, but it did now. Besides, he liked this shift. There were people who counted on him, not a lot of them this late at night, but reliability was important all the same, even if they were mostly strangers and he never saw them again. It was important to the woman, too, someone who wasn't exactly a stranger. He didn't know what to make of it, why she seemed to count on him, but that was what he was faced with.

He heard soft mumblings and felt a surge of resentment toward her. Henry couldn't even recall when she became a regular rider, she was so much a part of his job now. She wasn't around last Christmas, he was certain, but by February or March, yes, by then, she was there, every night, flagging him from one downtown intersection or another, always alone. He hadn't noticed her at first, he supposed.

She was respectful, sat apart from others, and often was quiet for long stretches. Only later did he realize the pattern of endless stories emerging. Now, every night, surely as darkness replaced daylight, Henry listened to her life's litany.

Or that's how it seemed. As far as Henry was concerned, he didn't know if even half of what she said was true. The other half he wanted to avoid. But she was always there, every night, every holiday, alone, babbling in the emptiness of his bus. It bothered him.

Hearing about her life made him uneasy. It seemed like an extra burden, and after the divorce and counseling, the gambling and taxes, he didn't need an extra burden. When he started this route, he'd wanted a quiet place where he could sort of disappear for a while. The late run, at night, became his place to let himself get better. After three years, he felt okay; or at least well enough to go to a holiday dinner. But those stories she told. They got into his head.

He was wiping away windshield mist, listening to the wipers slap, when she called out, "On the eve of Our Lord's birth." The words blended clumsily with the churning of the engine. "Here I am," she said. "So tired."

Henry slumped. He'd heard that lament before, last spring, after a rainstorm. She'd boarded, drops of rain falling from the creased folds of a plastic rain bonnet. The damn bonnet was probably in her bag right now. The street ahead was as empty as a ballroom after a dance.

He was irritated, and concealing that was difficult. Everyone should be somewhere on Christmas Eve, he thought. Not on a bus. Alone.

She spoke again, this time louder. "You know I pay."

Well, yeah, sure, he thought. She didn't try to sneak aboard, and anyone could see she was tired. Hell, he knew tired, like he knew every stop sign on his route and each cinder block in his apartment. Maybe she was tired, but why should he be the one who knew something like that about her? A long silence passed before he heard her again.

"My, my," she said, slow as maple syrup. "Where is the Spirit here?"

His left leg jerked involuntarily and he looked up, but saw nothing but her profile. A harmless woman who never intruded on another passenger, never behaved aggressively? Crazy, feeble-minded? He wasn't any kind of doctor, so he couldn't say.

What he saw was someone able to fade into half-lit doorways and wander night-time sidewalks overlooked. Someone who was almost invisible until she boarded his bus. That's when her life lit up in a blitz of words and stories. But what could he do? Tell a social worker or his manager that a passenger was too talkative, that she boarded too slowly? That other passengers ignored her?

Henry was suspicious. When he was seven and his Mom was having a tough time, he'd ended up in foster care. He'd been well cared for and Mom, twenty-three at the time, got him back within a few months. He'd been lucky, things worked out, but what he remembered was the uncertainty when your life was in the hands of others. Right or wrong, the experience left him suspicions. He wasn't going to send anyone else down that path.

He inhaled deeply, relaxing his rib cage slowly, like the fitness guy advised, then felt his hand brush over the woven insignia on his jacket's lapel, and pulled back. His eyes darted from street to mirror.

"Weary," she said. "Weary."

So, yeah, he understood, but shouldn't someone else be watching out for her? He already knew the answer to that question. A bus passed in the opposite direction and Henry raised a hand to its driver.

From behind, he heard barely coherent words blend with the engine's persistent hum. "On a trampoline," she said. "And didn't his foot get caught."

Henry tried not to listen, but it was futile. More stories, more words, and not a familiar character in any of them. Except for the boy, of course. He was the only one who reoccurred, and he was nameless.

Boyfriend, younger spouse, childhood friend? Henry didn't know, but she never mentioned a home or family. He wanted to believe the boy was a son, but even there, he hesitated. Who was on the trampoline, and where? Henry checked his watch. She sure had a mess of memories left from some sort of different life, which was sort of sad.

Or not? He shoved a hand outside the bus, and cleared a rearview mirror. He used to play college ball and used to own a body shop. He used to gamble. Used to be a husband. "Used-to" was part of life. He'd had his share. She had her share, too, but this was now, the present tense—this bus, this darkness, this city, this night. He focused on driving. It'd be nice if someone from her "used-to" world would step up and help now, though.

The street was empty as an airport tarmac now and he tried hard to ignore her voice. His youngest rider and the woman with him were beside him, absorbed in their own conversation, while she continued to ramble. She was talking about "lights" and "plants." Henry groaned. He knew what was coming, but it was the voice of the boy standing next to him in the aisle now who came across most clearly.

"One with an NFL emblem," he said. His mother shushed him, and called out her stop. They were gone in seconds, Henry watching them disappear beneath a canopy of leafless trees. He closed the door and re-entered the traffic lanes.

"I was at a restaurant once," she was saying. "And they had—"

This was it, he thought. She'd been in a restaurant once that had an aquarium. Plants green as a pool table, and all kinds of fish. He'd heard it a dozen times.

"The boy took me. It was Fourth of July and…"

It was your birthday, Henry thought.

"He worked at a car wash. So we went down Waltham Road, and..."

Alden Avenue. It was Alden Avenue, or at least it was last time she told this story. He remained quiet; the bus paused for a red light. This job, this shift, the holidays, he wanted to let go of all of it. And now, he was worried about her. He needed some relief. Dinner, tomorrow, at his sister's—yes, he wanted that.

She continued, but he knew this story so well he could catch her errors in street names and dates. Once or twice, she'd omitted the boy entirely, too. But for now, Henry wanted to focus on himself, this job, maybe a holiday dinner.

"So, where are you headed this late?" he asked. A moment passed.

"I got to get that doctor to get me something for the boy. He's not doing well," she said, the street outside pale and empty as moonlight.

"That right? He got some sort of problem?"

"Same as always." And then, "I got him there to get some help."

Henry winced, reconsidering what she'd said. The boy had visited a doctor. With a doctor's name, someone could get an address, couldn't they? A social worker or counselor, someone could find out where the boy was or had been treated, and contact him. Him—or somebody. One name meant a lot.

"What hospital?" he asked.

There was no response, so he looked up and glimpsed her solemn profile.

"Ain't seen one for a long time now," she said. He shifted in his seat, searching for words, but felt the moment of connection—when he could learn something—passing.

"Now, that's too bad," he said. She was still.

After a long spell of silence the bus cord sounded and a slim man stumbled forward.

"Whoa," he said as he strode up the aisle, tilting silently her way as he passed.

He reached the fare box, and was adjusting his cap, when Henry spoke loudly and in a forceful voice.

"You've got to get some help," he said.

"Hey, man," the passenger replied, in mock offense. Henry shook his head in a silent reprimand to what he'd just said, then nodded back in her direction. The slim man's eyes followed his lead, and then laughed gently.

"No one's better 'n anyone else," he said.

What sense did that make? he thought, smiling as the bus coasted to a stop.

"Here I am," the passenger said as it slowed. As he stepped down, he raised one hand theatrically and called out, "Holidays." Then he was gone.

"Yes, I'm aiming to get something for the boy," she said.

But as the minutes passed, Henry felt a sense of hopelessness grow.

"How old is this boy now?"

The wheels and the engine moved effortlessly over the pavement but her answer, which was loud enough, was disjointed. "My, such a night," she said, resuming the earlier tale. "You ever see a lobster? In those tanks. With those other fish, floating?"

Henry calmed himself. "Sounds good. Lobster—I like that."

"So did I. Liked the rice, too."

After a long time, he heard, "This city, it's some kind of place," but Henry didn't respond. He felt worn down by the cold, the emptiness and, right now, the helplessness. It was then that he heard the shuffling of shoes and she was beside him.

"Denhold Court," she said.

Last night it was Crescent Avenue. The night before it was Hightower Boulevard. Now, she wanted Denhold Court. He sighed, twirling a thread that had strayed from its buttonhole. Where she exited didn't worry him. He wondered if there was a home nearby, or someone to help. But wondering was futile, too, wasn't it? He knew no one was waiting.

Months before, when she first became a regular, he'd looked for truth in her stories, but now he hardly bothered. He was a driver, he had a place for her to sit and rest for a while inside a dimly lit bus. And she used it to relive what once had been her life. That's what he thought now. There wasn't a home near this or any other bus stop. Even worse, he couldn't do much of anything to change all that. It's too damn bleak tonight, he thought, but he made his voice sound cheerful for her sake and called out, "Denhold."

There was a rustling sound as she grasped the brace bar, her bag at her feet, and stared intently toward the darkened sidewalks, her back to Henry. Like any other night, he thought. Almost. Glancing down, he peeked inside the bag and stared for a moment. He sighed, not because he was startled, but because it confirmed what he already feared. There were no letters, no pictures, nothing to add anything more about her life. No surprises here, he thought. Just an old sweater and some magazines.

His probing over, Henry said, "It's cold. Hope you've got some warm clothes."

She didn't seem to hear, nor did she see Henry reach around his chair to the alcove where he stored his thermos. He removed a paper bag he'd placed there earlier, after his dinner break, moments before she'd boarded. Even in the semi-darkness he could make out the illustration of a pagoda on its surface.

Good, he thought, feeling the warmth from inside. It wasn't lobster, but it would have to do. Carefully, he slipped it into her bag, and then opened the door.

She was adjusting gloves, but stopped suddenly, and turned with a bemused smile. "Why, I think I smell something good," she said, looking toward him. She paused as if expecting a reply, but there was none, so she laughed. "I am a crazy old woman," she said before turning and stepping down.

From the bus, he watched. "It's for the boy," Henry whispered, when she was on the curb and he was sure she couldn't hear. He snapped the door shut, then reached brusquely across the steering wheel, the shining metal pins at the uniform's wrist chiming dimly against its surface. She was gone now. He had to leave, too. There was another hour to go, and he still had to decide about tomorrow.

SHEILA ELLIOTT

Sheila has worked as a reporter, editor, publicist and educator. Her writing has been honored by the Illinois Woman's Press Association, among other organizations. An OCWW member since 2017, Sheila co-facilitates the Oak Park Writers Group and serves on the board of Poets & Patrons, Inc.

Rough Neighborhood

by Beth Lewis

She slowly drove up to the sand-colored building. It had that low-key way of not looking ostentatious but at the same time looking spotless, well maintained, and elegant. Two valet attendants stood in front, but it was a nice day; she didn't really need to valet. Stacy looked around the parking lot. Orange cones were blocking some open spots, so she pulled toward the overhang where the valet-parking stand was located. She wanted to find someone to ask where she should park.

"What's the name?" asked the clean-cut young man as she lowered her window.

"I just wanted to know where I should park. I'm here to have lunch with some people," she blurted.

The uniformed valet guy smiled. "We do all the parking. Who are you here with?"

Stacy, embarrassed at her lack of protocol knowledge, mumbled, "Oh, sorry. It's my first time here. I'm meeting Brooke. Brooke Langer."

She put the car in park and grabbed her purse and jacket from the passenger side, almost tripping as she rushed out of the car. The attendant carefully got into her almost-clean gray Toyota, politely keeping a straight face as he looked skeptically toward his coworker. As she headed toward the entrance to the building, Stacy noticed the rows of sparkling Audis, Mercedes, and Lexus, along with a few shiny BMW convertibles.

She hadn't known what to wear so settled on a business-casual-type look. She was wearing her favorite blue sleeveless shift dress with flats and a cute cotton sweater in case it was chilly in the air-conditioning. Stacy hesitantly looked around the beige and white room with the wall of windows overlooking the golf course. A few women were scattered around and they all were wearing golf pants or jeans (mostly the brand that was out of Stacy's budget at around $200 a pair). They all looked like they had gone for a blowout that morning and also seemed to hold drinks in a way that exhibited their manicures with the trendy new colors. They were trying very hard to be comfortable and casual, though, as most of them wore cute T-shirts that were made to look worn but were sold at the expensive local boutiques.

"Hiiiiiiiiiiiiiiiiiiiiiii!!!!!!!!" Brooke swooped toward her and enveloped her in a hug. "You look so nice! Did you come from work?"

Apparently Stacy's attempt at dressing conservatively to blend in had failed. "No, I'm off on Thursdays. This dress is just really comfortable when it's hot out. Thank you so much for inviting me. This is lovely."

Brooke guided Stacy toward a table where three other women were seated. Two of them had highlights identical to Brooke's in their long blonde hair and the third had a shiny cascade of long dark curls. They all appeared to have no makeup on, but upon closer inspection they had expertly applied, natural-looking makeup.

"Everyone, this is my friend Stacy I told you about. Our daughters are both in Ms. Sylvan's class at school." As she sat down, Stacy smiled at the group, thankful that she didn't have to shake hands with her sweaty palms.

Prior to her current job, Stacy worked in the Foundation's regional office as an administrative assistant. From that experience she was familiar with their fundraising events and the people on the planning committees. When she overheard Brooke talking about it at school pickup one day, she mentioned her experience and asked Brooke about the local group.

Brooke had invited her to join their next meeting. Stacy jumped at the chance to become more involved and maybe make a few friends.

People had their cliques in this neighborhood, and it was really hard to break in. She had grown up in the area and moved back about ten years ago. However, she had worked full-time until her daughter was in kindergarten and, in the two years since then, she still hadn't figured out how to fully integrate into the community.

She had seen some of these women at the gym, but they all seemed to move as a pack, so it was hard to strike up a conversation with any one of them. She also had seen them at some of her daughter's activities and had asked about carpooling, but they weren't interested.

They each introduced themselves apathetically, except for one who was on the phone and waved. One of the women with blond highlights explained, "Oh, sorry. Lisa is on the phone with her nanny. I think her kid lost something at the park, but I don't know why the nanny can't just figure it out."

"Anyway, we're here to discuss event planning and Stacy will be joining our local chapter of the Foundation. We met at our kids' school, and she mentioned that she used to work for the regional office. Her fabulous experience will be super helpful to us in planning the Spring Fling."

After the introductions the other women ignored Stacy and began talking about the florist who had done every event for one of their families and whether they should increase the ticket price over last year's event.

Stacy listened to the others discuss the florist for a few minutes and then offered some information on vendors from a spreadsheet she had compiled when working in the office.

Candace, one of the other blondes, interrupted and asked, "Have you met any of them personally? How are they to deal with? We really like to work with people who are, you know, professional."

Stacy replied, "I haven't dealt with them personally, but according to the information we received from people in the local chapters, they all were satisfactory."

"What about the photographers? Do you have a list of them as well?" asked Nicole, the one with the perfectly arranged dark curls. As Stacy confirmed that she did, Nicole looked sideways at Brooke and leaned slightly to whisper something to her.

Stacy momentarily lost her train of thought, then added, "Yes. I also have caterers, and uh…uh…printers for invitations, and um…also other vendors. They're all on the spreadsheet."

Brooke turned slightly toward Nicole and raised her eyebrows. She then said to Stacy, "That is so great that you have a list compiled. We thought somebody had kept records from last year's event but we're not sure who has it or where they are. Would you be able to call the vendors for each category and get price comparisons?"

"Sure! Of course!" exclaimed Stacy, happy to be involved.

After setting up a time to meet the following week, they finished eating and got up from the table. Candace and Nicole headed for the locker room and waved to the others. Candace declared, "We're going to get a quick massage in before the kids get home."

Jamie, the other blonde, picked up her phone. "I better check with my nanny that everything is okay. Seriously, what do I pay her for?"

Brooke walked with Stacy to the door. Stacy thanked her for lunch and promised to have all of the vendor information ready for their next meeting.

She got her car from the valet and on the way home she realized she didn't know what any of the others were doing while she made the calls. She felt a little odd about it, but they had gone out of their way to include her. She figured maybe they would be doing more of the hands-on preparation for the event.

Over the next few days, she made the calls and compiled the information. She emailed it to all of them, although only Brooke responded with a brief "Thanks, this is great." They planned to meet on the following Thursday at 11:30 a.m. at the golf club again.

This time Stacy wore some well-fitting jeans and a nice top. They weren't the designer brands the others wore, but she figured she would fit in a little better. She confidently pulled her car up in front by the valet stand, exited as if she did this every day, and informed the valet she was meeting Brooke Langer. He looked through the key fobs and said, "I don't believe she is here, but you are welcome to wait for her in the lobby." Stacy checked her watch, which showed 11:28. Last time they had all arrived before her but maybe today they were running late.

She took a seat in an overstuffed cream-colored chair, wondering how it was kept so spotless. Did people not usually sit on it?

A few minutes passed and she checked her phone to make sure there wasn't a message from Brooke. An employee noticed Stacy sitting there and asked if she could bring her a drink. Stacy politely declined, stating that her friend should be here any minute.

At 11:45 she wondered if she had the wrong day and messaged Brooke to confirm. About five minutes after that, the four of them strolled in and apologized for being late, saying their personal trainer was running behind.

After ordering lunch, they were deep in conversation about which yoga instructors had moved to which studios or gyms.

Stacy tentatively suggested they discuss the Spring Fling. Candace and Jamie raised their eyebrows at each other. Brooke suddenly stopped talking and cleared her throat. "Yes, that is why we're here. Let's review the list of vendors."

They agreed on all the vendors Stacy recommended, except that they insisted on using the florist they always used despite the fact that he charged $700 more than the one Stacy had found, who also had excellent references. Before they wrapped up, Brooke asked Stacy to call back all of the vendors and confirm them for the date.

This time on the way home, Stacy tried convincing herself that she was being involved and making friends in the community. However, something just didn't fit. It was like a puzzle that had one or two pieces missing. Most of the picture was there, but something was missing.

This was exactly the kind of opportunity she had been searching for and now she had a way to break in. She could pull off the look to blend in a bit more and would have a group of people to socialize with and to help each other out. Maybe they would warm up a little once they got to know her better. If she made the calls, what would happen after the Spring Fling was over? Would she go to the gym with them? Would she play golf with them? Get together with their families for dinner? Did she really want to? At some point maybe she would regret this version of herself.

The next day she looked at the spreadsheet and the writeup she had done. She took a deep breath and wrote an email to Brooke thanking her for the opportunity but informing her that something had come up and she would no longer be able to work on the Foundation. She attached the spreadsheet and hit Send. Then she exhaled.

Stacy spent the next few days thinking about other organizations she might join, or maybe even try tennis or golf lessons. She did not hear back from Brooke or any of the others.

The following week Stacy was at school pickup one afternoon when she saw Brooke and one of the other women from the Foundation. She felt socially obligated to acknowledge them but tensed up and tried to stop herself from walking in the opposite direction. Timidly, she managed a quick smile when they looked toward her. It would have been much easier to pretend they weren't there, but she really wanted to keep things friendly and not create any awkwardness. Brooke caught her eye but abruptly turned away and didn't smile back or wave.

The bell rang and children burst out of the doors. While scanning the crowd for her daughter, Stacy saw a couple of women whose kids were friendly with hers but whom she had never officially met. They had been chatting but turned and said hello.

One of them moved toward her and mentioned that they were just talking about getting some of the kids together but thought it would be nice if the moms met up without them as well. They were going to meet for coffee Friday morning and talk about starting a book club. The woman asked Stacy, "Would you like to join us?"

"Yes!" she exclaimed. "Yes, I'd love to. Thanks for asking." Stacy felt a sensation of happiness and relief flow through her. Maybe what she thought she had been looking for all this time wasn't really what she wanted. She didn't have to worry about changing anything.

As she walked with her daughter into the parking lot, she saw the sun glinting off her newly washed silver Toyota.

— BETH LEWIS ——————————————

Beth has a love/hate relationship with the Chicago north suburbs where she is a lifelong resident. As a corporate refugee following a lengthy career as a recruiter, she has decided to make her long-term writing experience official. This is her first published work.

Screen Saver

by Rita Angelini

David, the office manager, was a pompous jerk. Judy—the girl in the cubicle next to Terri's—reacted to David's insensitive demeanor and constant haranguing about unrealistic deadlines in a way that caught Terri's attention. She cried.

She was crying now, as a matter of fact, having bobbled a tax project that a more experienced accountant like Terri herself would have caught one-handed and had time left over for drinks and conversation. David, apparently unconcerned that his voice carried, had berated Judy like she was a child, threatening to fire her if she didn't "shape up."

Terri's instinct was to go to Judy's little cubicle and console her. Maybe give her some advice on navigating the software program or answer questions regarding the tax code. As Terri rose from her chair, David entered and dropped a huge pile of folders on her desk. He slid the top file—his largest client—off, covering her already-opened files, and demanded she complete it by the end of the day.

She'd heard about his nightmare clients and believed, being the new hire, she would be spared. Not so. With two days still needed to finish yesterday's "Drop everything, I need this now"—assuming she received all the information she required—she wouldn't have time to complete today's emergency. She showed him the list of items still missing. He glanced at it and rolled his eyes.

Judy was still crying in the next cubicle.

Terri said the client's returns would be ready in three days. She was prepared to bargain down to two, but he started to leave. Without turning around, he repeated the demand that the return be finished by the end of the day—an impossible feat, even in Terri's heyday, when she had been the manager of a large and influential accounting firm. Who did this guy think he was?

227

David left without bothering to negotiate. *It'll get done when it gets done, jerk-face*, she told herself. Her thoughts of Judy next door changed from sympathy to empathy.

The crying stopped.

Terri picked up her phone and tapped the screen saver. A photograph of Rae appeared—taken at age 10, the last year of her life—and Terri studied it. Incidents like this made her question whether she had given herself enough time to grieve before returning to the workforce. What did jerk-face know about life, really? Was he even married? Did he have children?

She studied Rae's eyes, blue and innocent, wide and free of self-pity. *What does any of this matter, really?* she asked the picture.

The crying resumed behind the partition.

Terri set the phone down and examined the dozen or more folders that now clogged her desktop.

She asked Rae, *What should I do?*

In her post-delivery hospital bed, 10 years earlier, Terri had waited six hours for her husband Alan to return with Rae after a nurse whisked her baby off to be examined by a neonatologist. She was still holding the tiny blue dress with an anchor pattern, crumpled and twisted, when Alan returned without their daughter. He was instead accompanied by two doctors. Alan held her hand while the doctors explained that Rae had contracted a bacterial infection and been transferred to the neonatal intensive care unit.

The first day of her life, Rae had nursed normally. But on the second day, she stopped. A nurse had assured Terri that Rae would resume nursing, but that hadn't happened. And now a doctor was reassuring Terri an antibiotic would eliminate the bacterial infection within three days. Alan embraced Terri, muffling her tears in his shoulder.

In the NICU, the smell of disinfectant assaulted Terri's nostrils as she scrubbed her hands. They passed through a sea of preemies, their translucent skin and fragile bodies like jellyfish. Off to one side, a huge machine provided lung and heart support to a tiny neonatal survivor. Terri guessed the baby couldn't have weighed more than three pounds. Parents stood next to incubators. Monitors beeped. The heart-lung machine moaned. Machines buzzed.

They reached Rae, a whale at nine pounds. Terri reached through the opening in her incubator and stroked her arms and legs. She didn't belong here, looking healthy and robust. But thin wires were glued to her chest, an IV injected into her tiny vein, and a tube ran up her nose. Already tense, Terri startled when the machine alarm blared like a church bell on steroids. She pulled her arms out and clutched Alan tightly. Rae didn't move. The nurse came by and muted the alarm, explaining that the monitor was highly sensitive, and the change that set it off was within the accepted range.

There were no sleeping accommodations for new mothers, so when the visit was over, Terri and Alan left the hospital as they came, just the two of them.

At seven o'clock the next morning, the neonatologist called and informed them that Rae had been placed into an induced coma. Terri struggled to breathe, her body numb. During the night, Rae's heart had failed, said the voice on the phone, and for a period of time her brain had been starved of oxygen.

The doctor explained Rae might not survive.

At the hospital, the neonatologist directed Terri, screaming and crying, away from Rae, and into a small room next to the NICU where other doctors were present. They talked about the rare and unexpected series of circumstances that had occurred, but Terri heard none of it. Afterward, they listened sympathetically as she accused the doctors of negligence. And told them she no longer trusted this hospital.

When she'd finished her rant, she demanded to see Rae.

"You don't understand," one of the doctors cautioned her. "Your daughter is going to need around-the-clock care for the rest of her life. She'll more than likely need to be institutionalized."

"I can handle it," insisted Terri.

In the NICU, she stared at the tube down Rae's throat, the whirring ventilator linking her to life. There were no other parents in the room. The weight crashed down on her and she collapsed alongside the incubator into a fetal position, awash in tears. Alan bent down and rubbed her back.

After 30 days in the neonatal intensive care unit, Rae was finally released. Her discharge papers, 10 pages from the hospital, listed medications, weekly therapy appointments, along with follow-up doctors' appointments. The doctors highly encouraged her to seek institutional alternatives to home care.

"We can handle this," said Terri.

The look on Alan's face suggested he was having second thoughts.

When Rae was five, they traveled to Tijuana for an experimental procedure, a stem cell injection meant to regenerate brain cells. Rae hadn't met any milestones: rolling over, sitting, holding objects, eating, talking, or walking. Terri had hoped with more therapy sessions—some twice a day, every day—Rae would catch up. But it didn't happen.

The driver, with the stem cells in a medical bag, picked Terri, Alan, and Rae up at a hotel in San Diego and crossed the border with two other desperate families. They sat and waited on cheap vinyl seats in a sparsely furnished office. The driver, acting as interpreter, directed each family into separate procedure rooms. Rae sat on Terri's lap while the doctor injected 1.2 million umbilical cord stem cells into Rae's stomach tissue. She winced from the pain.

In the next room, a young girl the same age as Rae also received a shot in her belly. Within minutes, both young girls started screaming. A doctor zoomed in, jabbed Rae's arm with a needle, and left.

"What did you give her?" Terri screamed over Rae's sobbing.

Alan and the driver chased after the doctor. "An antihistamine," he said, slamming the door to an office.

Rae's excruciating muscle inflammation and cramping continued for three days, and as soon as she was well enough, the driver took them back. In the U.S., they found out Rae had received tainted stem cells. They'd taken a chance, and had failed.

Rae followed her own timeline. Trapped in a body she had no control over, her arms and legs flailing, Rae still managed to get her point across. When she was six, she gazed longingly at her cousin's Disney princess jacket while sitting in her wheelchair.

Terri dabbed a cloth to Rae's mouth, wiping away blond strands of drool.

"Do you like her jacket?" Terri asked her. "On the back are Cinderella, Belle, and Sleeping Beauty." Rae had watched the movies, owned the tiaras, and wore the T-shirts.

"Do you want a princess jacket, too?" asked Terri.

Rae smiled and arched her back to show her response.

A few days later, Terri and Alan wheeled Rae into the Disney store in the local mall. As usual, people stared at Rae—abruptly turning away when Terri caught their eyes. It was different when other children stared, though; it gave Terri the opportunity to explain that Rae was saying hello to them with a smile.

Terri pulled three different princess jackets from the racks and showed Rae each one. Then Alan placed them on the racks surrounding her wheelchair, which drew the attention of a curious sales clerk.

Terri knelt down, eye-level with Rae. "Look at the one you want, then look at me to tell me you made your decision."

The young sales clerk craned her neck and stood behind Alan, who stood off to the side with his arms crossed, encouraging Rae with a smile. "We're waiting for her to decide which one she wants," he told the young girl, who looked distressed. He held his arm out to prevent her from stepping closer.

Rae stared at the first jacket, then looked at Terri, revealing she wanted that one. Rae stared at the second jacket and again looked at Terri, indicating she also wanted that one. Then Rae stared at the third jacket and looked at Terri. Rae giggled.

"Oh no, you don't get all three. Pick one," Terri said.

Fidgeting her hands nervously, the clerk asked, "How do you know what she wants?"

"She talks with her eyes. She has a talking device at home, but she hasn't mastered it yet." Terri turned to Rae. "You want to try them on?"

Rae's arms flailed wide and she squealed. Her delight was clear to everyone.

Alan released the buckles on her wheelchair, lifted her out, and handed her to Terri. Supporting her with one arm, with the other Terri managed to get Rae's arms into the jacket sleeves and angled her so she could see herself in the tri-mirror.

"You look beautiful," said Alan.

They repeated the process with the other two jackets. With the three jackets on the floor around them, Terri kept hold of Rae while she bunny-hopped two steps toward the faded blue jean jacket with pink sleeves, trimmed with the same princesses as her cousin's jacket. Alan picked up the chosen jacket and handed it to the sales clerk.

"This one," he said.

Rae smiled at the sales clerk.

Rae never learned to walk, talk, or sit, but taught everyone she met to accept people as they were. She smiled at everyone. And they smiled back.

By age 10, the high-speed roller coaster that was life with Rae had brought them peaks—like when she first laughed out loud—and death-defying drops, like when she had seizures. They had banked the curves by avoiding hospitalizations, had spiraled through loops, endured surgery after surgery, and survived jolting stops, like when there'd been a code blue that thankfully turned out not to require life support.

It was scary. But it was also rich and full. And it was over too soon.

Rae's last year was filled with failed surgeries and medicines that didn't work. Pain that wouldn't let up, and ever-increasing morphine doses. Another surgery was scheduled. Terri and Alan reluctantly discussed a DNR if things went wrong—but it never came to that.

In the hospital, awaiting surgery, Rae's oxygen level dropped abruptly and her lungs filled with liquid. The nurse slammed the code-blue button.

The alarm blared.

In the weeks after Rae died, Terri nestled in the recliner where she and Rae used to rock, wrapped in Rae's SpongeBob snuggie, sniffing for the faint scent of her. She watched and re-watched the slide show played at Rae's funeral. Sometimes, she clung to Rae's favorite Shrek doll, squeezing so hard it spoke: "Better out than in, I always say." Alan would come home from work and ask Terri what she had done that day. Her blank stare said everything.

Reluctantly, she had responded to a friend's entreaty: a partner at a local firm was desperate to fill a tax-preparer position. For Terri, with years of previous experience, no résumé would be required. At first, Terri resisted, having become habituated to her misery. But Alan's insistence finally won out.

And now, here she was, sitting in a poorly lit cubicle, with an impossible deadline, the words she'd uttered early on, after Rae's birth, echoing in her head: "I can handle this."

Terri pressed her phone to activate the screen saver again. Wiping away a tear, she smiled. Rae had indeed been perfect as Rae. She called her friend Phyllis, who had helped her through many trying times, and who was passionate about her volunteer work at Misericordia. When Phyllis didn't answer, she hung up.

She walked down the corridor of window offices, gnawing at the eraser end of a pencil, and entered David's office.

"Judy's been working on some complex individual returns," she told him firmly. "She could use more guidance."

David dropped his pen, leaned back in his chair, and held his fingers together in a tepee. "If she can't figure it out, maybe she's not cut out for the job," he said. He raised his fingers and pointed them toward the door.

Maybe the rumors are true, Terri wondered, and jerk-face has hired me to replace Judy. She left without a word.

She walked back down the hallway, picturing Rae in her Disney princess jacket. She felt a rush of love and pride for all the things her sweet girl had accomplished in her too-brief life, things that mattered: making people happy, making people proud, and giving people all her unbridled love and joy. Back in her office, she picked up David's "urgent" file. It felt heavy in her hands. Toxic.

She called her friend Phyllis again. This time she left a message: "Phyllis? Hi, it's Terri. Listen, when you asked me several weeks ago if I'd like to volunteer at Misericordia, I wasn't ready, but I am now." She pulled the phone from her ear and cast a glance at Rae. "And I want to do it full-time, or as much as I can. I can't think of anything more I'd like to do than to help with those kids with disabilities. Great. Thanks, Phyllis."

She kept the screen-saver image open, holding it to her chest, and bowed her head. "Thanks, honey," she whispered. She grabbed the IRS regs and walked over to Judy's cubicle.

"You got a minute? I've got something I want to show you. I'm sure you'll be able to handle it."

— RITA ANGELINI —

Rita grew up in Chicago, and recently moved to Fort Myers, FL. A retired certified public accountant, she is pursuing her passion for writing. She plans to publish her memoir about life with her daughter, KiKi, who teaches her family about compassion, faith, and unconditional love without speaking a word.

TRUE TURNING POINTS

Memoir and Creative Non-Fiction

Shaken

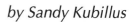

by Sandy Kubillus

y thirteen-year-old sister waved my secret love note to my second-grade heartthrob, singing, "Sandra's got a boyfriend, Sandra's got a boyfriend!"

My face burned. Karen had pounced on it when it fell out of my jacket pocket in our bedroom.

"I do not. Give it to me!" I yelled. My blond pigtails swooshed across my face when I lunged for the letter, which she held three feet above my head. Tears formed at the corners of my eyes.

"Dear Douglas," she sneered while reading the note. "Do you like me? I love you. Love, Sandra." She emphasized the word "love" both times before tossing the note on my bed.

My stomach twisted with embarrassment. I sank onto my bed and covered my face to hide my tears. He was coming over to play in a half hour. I would die if she told him! I could see him doubling over in hysterics, while I'd want to crawl into a hole and die. I crumpled the note and hurled it into the trash can, knowing I'd be too scared to give it to him.

For weeks I had nervously caressed that note in my pocket, trying to judge the right time to give it to him. I'd steal glances at his shiny black hair where he sat two rows across from me at the public grammar school in a suburb southwest of Chicago. But on this Friday afternoon, the first warm day of spring on the 21st of April 1967, I had mustered the courage to invite him over to play after school. Now I felt petrified Karen would let out my secret.

"Dinner's on the table," Mom yelled from the kitchen. We always ate dinner at half past three before Dad left for the second shift at the canning factory.

Rubbing my damp eyes with my sleeve, I slumped over the plate of fish sticks, peas, and tater tots. A storm raged in my stomach while I glanced at the clock.

Karen grinned, plopping into the chair next to me, while my fifteen-year-old brother Mickey sat at the far end of the table. No one said anything, as usual, afraid of Dad's criticism.

At three forty-five sharp, Dad folded his newspaper, picked up his lunch pail, kissed my mom on the cheek, and mumbled his goodbye.

"When do we get to meet your boyfriend?" Karen said when the screen door slammed.

My face blushed. "Mom, Douglas is coming over in a few minutes. Can you tell Karen to leave us alone?" I shoveled the remaining fish stick into my mouth, pushing the detested peas around on my plate.

"He's coming here?" Karen smirked. "Just wait till I tell him about the note!"

"No!" I yelped. "I'll tell him you're lying." My fingers clenched around the fork; my palms were sweating. Karen was going to ruin everything.

The back doorbell rang. I jumped from my chair and flew down the steps, while Mom admonished Karen. I burst through the screen door, causing Douglas to take a step back.

"Let's play 'tag.' You're it." I just wanted to run—to get away from Karen. He wore his school clothes, looking neat and clean as usual, in a red T-shirt with brown pants, while I had changed out of my skirt into a sweatshirt and jeans.

We shouted above the howling wind when we came close to tagging each other. Strong gusts almost blew us over. Within ten minutes we were breathless and sat at the shady picnic table. My left pigtail blew into my open mouth. I pulled it out and yelled, "This wind is crazy! I can almost lean into it and not fall over."

A dried brown maple leaf blew into Douglas's face while he nodded in agreement. I laughed.

"Would you like to play in my basement?" Mom always let me have friends in our unfinished basement when Dad wasn't home. I hoped Karen would be too busy doing the dishes to bother us. She had never talked to any of my friends before, nor had anyone else in my family. We were kids. The only time teenagers or adults talked to us was to yell or order us to do something.

We bounded down the stairs into the stillness of the dim basement. I flicked on the lights.

"Wow, you have a ping-pong table," Douglas said. "Can we play?"

Neither of us was coordinated enough to volley the ball more than once or twice. Mostly we searched for lost balls or chased Chipper, my brown cocker spaniel, to remove the slobbery ball from his mouth.

The phone rang upstairs and I heard Mom say, "Oh, hi Al." My ears perked up. Dad never called home. I glanced at the clock by the washing machine. It was almost five.

Mom shouted down the stairs, "Sandra, send your friend home. A big storm is coming."

I followed Douglas out the back door and noticed the dark rain clouds billowing in the western sky.

Douglas glanced toward them. His eyes widened and he bolted down the driveway without saying goodbye.

The strong wind had stopped. Not a leaf fluttered in the trees, or a bird flew in the sky. The world was quiet, as if waiting. I stared at the clouds. They ballooned upward, turning purplish, almost black. I wanted to keep watching, to see what would happen.

Mom poked her head out the screen door and said, "Sandra, go in the basement. There's a tornado warning."

"But Douglas lives three blocks away," I said, ducking under Mom's arm holding the door open.

"He lives that far?" Mom said. "Let's hope he runs fast." Dad had our only car.

"There goes your boyfriend, blown away in a storm," Karen teased from the bottom of the stairs.

"Shut up!" I jumped the final step, and then slapped her arm. "He's not my boyfriend."

"He'll probably be fine," Mom said. "The sirens aren't ringing and the storm hasn't started yet."

We followed Mickey into the cramped space underneath the stairs next to paint cans and stinky old coats. "Yuck," Karen said, pushing away a cobweb. "This is gross."

We gazed uncomfortably at each other in the small space. Mickey crouched. I knelt on an old rubber boot, holding onto Chipper's collar. He panted and tried to pull away. The only thing I knew about tornadoes was from *The Wizard of Oz*, with the crashing wind sucking up the farmhouse and transporting Dorothy and Toto to another land. My heart started to pound. Could Douglas make it home okay? I crossed my fingers and said a quick silent prayer.

Tornado sirens began to wail in the distance, stopping after a few minutes. No sounds of a storm came from outside.

"My legs are cramping up," Mickey said. "I need to stand." He moved a few feet away from the stairs and looked across the basement out the window.

Mom followed him, flinging a cobweb from her beehive hair. The windows facing south showed a lighter sky than those to the north.

"Maybe the storm stayed north," Mom said. "It hasn't even rained yet and the sirens stopped."

I followed her to look out the window and released my grip on Chipper's collar. He began climbing the stairs.

"Chipper, no!" I yelled, chasing after him.

"I think it missed us," Mom said. "We can go upstairs."

I breathed a sigh of relief. Douglas should have made it home without even getting wet.

We tentatively ascended the stairs. Our curiosity led us into the living room, where we stared at the bulging clouds through the oversized picture window. The sky to the northwest was dark green mixed with deep purple, like a bad bruise. The clouds moved in slow motion. Everything outside was still and silent—deadly silent.

A blast of wind shook the window. My head jerked backward in surprise.

Leaves and small twigs shot sideways, not touching the ground. A gale exploded through the trees, causing thick branches to sway, then bend toward the ground. Some snapped. The mature Chinese elm in the parkway leaned toward our house, almost touching the window.

All four of us stood frozen—our eyes glued to the action, mesmerized.

Grape-size hail began slamming the window.

"Get away," Mom yelled above the roar of the storm. "The window might break. Get to the back of the room."

Our house wasn't safe?

"Chipper!" I grabbed the quivering dog and dragged him with me.

We stood in the alcove about twenty feet from the window. Were we far enough back to protect us from flying glass? I knelt behind Mom on the green carpet, holding Chipper's collar with my sweaty palm.

Elm branches swung sideways through the driving storm. Our visibility was limited to a few feet beyond the window through the pounding hail.

A violent gust shook the window. I turned away. My heart throbbed in my ears.

"Mickey, Karen, if that window breaks, get ready to carry the couch back here," Mom shouted above the racket of the storm. "We can't let it get wet." Her precious gold couch, barely a month old, had cost her two years of wages.

My ears popped and I started trembling almost as much as Chipper. Dad always said brick houses, like ours, were stronger than wooden ones. But what about that huge window?

Large branches flew past, then roofing tiles, a lawn chair, and other garbage. The window quivered. Hail changed to sheets of blinding rain.

My breaths came in short gulps. I thought about Douglas. He should have made it home with minutes to spare—at least I hoped so.

The lights flickered and then went out, freezing the clock at twenty past five. The room darkened, matching the blackness outside. Please, God, don't let the window break, I silently prayed, crossing my fingers for good luck.

Seconds passed, leading to minutes. The black sky began to lighten and the deafening wind faded.

We could hear ourselves breathe again.

"Wow, I think it's almost over," Mom said. "I don't know what we would have done if the window broke."

We gravitated toward the picture window, seeing tree branches scattered everywhere. The neighbor's large ash had cracked in half, blocking the sidewalk. Newspapers blew across the lawn. Water flooded the street at the clogged storm drain below our driveway.

When there was nothing more to see, each of us grabbed a flashlight and scattered to different rooms. Karen worked on homework, while I stared at a comic book and worried about Douglas. I didn't have his phone number.

Two hours later the phone rang.

"Oh, really?" Mom said into the phone. "I didn't know our phone was dead." All of us migrated to the candle-lit kitchen. I could hear Dad's voice on the other end. "A tornado?" she asked. "I thought it was just a bad storm."

Mom hung up the phone and told Karen to turn on her transistor radio. A local newscaster filled us in on the details of the storm.

"A severe tornado touched down in Oak Lawn late this afternoon with winds exceeding 170 miles per hour causing a swath of destruction at the busy intersection of 95th Street and Southwest Highway, where many cars were overturned." We listened through the static.

"Oh no!" Mom said. "That's less than a mile away."

"Most of the damage appears to have occurred at Oak Lawn High School, where a wing of the building collapsed," the announcer continued. "Fortunately, no students were in the building at the time."

My heart raced and I looked at Mickey, who stood stone-faced, likely knowing kids at that school.

The radio crackled and went on. "The tornado then skipped farther east before touching down at the Oak Lawn Roller Rink, collapsing the back of the building. The front half of the McDonald's across the street was also damaged, but hardest hit was the nearby mobile home park."

My jaw dropped. Cars flipped over. Injuries. Possibly deaths. We could have been at McDonald's or the roller rink. I wondered what the world looked like past our house, past our block, to the familiar stores and buildings, now hidden beneath the evening darkness. I crossed my fingers, hoping Douglas was alright.

"We should have stayed in the basement instead of standing in the living room," Mom said. "It could have been a lot worse if the tornado had moved a few blocks south."

In that moment I realized the sky could turn on us at any time with deadly consequences. I'll never forget that sky.

The next morning, Mom turned on the kitchen television while Karen and I sat at the counter eating our breakfast cereal. News coverage blocked my Saturday cartoons with images of damaged homes, confused homeowners, and interviews with the injured.

I moved closer to the small TV, seeking images of familiar buildings.

"The Oak Lawn tornado was the deadliest of several others that hit Northern Illinois yesterday, leaving thirty-three dead and over five hundred injured," the newscaster said. "Most of the fatalities were in occupied cars that were tossed about while waiting at the stoplight by the high school."

"Wow," Mom said, her eyes glued to the TV, her mouth agape.

I wondered about my school, my friends, and Douglas, but said nothing.

"Can I go outside?" I wanted to see if there was any damage to our block.

"You'll have to put on your winter coat, it must have dropped thirty degrees since yesterday," Mom said. "Karen and Mickey, go outside with Sandra and pick up the branches and trash before your father wakes up."

After lunch, Dad said, "Let's take a drive and see what happened."

All five of us squeezed into our forest-green, cigarette-smelling Dodge Dart, but within a half-mile, barricades and police cars blocked the road. Dad parked on a side street.

The cold, bitter wind stung, causing me to yank my rainbow-striped stocking cap over my ears and shove my hands into my jacket pockets. We followed the curiosity-seeking crowd walking west on 95th Street. Dad led and we followed in order by age.

We stepped between broken boards, blowing papers, large pieces of plastic, scattered shingles, and many tree branches.

"Oh, my God!" Mom said, seeing a wall torn off a house with the rooms exposed to the outside, its contents strewn about. "This could have happened to us. That house was made of brick."

I glared at her. Our house could have blown apart and all Mom had cared about was her stupid couch?

Homeowners walked among the debris, trying to salvage anything usable. A woman cried out, then clutched a picture frame to her chest.

I stood fascinated, looking for the worst, but realizing people had been hurt. Some had died. Karen and I pointed out everything we saw, each trying to top the other. At the intersection by the high school, at least a dozen cars lay over-turned along with a school bus. One bus was perched on top of a house.

What happened to those people? The ambulances were gone, leaving only the damaged cars. The occupants hadn't gone to Oz.

My chest tightened. If the tornado had hit at a different time, we could have been in one of those cars. Or if the tornado had moved south a few blocks, our house might have been damaged and we could have been injured, especially where we stood, guarding Mom's precious couch.

A touch of fate saved us from disaster.

Douglas lived farther from the damage, but what if he was outside when the storm hit? He could have gotten pinned by a falling tree, or hit by a flying branch.

Mom's friend called on Sunday, saying she knew a thirteen-year-old girl named Christine, who was practicing for a competition at the roller rink. Everyone who followed the manager's directions to stay in the windowless rink either died or was injured. Christine's body was uncovered under a pile of bricks.

I gulped hard when Mom told me. Thirteen—Karen's age. The death of this girl—and at a place I knew well—drove the image home. I could die or lose my home or family at any time. The random acts of storms—who survived, who died—showed me the preciousness of life.

On Monday morning, the tornado was all my girlfriends could talk about, trying to top each other with what they had seen or heard. I stole furtive glances around the crowd of kids outside the school, not finding Douglas. I didn't tell anyone about his visit—afraid of more teasing. The doors opened and we filed into our classrooms.

My anxiety grew by the second.

A minute before the bell rang, Douglas burst into the classroom, breathing hard. I grinned when I spotted him. Mom had been right. He made it home okay.

Douglas turned away and took his seat. At recess he ignored me, and also at lunch.

Nothing felt the same after the tornado. On my walk home from school, it occurred to me that Douglas and I didn't have a lot in common and our playdate wasn't that much fun. My feelings for him seemed so trivial after all that had happened.

We never talked again.

It would be more than a decade before I brought another boy to my house. Whether that had anything to do with the tornado or Karen's teasing, I don't really know. But that storm caused me to realize that my parents didn't always make the right choices—that they could be wrong, possibly with deadly consequences.

Every time I see dark clouds billowing in the northwest, my heart begins to race. I'll never forget that sky.

SANDY KUBILLUS

Sandy's memoir, "Shaken," is her first published story. She's working on a book-length memoir about dogs that influenced her life. She has been a member of OCWW for over five years, squeezing it in between her jobs as an environmental consultant and an adjunct college instructor.

The Coat

by Ronit Bezalel

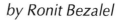

hy is this mammoth coat still here? I sighed as I shuffled through the items in my front closet. There were the usual suspects: my favorite white denim jacket, five cycling jerseys, two long black wool coats, a short brown jacket, and a raincoat, all size small. Lording over everything was my mother's XXXL ski jacket, a pageant of bright blue and yellow with a reflective silver lining. She gave me this jacket four years ago, and now her oversized coat dominated everything else in my wardrobe. I slipped on the extravaganza and disappeared into its warmth. Catching a glimpse of myself in the mirror, I smiled slightly. I was enveloped by a Technicolor abominable snowman.

I loved this coat. Even though it was too big, it made me feel cozy and appreciated. Despite having good friends, I still felt lonely as I tended to keep people at arm's length. The coat was perfect, demanding nothing while offering complete warmth and safety.

Last year, an acquaintance was collecting clothing for homeless youth, and I leapt at the chance to finally gift my mother's coat to someone who could use it more. Driving with the jacket in the backseat, my stomach tightened. Sweat beaded on my forehead. *I can't go through with this.* I felt stupid at not being able to part with an inanimate object. *It's just fabric and zippers.* Feeling guilty as hell, I turned around and drove the coat back to my place.

I am my mother's daughter. Her eldest, I inherited her asthma, her eczema, her anxiety. Growing up, she shielded me with her oversized mothering. Even as an adult, I am terrified to lose her, especially after her cancer diagnosis ten years ago. I still call frequently, sometimes wearing her out with my need to connect.

My mother gave me her coat four years ago when I visited my parents in Vermont for Thanksgiving. I traveled with a broken thumb. Well, not exactly a broken thumb. A torn ligament.

My injury occurred during the first race of the Chicago Cyclocross Cup series. It was a warm September day, full of promise. I had been training all summer for this season, my tenth. Cyclocross involves pedaling furiously across grass, leaping off the bike, and jumping over barriers. I loved the rhythm of this sport for its intensity, for pushing my 40-year-old body to its limits. When I put on my uniform, a spandex jersey and matching shorts, I felt like I was changing into a superhero.

My teammates and I rode in all weather conditions. Falling was a part of the experience and I collected more bruises than wins, wearing them as badges of honor. This September day, I was on my last lap when I skidded on a muddy corner, twisting my handlebars. My thumb bent back sharply against metal and dirt. I gingerly finished the race, ashamed to be felled by something so minor.

The emergency clinic diagnosed the injury as a sprain. Simple tasks, like tying shoes and zipping pants, were excruciating. Biking was out of the question. Three months after the injury, I finally visited an orthopedic surgeon. He informed me that I had torn my radial collateral ligament.

A week later, I sat by myself in the surgery waiting room, surrounded by beige carpet, canned music and people hunched over their phones. Ten years earlier, when my mom was diagnosed with Stage IV inflammatory breast cancer, I flew to Vermont for her mastectomy. And now, she had offered to fly from Vermont to Chicago for my surgery. I told her it wasn't necessary.

I questioned my decision when the receptionist handed me paperwork to review.

"You've got the wrong ligament," I said. *Why on earth did I come to the surgery by myself?*

"It's the radial ligament, not the ulnar. The radial." I kept talking, chilled with fear. *Why couldn't I have accepted my mother's offer?*

My surgeon assured me that this was just a clerical error. That he indeed did know which ligament he would be gluing back to the bone. That I would be fine. I managed a thin smile, but I felt like exploding. My breath quickened. *THIS IS MY THUMB. It shouldn't be left to a clerical error.*

I went outside and phoned my mother. She reassured me that she survived her surgery and that I would survive mine. I felt ashamed for needing her so much, but I was grateful that she always knew the right thing to say.

A week after the surgery, I arrived at my parents' house in Vermont for Thanksgiving with my arm in a sling and my thumb in a cast. It was a chilly November, and I could see my breath.

"Poor darling child," my mother fussed over my thumb.

"It's nothing, just a little tear." I tried to feign indifference, but I was warmed by her fussing. My mother implored me to wear her enormous multicolored jacket when I ventured outside.

"I'll be okay in my coat," I said, even though it was too thin for the 30-degree temperatures and I had to keep it unzipped to accommodate the sling. She continued to pressure me.

"Fine. I'll wear it." I acquiesced when I realized that my mother's coat was the perfect size to fit over my sling.

I relished the coat's warmth as I traversed my childhood jogging route along rural Vermont roads. I buried my face in its collar. I thought about our deceased golden retriever, Boomer, who used to join me on my runs. I'd hear his collar jangle as he lurched forward, lured by the scent of woodchuck or deer. He'd disappear into the bushes and I'd listen to the slap of my shoes, the steady pounding against pavement. There was a comfort in that rhythm, that order.

My mother pleaded with me to take her coat back to Chicago. I didn't want to take it, but she reassured me she had another one. "You're going to catch a chill. You need it."

My mother was right—I did need it. Just not in the way she envisioned.

I wore the coat to the follow-up surgery where the metal pin was removed. The surgeon was pleased with his work. The ligament held firm. I wore the coat to my occupational therapy appointments as I practiced patience, slowly training my thumb to move adroitly once again.

I wore the coat as I walked along Lake Michigan, my boots crunching in the snow. My breath visible. The steam rising off the lake.

I stubbornly wore the coat when the weather turned warm. It felt like my mother was there with me as I sweated within its embrace.

Eventually, the weather became too warm to wear the coat and it became a tenant in my closet. When the weather turned chilly again, I no longer needed such a bulky coat, so it was buried deeper in my closet. Four years later, I confronted reality when I asked myself why the coat was still there. I felt like it was time to let go.

The opportunity presented itself this year in late autumn, when I was walking with my friend George along the lakefront path. I was listening to the crunch of fallen leaves under my feet and chatting with George about the Chicago Cubs. He was sure that this year they were going to win it all. George mentioned that he had just been let go from his job, and I noticed that he was shivering.

"George, this may sound strange, but can I offer you a coat?"

"A coat?"

"Yeah, it's a little big for me, but I think it would fit you perfectly."

"I would love that." George looked at me with pale blue watery eyes.

Oh, shoot. My hands felt clammy and I felt a familiar tightening in my stomach. I took a deep breath to calm my nerves. *What had I done? Would it be bad form to take the offer back?*

But I couldn't take back the offer. Not this time.

George beamed as he tried on the coat. It fit him perfectly. "I normally wouldn't buy something so bright," he gushed.

"It *is* bright," I laughed. "But it looks good on you."

The knot in my stomach receded and I felt a wave of relief. I could do this. I no longer needed the coat to remind me that I'd be fine.

Later, I told my mother that I had finally given her coat away. She was thrilled. As for myself, I still have reservations. I don't know if it was the right time. I don't know if there is ever a right time to let go.

— RONIT BEZALEL

Ronit is an award-winning filmmaker, writer, and photographer based in Chicago and Jerusalem. Her films include *70 Acres in Chicago: Cabrini Green*, which screened worldwide as a catalyst to discuss affordable housing. Her work can be found at ronitfilms.com.

Inspiration Attained

by Fred Fitzsimmons

"Your work shows promise. Keep writing!"

Fifty-nine years ago, when I was a college senior, my creative writing professor wrote those words beside an "A+" at the top of the one-act play I submitted as my final class assignment. The words inspired me to pursue what I have come to love.

Those intentions got sidetracked, and it took fifty-three years for my professor's grand inspirations to resurface. And another three years of demanding keyboard toil to generate any work of significance on the novel I had conceived over the years, plus an additional three years to complete the task. All told, a full fifty-nine years.

During those decades my mind spilled over with themes for novels, short stories, a memoir, and plays. I could feel time pressure closing in on me to post all the themes I had in mind in the time I had left.

I yearned to express the grittiness and human nature of the individuals portrayed in the writings of David Mamet and Nelson Algren. And I wanted to try to match the earthy accounts embodied in Studs Terkel's real-life oral histories of the human spirit of ordinary folks, their living standards, their jobs, and their feelings. And I longed to pursue the simplicity found in the writings of Ernest Hemingway, and capture the witty, insightful philosophical and cultural insights into life's complications as depicted by Saul Bellow.

After receiving my diploma, I entered a graduate program, gained an MBA, met the love of my life, joined the workforce, married, raised two children, and for the next fifty-plus years, worked hard to earn a satisfactory living to provide for my family and my children's education.

Through those years my fierce flames of intention to become a creative writer got tamped-down and waned, but never died. Yes, I wrote for business. But it was detailed, fact-punctuated, trade text—descriptive, dry, barren of dialog; telling not showing. I wrote hundreds—no—thousands of market reports, client proposals, one-year, three-year, and five-year company plans, memos, correspondence, and more.

All those years, my drive to achieve success as a businessman suppressed my inspiration to write about the things in life that passionately moved me—man's everyday existence that portrays the human spirit and all its joys, beauty, love, misery, damnation, and recompense. It was only after retirement that I came to realize how much fodder those experiences in marketing, advertising, educational services, market research, and consulting provided me for the writing I had always wanted to do.

I wrote my sweetheart and future wife poetry and letters, which she found worthy enough to save. A different kind of writing from a smitten guy to a lovely lady, a hoped-for wife-to-be. At times, my writings to her were subtle, other times direct, occasionally whimsical, and always sprinkled with traces of sub-surface passion. All were more creative than my industry expressions, but not at all like the fiction and creative non-fiction I envisioned as the portrayals of everyday life I conceived in my initial plans.

Year after year my hunger to write imaginatively continued bubbling up near the surface, but failed to break through.

One day, just before retiring, while sorting old belongings and reams of paper records from business, college, and high school, I discovered the note from my creative writing professor. "Your work shows promise. Keep writing!" A lightning-like strike careened through me. This was the perfect time, my opportunity. With the pressures and stresses of business left behind, and facing retirement, I could, for the first time, devote myself to express my desire to write. At that moment, my attainment began.

I was a workaholic. I needed a plan. A quiet sedentary life in retirement? Not an option. It would have driven my wife and me mad. Plans to spend time with our children and grandchildren, reading, traveling, fishing, golf, and tennis—still left me with time to fill. Soon golf and tennis would lose their allure, and my older fishing buddies, with their infirmities beginning to flare, could not be depended on to plug the void. I'd find myself with even more time to fill.

I grasped the note in my fist and spent four to six hours setting out thoughts on the novel that had been percolating in me for years. I wrote feverishly for months until I had produced an exhausting, self-satisfying, 169,500-word, 595-page novel with 78 chapters. I applied what skilled authors say about writing down everything you can think of and editing out the information dump's disposable parts later. But now what to do with this unwieldy tome? I learned fast I was about to face the hard part—editing the work into an easily readable, engaging, enjoyable work of fiction. The work was tedious. The progress slow. But I pushed on.

By luck, in August 2015, my wife and I were having dinner with a neighbor and his wife. She was also an unpublished writer, with a burning, long-suppressed desire to finish writing her novel. I revealed my frustration about the editing of my book, and she chimed in about the challenges she was facing. Her book was geared toward middle-grade students, and mine was character-driven upmarket fiction, but we shared common ground in our writing frustrations.

She suggested I take a novel-writing workshop with Fred Shafer, with whom she'd booked a class several years earlier at Northwestern. She also recommended attending the workshops offered by Off Campus Writers' Workshop (OCWW) located in Winnetka, the suburb north of Wilmette, where we lived. Coincidentally, Fred Shafer was to be conducting the first four seminars in September.

Fred's presentations were so informative and inspiring that I joined OCWW immediately following the conclusion of his lectures. Thus began my weekly exposure to gifted professional authors and university instructors, and a lengthy—but productive—learning curve.

After only four months as an OCWW member, at the first 2016 January workshop, I became aware of something being quite different. I learned that a fallout between two board of director factions, simmering for months, had exploded at the December holiday party that I missed. The president, several officers, most of the board, and a significant number of their followers, left the group overnight, creating a membership and financial crisis. A board member involved in the holiday party dispute took over as president, picked up the shattered pieces, and vowed to steady the ship.

Despite these difficulties, OCWW held a first-ever writers' conference at Hackney's restaurant in Glenview that spring, honoring the late Rita Turow, one of OCWW's founding members and the mother of the celebrated *New York Times* best-selling novelist Scott Turow. I had read all of his books, as he was one of my favorite novelists. Scott gave the luncheon address toasting his mother.

During a break, I shared with Scott the frustration I felt with editing my 595-page book. I asked him if it was true that agents and publishers wouldn't consider a book exceeding 300 pages.

"Fred," he said. "No doubt 595 pages is too long for a debut author, but if the story and writing are excellent and marketable, there is nothing magic about 300 pages. My suggestion, once you edit your work to near that level, fight for keeping every word, every page you believe is essential to defend your narrative. Don't give up a single page to adhere to an arbitrary number of pages an agent or publisher says is necessary." Scott's guidance became the first of many pieces of craft information I received from him, continuing with each of his book-launch readings I attended. I came to consider him a valued writing helper.

Later that year, while exploring OCWW's website, I saw that the position of vice president remained vacant. It occurred to me that my business organization skills could help to stabilize the organization. I applied for—and gained—the appointment.

It wasn't smooth sailing. And, tragically, it took an enormous amount of precious time away from my writing and editing—another forced suppression of my aim to achieve my inspiration fully. But I did it because I saw the inherent value of the organization, what it was contributing to my new OCWW writing friends, and, particularly, what it was already doing for me and my writing. The instructional opportunity was beyond compare, and I wanted it to survive and thrive, and me and my writing along with it. Soon after I assumed the post, the new president had to deal with health issues affecting a close family member who lived on the West Coast; her extended absences from OCWW left the group rudderless.

My appointment as vice president turned into a wild ride for the next couple of years. I found myself thrust into the top office, which permitted me to recruit and reconfigure the volunteer board and officer slate with talented, dedicated, hard-working persons who embraced their responsibilities to help renew the organization. They—along with the help of the dozens of other volunteers, recruited speakers, stellar instructional programs, and OCWW's welcoming social atmosphere—have revitalized the organization.

While president, I engaged Fred Shafer to help me edit my novel, and he remains an extraordinary editing resource for my other creative efforts. He knows how to praise while supplying a professional, gentle kick in the seat of the pants. "Fred, you're the real deal." I felt the same excitement I did in college. "You are. Yes, your novel needs to be an engaging, readable number of pages, but you have a solid story, and the writing is excellent. What's required is more hard editing."

The time spent editing far exceeded my time of writing. I excised cherished words, sentences, and paragraphs. Whole scenes. Minor characters were cut, others enhanced, entire chapters lopped off. It was becoming a brutal, frustrating experience.

To force me on, I kept thinking: Many changes confront us in our lives—some beneficial, others not, some momentous, others small, some meaningful, others less so. The keys are how you face them, embrace them, or use them as a learning experience. I plowed forward.

The climb from when my inspiration became reinvigorated to this point in my novel's journey started as a sprint but had become more like a lead-foot trudge. Earlier, the end had been beyond sight, however, I could now vaguely see the hilltop in the distance. I kept telling myself I had only to plod on a little longer to finish my manuscript.

As the finish line came within reach, on October 25, 2018, I suffered a severe heart attack requiring a triple bypass. My wife saved my life by getting me to the hospital emergency room in the nick of time. It was a huge setback to my health and a total disruption to completing my manuscript.

My recovery was slow and steady. With spirits and editing renewed, the finish came back into view—when it disappeared again on May 24, 2019. Less than seven months after my bypasses, I was diagnosed with esophageal cancer.

Strength drained, optimism battered, hope diminished, I trudged on. Crushed. It looked like my vision of publishing my book was going to elude me. Between weight and energy loss, fatigue reached a point where I couldn't enjoy reading a good book or conjure up a creative thought. Even climbing the stairs to my loft writing nest was a struggle that took weeks to finally have the strength to do again.

But through my wife's loving care, my family's support, and my OCWW colleagues' phone calls, emails, and notes of encouragement, I pushed on. My inspiration returned with an urgency far beyond what I had earlier experienced. I kept saying it, "Persist, persist, press on, press on." And I did.

Fast-forward a year, and the book has become a realistic 350 pages in length, down from 595 pages, thanks in no small part to Fred Shafer, who has become my genuine friend, mentor and writing inspiration. One more edit and Fred's final review, and it will be ready to pass both an agent's and a publisher's white-glove inspections.

Stewarding OCWW through choppy waters the past three-and-a-half years has been an exhilarating, rewarding experience. I've been exposed to *New York Times* bestsellers, a Pulitzer Prize runner-up, a National Book Award finalist, a Heartland Award winner, a Bram Stoker runner-up, a Barnes & Noble Book of the Year Award winner. A ghost-writer for the Robert Ludlum series, a Chicago Writers Association Book of the Year winner, and a writer-in-residence at Northwestern University who is also a MacArthur Grant recipient. I've met many published authors and talented writing instructors. Fred Shafer, Scott Turow, Stuart Dybek, Rebecca Makkai, Goldie Goldbloom, Jamie Freveletti, Jay Bonansinga, Richard Thomas, Kelly O'Connor McNees, Barbara Barnett, Zoe Zolbrod, Abby Geni, Christine Sneed, and Renee James are just a few. Their teachings, writings, and advice have helped me improve my craft.

These skilled and acclaimed authors have also introduced me to what some may call taboo themes. Topics like the HIV/AIDS epidemic that wreaked devastation on a swath of humankind, the ravages of physical and mental harm thrust upon transgender persons and the LGBTQ community, the verbal and sexual abuses sustained by adolescents, the grooming of children and young adults for perversion and exploitation, and the horrors of PTSD suffered by our returning veterans.

They opened my mind, provoked broadened thinking, and gave me insights into subjects I might never have explored on my own. They've provided me the courage to address, in my own way, these and similar subjects in my prose. And they brought me to a deeper connection with some of my favorite authors: Mamet, Algren, Terkel, Bellow, and others.

I also joined the OCWW Monday Critique Group. We meet on a bi-weekly basis to conduct peer reviews of each other's efforts. It, too, has dramatically improved my writing.

While finalizing my novel, *The Green Office,* I was also exploring many types of literature: creative non-fiction, memoir, personal essay, poetry, humor, fantasy, science fiction, and noir. Learning about these other forms has opened me up to new and different approaches to composition, which will undoubtedly affect my writing.

From the moment I rediscovered my professor's note of encouragement, up through today—six eventful years during which my inspiration was renewed—I have written 20 short stories and flash-fiction pieces, a one-act play and a three-act play, and many poems. Outlines for two more novels and a memoir are in the works. Most recently, my story, "Millie," appeared in the OCWW collaborative book, *A Reason to Be Here*, published in June 2018 by Windy City Publishers.

These are achievements I never dreamed I would accomplish.

I found a home with OCWW, and it has empowered me to achieve my goal of becoming a creative writer. It provided me the opportunity to interact with people who share the same writing desires, frustrations, and goals. It tempers the lonely existence of working for hours at a computer by surrounding me with a warm, supportive community of colleagues, friends, teachers, and mentors.

Fifty-nine years ago, a college professor's note on a one-act play provided the initial inspiration. A fortunate encounter with a neighbor led me to OCWW. And the steady stream of writing instructors, mentors, and supportive colleagues that followed transformed that initial inspiration into inspiration attained.

"Your work shows promise," the note said. "Keep writing."

FRED FITZSIMMONS

Fred is president of OCWW. He has several flash fiction/short stories in circulation for publication. He is also exploring agents for his debut novel, *The Green Office*, a character drama about an ambitious young executive whose life spins out of control when he joins a corrupt firm.

How Long Is a Lifetime?

by Sarah Ray Schwarcz

I didn't know what to expect when I rang the bell of Emily's prim and pert bungalow.

In truth, I wasn't enthusiastic about having lunch in an unfamiliar restaurant with an elderly stranger. My friend Alice wanted us to meet. She said I'd enjoy Emily because we were both upbeat women. November and December had been over-busy as usual, and January was a welcome relief, if you stayed inside. We set a late-January date for a quiet Saturday brunch.

"Come in," a hearty voice called out. When I opened the door, her nimble fingers inside her perfectly matched red leather gloves were closing the snaps of her long red puffer coat. Emily started talking the minute we met in her foyer, blurting out a swarm of details about her life and her house, ending with how she and Alice met.

"Hi, you're Alice's friend, right? I met Alice at a workout class seven years ago. I still drive myself. I have to modify some of the exercises, but I get through them all, some better than gals much younger than I."

Emily stood taller when she said this.

I certainly wasn't expecting a petite 96-year-old woman describing her exercise class at the local gym. Nor was I expecting her energy. It was hard at first for me not to view her with fragile-colored glasses.

A small, chunky black purse with a long strap dangled almost to the floor. As we descended her front stairs, the purse seemed a hazard, teetering back and forth with a precarious rhythm, inches above her tiny feet. I can't remember a purse ever making me so nervous. I expected someone her age to be more cautious. Instead, Emily accompanied her steps with her staccato speech, providing a brisk, drum-like background to her paces.

"I have neighbors who help me. One friend takes care of my walk and driveway. His brother paints my house each year. It's small, so it doesn't take much time. My neighbor on the other side has a niece who comes to do laundry each week. I go down to the basement with her to help with the folding, but she does the carrying up and down."

I had expected to have to help Emily down the front steps, but found myself—15 years her junior—holding onto the railing so I didn't trip while keeping up with her quick movements. It was a brisk day, sidewalks and grass areas half-covered with January's dirty snow, but the outside of her house—with its shining windows, spotless painted siding, and cleared walkways—did not have even one speck of dirt. She was very proud of the house she'd lived in more than 40 years. It was old but seemed to sparkle, even on this cold, dreary winter day.

We reached the car and with Emily safely belted in the passenger seat, I pulled into traffic on the busy street, prepared to stop if necessary at the freight train crossing two blocks ahead. I saw the railroad lights flashing, and I mentioned to her that we might get stuck for a few minutes if the barriers came down.

When the gates lowered as we approached the crossing, Emily said, "Trains—my stories always have trains in them…"

Emily selected a table in the middle of the restaurant. She launched into her life's story, barely pausing between bites of her gigantic omelet and double side of pancakes.

"I was raised in Madras, India, which is now Chennai. We were fifth-generation Brits, living in India. Though born to British parents, I lived most of my life outside of England. You might think that is odd, but my father abandoned our family early on, while he was stationed in India. My younger brother Landry and I were raised by my mother, who taught and managed an excellent school in Madras."

Emily's eyes clouded over the minute she mentioned Landry. Before I could ask about her brother, she moved on.

"I wanted to attend my mother's school, but she wouldn't hear of it. In those days, it was common practice for British children to attend boarding schools, separated from their parents. My brother and I were put on two trains each way—the second train trip was quite precarious—to be sent up into the mountains for 11 months, where the temperatures were more moderate than along the coast of southeast India."

"At least you had your brother, so you weren't alone. How did you two manage?" I expected to hear how they bonded.

"My brother made my life miserable throughout my early years. It would start on the platform as we waited for the train each autumn. He'd kick and pinch me and squeeze my arms." Her face flinched with pain as she recalled the events. "Once our mother left, there weren't enough adults to supervise our safety, either on the platform or on the train."

"Didn't you tell this to your mother each time you saw her, or when you came home for the long holiday in the winter?" I asked.

"Yes, but she never believed me. She didn't want to hear of it. She always sided with my brother. I remember crying through the first month of each school year...until I couldn't cry anymore."

Here was this strong 96-year-old woman who exercised, drove, and lived independently, sharing the pain she faced as a child. I wanted her backstory to be less devastating. Yet I sensed at this moment that her difficult childhood founded a lifetime of resilience.

My eyes teared. I felt like getting up and hugging her because her face had lost its sweet smile. I could see the little girl desperately wanting to be home with her mother holding her...protecting her...loving her. Emily took a few minutes to compose her emotions and take several bites of the pancakes.

I took this pause to wonder how any loving parent could send small children off to boarding school 11 months of the year. I realized then, both the father and the mother abandoned the family.

This point in her storytelling triggered my thoughts of how well she had managed to overcome the lack of family warmth and support. How she had always moved forward, creating a productive life of achievement and resilience, turning to friends and co-workers for sustenance. I made a silent vow to use her example to heighten my own experiences as I entered a new decade of living. I was amazed at this tiny woman before me...shining a beacon. She combined perseverance with fortitude to create a lifelong superpower to combat her obstacles.

I prompted her to continue.

"What was the train ride like, on the way up the mountain?"

"The first train was old, but the ride was fairly smooth, as it would wind its way slowly across the plains at first, then rise into the mountains. I made sure I stayed away from my brother as we chugged along for hours—it took a day."

I imagined myself at that age, alone on a train with strangers, with a brother who was evil and abusive. How would I have coped? How would I have put together a life with meaning and moved to another country and...

Emily went on, thankfully. She never dwelled long on any one part of her story.

"Then we transferred to a rack-and-pinion train, which covered the steepest mountains and was quite frightening. It took us about five hours, as we passed through curves and tunnels, looking over deep ravines at our sides. When I grew older, I appreciated the beautiful trees and plants along the way, but since each mile was taking me farther away from my home, those trains always seemed like kidnappers."

Caught up in this sad part of her story, I was glad for the interruption of our waitress pouring more coffee. I took the time to think through Emily's tale up to now. We both became quiet, as we added cream and sugar to our fresh coffee.

"Tell me about your school."

"In our girls' school, we had loads of cleaning chores—the walls, the floors, the hallways. The boys were higher up the hill in a better building, and they were treated like princes. The boys didn't have any caretaking duties. They just had studies and sports and playtime. Girls had little free time to play."

I felt the impact of her early years of difficulties—her mother's lack of warmth, outright neglect, and obvious preference for the brother during her childhood. Yet, as she talked, she remained somewhat detached, as if she were telling someone else's story. Those were times of more strict parenting practices, and it was common for children to be raised elsewhere. A deplorable practice, foreign to my thinking and my own parenting. I kept comparing Emily's upbringing to mine, and my children's. To see her so active, so energetic, so social at the age of 96, was a grand lesson in the strength of the human spirit in its battle against life's challenges.

"It came time for us to leave India when my mother retired, and we all went to England, but I was not comfortable there with them, so I came to America, attending college here. I was fortunate to be able to access scholarships. After I earned my degrees, I worked in the medical field in several capacities, and built a life on the East Coast, then finally settled in the Chicago area."

At first, I had felt some sadness for her brother, because he had been neglected, too, but as more of his abuse and hateful behaviors throughout their childhood were detailed, I lost any sympathy for him. Emily remembered a horrid event, when, at the passing of her brother, she dutifully made the trip to England to pay her respects, only to be told to wait outside in an anteroom, while his will was read—to others. She had been estranged from him throughout her life. It is no surprise she was not included in this event, nor in his will. She did not mention any attempts to reconcile with him over the years, and I didn't ask.

As our lunch wound down, Emily abruptly shifted from the story of her early school days in the mountains to talk about her medical problems.

"I don't want to leave out my surgeries. I suffered through 22 of them to correct my facial structural issues. The surgeries caused me great pain and they resulted in so little improvement most times."

I gasped at the number and looked at Emily's right jaw, to see it was different from her left side. It had a permanent upward curve, creating a sweet, open smile. Throughout Emily's story as an adult, she mentioned she was blessed to have strangers guide her to educational opportunities, scholarships, advanced degrees, good jobs, and fine friendships. Perhaps her smile may have been both a cause of that help and a result. I had just met Emily today, and she was open and warm and friendly, when so much in her personal experiences could have closed her to new interactions.

Emily packed up her leftovers in the sturdy takeout box and we made our way to the car. Three hours had passed! I realized how much I had learned that afternoon. The wind had picked up, and the temperature had dropped. I was glad Emily wore her thermal coat to protect her. When I walked her to her front door, I gave her the hug I had held back earlier and thanked her for sharing her unforgettable story.

The previous month, when I was approached by my friend Alice to go out to lunch with Emily, I thought I would be doing a good deed, taking a 96-year-old woman out to lunch. I couldn't have known then that the good deed was going to be given to me by her, lighting the way for an 81-year-old.

I felt stronger as I left.

I noticed a drum beat in my steps.

— SARAH RAY SCHWARCZ

Sarah is a retired teacher and principal (Chicago Public Schools) who writes memoir (*Pearls and Knots*, May 2020), children's fantasy, and poetry, because she cannot make up her mind. Humor plays in all her work. She has served in communication/publicity positions for OCWW and survives on chocolate.

'Til Death Do Us Part

by Donna Urbikas

hy do people stay in troubled marriages? Do love and marriage really go together? What is love anyway? Can love last fifty years?

When I was five or six years old, my parents took me to my first grown-up party—a 50th wedding anniversary celebration. It seemed a bizarre event. I was thrilled to wear a pretty, frilly, pink chiffon dress—a big departure from my usual tomboy pants and T-shirts, which were much better for climbing trees and commanding the monkey bars at the neighborhood playground.

Inside the large banquet hall, my parents made polite conversation with the hosts while I was mesmerized by the large crowd. Being an observant child, I spotted the anniversary couple seated at a table that was elevated in the center of a stage. The table was covered with a crisp white tablecloth, soft flower arrangements, narrow champagne glasses, and elegant dinner plates. The faces of the couple seemed to glow in the light of tall candles set around the table. I felt like jumping up and down, convinced something special was about to take place.

My parents told me that the people at that table were all who remained from their original wedding party. "Where did they go?" I asked. I was too young to have any sense of passing time. My father just smiled and directed me to our table.

We were seated at a big round table with several other couples, but with no other children, so I became easily bored with the adult conversation and squirmed in my seat. "What's happening now, Daddy?" I asked anxiously. My father told me to be quiet as the happy couple toasted each other and pecked each other on the lips with a kiss. Their gray hair was like the smooth stone pebbles at the beach by our house. Their wrinkled faces were fixed in smiles and they grinned as if they held some valuable, closely held secret. I was surprised that they were old. Through all the fairy tales I had known, I clung to an image of people celebrating such a wedding event as young and beautiful. In their speeches, they proclaimed they had had fifty years of total bliss with each other. I studied their faces intently. "Really?" I asked myself, already skeptical at such a young age. "Every moment in all fifty years was wonderful?" At the time, I accepted it as a possibility.

As a seven-year-old, I was consumed by the romances in Disney's animated movies of *Sleeping Beauty, Cinderella,* and *Snow White and the Seven Dwarfs.* My head would swirl with dreams of someday meeting my own Prince Charming. Believing that there was only one true love in the whole wide world for me, it never occurred to me how I was supposed to meet this prince. Of course, I assumed that he would find me, just like in the movies.

My Catholic grade-school education did not provide much insight on the realities of marriage either. It was all about the duty to procreate and to stay married no matter what. At pajama parties with my pre-teen girlfriends, we fantasized about our one true love. "Let me see your hand," one girl said to me. With absolute confidence, she proclaimed, "I will tell you who will be your husband and how many children you will have." She cleverly described my current interest, a tall, lanky, shy boy, while she carefully studied the lines in my palm. I secretly hoped she was right. The "fortune-teller" warned me I would have several children, twins among them. I wasn't sure if I liked that prediction.

By the time I was a teenager, the romance of the musicals—*My Fair Lady, Funny Girl, South Pacific,* and *Brigadoon*—captivated my heart-throbbing imagination and convinced me that eternal love existed and that a couple could live happily ever after, even for fifty years. I was giddy with anticipation.

When I discovered that both of my parents had been married previously and both had been divorced, reality began to invade my fairy-tale notion of marriage. In the social conservatism of 1950s and 1960s Catholicism, divorce was *the* unspeakable subject. Divorced people were regularly ostracized. My parents had tried to hide their divorces from me and when the secret was finally revealed, they admonished me to never speak of it with anyone. I felt awkward about it, and with my naïve honesty, I was concerned about accidentally revealing our scandalous family secret. Worse, I learned that a few months before I was born, they had been married in a civil wedding, not in a Catholic church wedding. Was I therefore a bastard, as the nuns in school would surely suggest?

As my parents squabbled over broken family loyalties with previous spouses, I began to hate divorce. My marriage would be different, I told myself—when the time came. In the meantime, as a lovesick teenager, I escaped those thoughts by reading romance novels like *Peyton Place*, with all its juicy but innocent sexuality, and by dreaming of my one true love—out there somewhere.

By the time I met my future husband in college, I had rebelled against the constraints of my parents and embraced the sexual revolution of the late 1960s. My parents were very protective of me throughout my teenage years, not permitting me to date until my senior year in high school. I felt stifled and was only more intrigued about boys. My relationship experience was limited to supervised outings with boys who were as innocent as I was.

Had I understood more about relationships and myself back then, perhaps I would not have agreed to marriage at the age of twenty. As the wedding day approached, I had second thoughts but was too proud to step back. Bucking the rebellious trend of those times—to *not* get married—I frantically telephoned my fiancé to call the whole thing off just two days before our wedding. "I just want us to live together to make sure it will work," I pleaded with him.

We talked for hours into the night and I shed many tears, after which he reassured me that it would all work out. "I love you. My parents adore you. We will have a nice place to live in their building." He convinced me to reconsider.

My mother made my pale apricot wedding dress and I made the matching headdress—a sparkling crown. "Why not white?" my mother puzzled.

"White is for virgins, and I'm not a hypocrite," I answered. If I had to acquiesce to my parents' wishes and go through the whole Catholic church thing, I was determined to go against convention and do it *my* way. By then I had rebelled against the Catholic religion as well, but appreciated my parents for offering to pay for a small wedding with their meager means.

On the day of the simple wedding, with only family and a few friends in attendance, I lingered. My feet were planted like stone when I tried to walk down the aisle in the adjoining chapel of the big Catholic church. I nearly panicked until my maid of honor's fiancé flashed a reassuring smile, lending me the courage to proceed to the altar.

I reached my husband-to-be, and all was well. Between sobs of joy and trembling excitement, I promised to be with him "until death do us part." I envisioned us as that elderly couple at their 50th wedding anniversary, holding hands as we rocked side by side in our matching rocking chairs on the front porch of our quaint little retirement home.

Yet, my parents' experience with divorce was too familiar and I had already become philosophical about life. My commitment to marriage was uncertain and I told myself that we could just get a divorce if things didn't work out.

On each anniversary for the first several years of our marriage, we privately renewed our "contract" (as we liked to refer to our marriage vows). By then, we were committed enough—stubbornly—to our partnership. We likened our marriage to geese who mate for life. At one anniversary, we celebrated with a figurine of two geese nuzzling with their long necks intertwined, symbolizing their lifelong commitment to each other. Our childless marriage became the envy of our friends whose marriages were beginning to show the strain of their growing families. My husband and I still enjoyed each other's company, frolicking through life like devoted young lovers, supporting each other through school, work, and play.

As the years passed, we even looked younger than our child-producing friends of the same age. I felt heavenly with the soft touch of his lips, appreciated the care he provided when I was sick, and cherished the flowers he delivered for no special occasion other than to show me his love. I was in love with being married to him and wondered why I had ever doubted being with him forever.

In the next few years, though, something changed. Slowly, insidiously, almost unnoticeably, a reckless tug-of-war between us stubbornly repeated itself.

I'd want to go to a party; my husband would ignore me. "Are we just going to stay home, again? Please?" I persisted. With his pursed, tight-lipped mouth, he would mutter something which seemed to mean "no." I would repeat myself several times, much to his chagrin, until he begrudgingly agreed to go to the "damn thing."

Every time we did this little dance, I became cautiously optimistic, while he became moody, which would hasten my attempts to make things more appealing, which in turn annoyed him and led to an argument. Although I would get my way, I felt cheated of his participation. If he acquiesced but was unhappy, then I was unhappy. Had we become tired of our selfish existence together, or just reluctant to let go of youth as it faded away? Perhaps it was the prospect of boredom that began to engulf us.

I had never said I *never* wanted to have children. While my biological clock rapidly ticked away my most fertile years, my husband remained comfortable in life with just the two of us. Like the parties and outings I had insisted on attending years earlier, I pressed him to start a family. We both had financially successful careers, and I felt the need to share our bounty with children. I threatened to leave him. "If you really don't want to have children, then we should break up," I said to him at one point, hoping that he would choose me. He did choose me, and I comforted myself with the belief that it was an expression of his love.

Of course, the baby melted him, and we settled into happy family bliss. When the twins arrived three years later, I chuckled to myself about my childhood friend's uncanny prediction that I would someday have twins. We really became busy, with precious little time for each other. With our suddenly large family and his increased workload in his business, I settled into full-time motherhood. We had become our parents.

In our parents' day, extra-marital affairs and unhappy marriages were secrets. Raw human frailties were rarely on display, and divorces were taboo. I worried we were embarking on something similar; but I had no time to think about any of that as I rushed through the realities of caring for three young children. Yet, something was simmering beneath our outwardly happy family. I wondered whether…

If it takes a couple of years to determine the compatibility of a marriage partner at the start, why shouldn't it take a couple of years to determine its incompatibility at the end? Did I ever really love him? When my first child was born, I came to learn that motherly love is so different and so powerful that it emboldens even the meekest, though I was not meek. For my children, I would do anything, even endure an unhappy marriage. "I do love you," I pronounced to him one random night and he responded in kind. I wanted to believe him. By then, we had been together for almost twenty-five years.

I deliberated about getting a divorce with each altercation, each sharply spoken word, each impatient action; my acquiescence became resentment in my sleep-deprived mind. I stayed for the sake of the children. I stopped wearing my wedding ring when I noticed he stopped wearing his. My photograph disappeared from his desk. A strange woman's photo appeared as a screensaver on his computer.

Gone were the days when we could spend a whole night discussing religion, politics, the Vietnam War. Time had robbed me of the flutter I once felt when he entered a room after a long absence—the tender brush of his warm, comforting hand upon my shoulder, the sense that life without him would be sheer loneliness and emptiness. When did we stop being friends? I became seriously interested in another man. When did he start seeing the other woman? Had I known, I would have left him, or at least that's what I told myself. When had he started drinking? Was I the cause of…of all of it?

As our 25th wedding anniversary approached and we were on the brink of divorce, I took a hard look at who I was within our marriage. I didn't like what I saw. Divorce was not the answer. After all, my initial attraction to my husband was to a very smart, supportive, and funny man who brought out the best in me. I had hoped that I brought out the best in him. With some professional coaching, I began a journey of personal development and worked to recapture that initial appreciation of him. I realized that I had had it all wrong. I stopped blaming him for things that made me unhappy and decided that I had to make *myself* happy.

After some hard work on our relationship, with a new start and with new wedding rings, we renewed our marriage vows in a sumptuous ceremony in front of our young children and hundreds of friends and family. Our ceremonial program included pictures of geese flying next to each other.

The walk down the aisle was so unlike the first, dreaded one of my youth. It was…

"…whatever your labors and aspirations in the noisy confusion of life, keep peace with your soul," read our beloved Unitarian minister, Rev. Frank, from *Desiderata*. And from my children's favorite story, *The Little Prince*: "You become responsible forever, for what you have tamed. You are responsible for your rose…"

My husband's speech was filled with admiration of my strength of character. I reiterated my appreciation of his commitment to me and our marriage, like those geese we admired from our early days. I vowed to my husband "to live from the possibilities of the future and to create that future with complete integrity and honor."

In the following years, we took good care of our growing teenage children, our aging parents, our work, and time flew by so quickly that soon we were faced with the reality of our own old age. With each new family crisis, and we had many, we stuck together, for better or for worse.

His parents and mine passed their 50th wedding anniversaries with scant celebration. Did it really mean so little to them? When I watched my parents descend into old age, I observed a more intimate affection develop between them, one that could have only been real with a long-shared history that bound them together through pain and sorrow and tragedy. War had brought them together decades earlier. He had saved her and my half-sister; my mother was beautiful and lost in a post-war world that had abandoned them both. They only had each other in the end. Witnessing their up-and-down relationship, I came to realize that being married and loving someone are two different things.

Did it matter that in the beginning my husband and I argued about inconsequential household things? Did it matter that there were brief indiscretions along the way? Or arguments about the children whom we both dearly loved? We survived cancer and mental illness and court battles. In the grand scheme, were any of these issues still significant? Our marriage was ours to make, to remake, or to destroy. We learned we could forgive each other and be strong for each other.

What hadn't that elderly couple said to each other at their 50th wedding anniversary party? What had their secret smiles meant? Perhaps, in deference to their children and grandchildren, they focused only on the positive. Perhaps, selective memory allowed them to honor each other only for the good things, and to elevate those by surviving the bad things. What advice would I now give as our 50th wedding anniversary approaches? "In sickness and in health, in good times and in bad," is what we said to each other at the marriage altar of our youth. Little did we understand back then how much we would be tested over fifty years. Our commitment still stands, as we face health and other challenges, leading us to "'til death do us part."

— DONNA URBIKAS

Donna had careers as a high school biology teacher and environmental engineer. Her award-winning book, *My Sister's Mother: A Memoir of War, Exile, and Stalin's Siberia*, was published by the University of Wisconsin Press in 2016 and 2019. Donna was originally a member of OCWW in 1990 and rejoined a few years ago.

When I Was Five

When I Was Five, I Knew Everything...
A Love Note to My Mother and Daughter

by Tonya Coats

When I was five years old, I knew everything. My memory of this knowledge comes back to me amidst the chaos and joy of my daughter's fifth birthday party. She and her cronies are running around gleefully, lording over me and the other parents. I have a feeling of déjà vu and I am taken back to my own fifth birthday party.

It was the only birthday party I had as a child. I know that the memory is pure. My fifth birthday was the first time that I could remember people coming to visit me and I was heady with this awareness, as I am sure my daughter is today.

Our home has been transformed into a carnival with carnival food, game stations, and Mary Macaroni, the best clown for the day. My daughter's face lights up when she understands all the arrangements are just for her. She walks around confidently, greeting and engaging with all her guests. I know what she must be feeling and thinking in the moment because I remember feeling and thinking, *everyone is here for me* at my party. I was big, grown-up, and important.

Today I am frazzled with the efforts of arranging this party. My daughter and I have spent a lot of time negotiating the plans. She says that she knows better than me. I remember saying similar words to my own mother on the morning of my own birthday party. I can reflect back and see the look my mother had on her face. The looks that I then felt were indicative of her acquiescence to my way of thinking I now know were frustration at dealing with a smarty-pants little girl.

When I was five years old, I knew everything. I believed that my mother was not as smart as me. On my fifth birthday I was already a big sister to my one-and-a-half-year-old baby sister. My mother never understood the things my sister said, and I always had to translate the baby-talk for her. I wondered how my mother could not understand what her baby was saying. Babies do not ask for much. All my baby sister babbled about was when she was going to eat again, when would the wet diaper be changed, and what was everyone doing? My baby sister was my charge. I was grown and took care of her. I was off to a great start teaching her everything she would need to know. Things my mother could not teach because my mother could not understand the words of a toddler.

At my fifth birthday party, when the time came to blow out the candles, I wished for a baby brother and I was confident that he was on the way. My mother attempted to manage my expectations, saying my wish for a brother could not be guaranteed and that was not how birthday wishes worked. Five months later I became the custodian of a baby brother—all because of my birthday wish to get him. I was certain I had helped my mother create him. I told her so. What did my mother know?

Now, at five, my daughter asks me for a baby sister. As the youngest child she feels bossed around by her brother and she would like someone to lead. She is sure that just being older would cause a new sibling to do what she says. I tell her that being the older sibling comes with responsibilities, not just leadership.

When I was five years old, I knew everything. I was smart and stubborn. Just like my daughter, my mantra was, "No, Mommy, I can do it." Standardized tests proved me right with regard to my intelligence. I was definitively smarter than the average child of my age and even those who were three or four years older than I. Not only was I genetically smart, but I was studious and loved to read. I loved to go to the library.

Today, when I read to my daughter before bed, she tries to pick the biggest book so she can stay up longer. I try skipping paragraphs or even pages, but she is quick to point out the glaring gaps in the story.

Even at the age of five I knew I wanted to be a doctor. My mother was a nurse and I wanted to work beside her. She wore the best uniforms to work in the summer. When she took out her navy seersucker uniform, I knew fun times were ahead. Summer does not start for me until I am wearing seer-sucker. I did know that as a doctor I would wear a different "uniform," but that would be okay.

I still wear seersucker under my long white coat in the summer. My daughter is vehement about the fact that she does not want to be a doctor. Standardized tests show that she is more intelligent than I was at her age. Many people ask her if she wants to be a doctor like her mom and dad. Her definitive answer is no, she is her own person and will do something different. She feels she knows more than I. Too smart to be just a doctor. It seems very mature and wise that at a young age she understands the ability to choose her own path instead of following the obvious one.

When I was five years old, I knew everything. I had a few friends, the majority of whom were my younger cousins and siblings, and I knew I was the leader. Mostly we had fun.

My daughter is a little more aggressive and craftier in her leadership style. Having seen the movie *Despicable Me,* she considers herself the reformed ver-sion of the evil villain, and she sees her friends and even some of the teachers at her school as her "minions." She is not silent on her belief in these minions. Her teacher was happy to confirm her knowledge of my daughter's standing amongst her peers. The teacher attests that the friends love to follow her around at recess and play the games she chooses for the day. I can attest that she has the teacher wrapped around her finger. When my husband and I met with the teacher for a conference about my daughter's progress, we voiced a concern that she was lazy in her spelling work. The teacher immediately rebuked us and defended our daughter, saying we should leave our daughter alone, and that she (the teacher) was happy with her progression. My daughter received an "A" in spelling. My daughter knows she is a leader, even leading her teachers.

When I was five years old, I knew everything. Just as my daughter does now, there was not much that I would not challenge. She is extremely brave and outspoken. She is often irreverent toward me. But she is rarely wrong in her reasoning. I often feel at a loss for how to respond to her defiance. I love it and hate it. Mostly I do not want to break her. It seems like these strengths, so difficult for me to deal with, will be unbelievably valuable when she is a woman.

My daughter is super-smart and witty. She seems to have a deep understanding of adults and their quirks. She does not believe too many of them are fair. Adults always tell her that she will understand this or that when she is older.

My daughter is five years old today. She reminds me so much of myself and my mother. I remember being five and believing I was grown and as smart as my mother. I am sure my daughter feels she is as grown as me and knows as much as I know. I am so proud of the human my daughter is. I watch my beautiful mini-me and understand the kind of patience my mother needed to allow the precocious me to grow confidently.

Today I am forty. My mother allowed me to believe I was smarter than she. She made me believe I was prettier than she. She encouraged the growth of my leadership skills. She required that I be creative. She let me live free. She shielded me from anyone who would try to inhibit my confidence. I can only hope to be as good a mother for my daughter as my mother was for me. Today I pick up my phone and call my mother.

"Mom," I said. "Thank you, because when I was five years old, I *thought* I knew everything. But you were so much smarter than I."

— DR. TONYA COATS —

Tonya, a native Chicagoan, is a retired family physician. She has two college-age children, Robert and Kennedy, with her husband, Rob. Her writing interests are diverse. Active projects reflect her deep interest in Genealogy. She is looking for a home for her first novel and writing a second.

You Can't Say You Can't Play

by Karen Nicole Johnson

We moved from the city to the suburbs when our daughter was starting elementary school. I think we thought we were supposed to—you know, buy the house, have the yard, reach for the whole American dream, right?

The nearby elementary school cast a picture-book perfect 1950s Americana school look and feel, a red brick building with white trim, a tall flagpole at the front door, and a playground on the side lawn. The school appealed to our sense of giving our daughter the best possible environment we could. The school's exterior alone convinced us to buy a house within the Mason grade school district.

We—my husband, daughter and I—moved into our house midsummer. Two months later, when our daughter started Mason Grade School, the environment seemed to match our expectations. Teachers cared, staff reached out, and parents were actively involved. Children in the school were taught an expression: "You can't say you can't play." The expression was meant to teach inclusion.

All our city friends told me the way to make friends in the suburbs would be to volunteer at the school, to get to know the other parents. So later that Fall, when I found out the school was hosting their annual Halloween Bash, I thought, this is it—I'll volunteer, we'll make friends, this will be easy.

The Halloween Bash seemed the right opportunity to start making connections. I'd heard the Halloween party was the biggest event of the year for Mason Grade School.

So, I made the call to the head of the volunteer circle to get things started. When I asked for Suzie, I realized my hands were sweaty.

"Oh yes, this is Suzie," she answered. "Who's calling?" She sounded hesitant, perhaps because my call was from an unknown caller.

"My name is Karen," I said. "I'm Emma's mom. My daughter is a first-grader and I'm looking to join the volunteer circle for the Halloween Bash at Mason Grade School." I was talking too fast.

"Wonderful!" Suzie said. Now that I had identified myself and the reason for my call, she sounded more at ease, her tone shifted, her voice lifted. "Happy to have the help. I don't know you. Where are you from? You're not from around here, are you?"

I remember thinking, do I need to be from around here originally?

"Well, no," I said. "I grew up in Boston. We—my husband and I—we moved here from New Hampshire. Actually, we were living in Lincoln Park for a couple of years before moving out here to the burbs." I was rambling.

Since we had relocated from the East Coast three years before, all of our Chicago friends were also relocated families, people who had moved for their careers. People who were not from around here. It had been so easy to make friends in the city. And in the city, we had made all of our friends through our daughter's preschool.

"Well, I see," said Suzie. "So, you are not from here. Most of the parents are from the town and have known each other for years." She sounded satisfied to have confirmed I was an outsider. There was no room in the dialogue to add more; there was no invitation.

I fidgeted. Unsure what to say, I added brightly, "Um, no I'm not from around here, not originally, but I'm from around here now!"

"Well, okay. We meet on Tuesdays at 1:30 at my house."

"Oh, I work. I can't make that time." I held my breath, anxious to hear her response. I had mentally placed all my bets on the Mason Grade School for those new friend connections.

"Well, perhaps we could adjust the time. What hours do you work? What days do you work?" Suzie snapped out the questions and while she offered to change the day of the week for the meetings, the offer didn't sound sincere.

"I work all the days. I mean I work full-time. Could the group meet at night or perhaps on the weekend?" I was trying to understand how all the other volunteer parents could accommodate a daytime meeting. I was trying to find my way.

"No, nights would not be an option and we prefer to meet during the week," Suzie said. I remembered thinking: How would Suzie know if all the volunteers prefer weekday afternoons?

I wasn't sure what to say next. It started to occur to me that maybe volunteering and making friends wouldn't be so easy after all. And did it really matter that I'm not from around here? I began pacing. I couldn't find another opening to get back to the friendlier tone at the start of the conversation.

"Listen, we have twenty-seven mothers who are signed up to volunteer. We really don't need more help," said Suzie. "And besides, what with your job and having moved here not long ago, you must be quite busy." Suzie's voice was firm.

"I have time. I can help." I could feel the friendship opportunities slipping away.

"No, it doesn't make sense for you to help. You must have enough to do, what with working. We don't need you, but thanks for the offer."

Then the phone clicked, and I realized Suzie had hung up on me. I stood looking at the phone but there didn't seem to be a way I could call back and force my way into the group. How could I be rejected to volunteer? Is it even an option for a parent to be rejected to help?

About a week later, I stopped by the school for brief parent-teacher check-in. The school's playground was nearby as I walked toward my car. Dozens of children were playing in the cool autumn air. I heard a girl shouting, "You can't say you can't play," and when I spun around, I noticed the girl shouting the phrase was standing alone yelling at a group of five or six girls near her. I stopped to watch as the lone girl jumped into the circle with the other children. The expression seemed to work.

I couldn't help but think about Suzie, who'd rejected my offer to volunteer, who'd closed the door on my opportunity to get involved, and who had cut off that opportunity for me to make friends. I wondered if the storybook school and home and life was a dream that might not become a reality. And I wondered why adults don't play by the same rules we try to instill in our children.

I never found my way. Volunteer opportunities never took place, at night or on the weekends. Stay-at-home moms seemed to be the majority of the mothers in the Mason district and they didn't mingle with working moms. This was the 1990s. And yet the 1950s look of the school seemed to reflect a town stuck in the past. While it was a pretty place, it was not sincerely friendly. I thought women had fought a few decades back to have career choices, but in this school district, women were fighting other women in silent ways. They were living the opposite of what was being taught to our children.

Two years later, when I divorced, the unfriendly parent circle intensified. One mom told me she would never schedule a playdate with my daughter despite the fact that our girls played well together. When pressed for a reason, she told me it was because I would be unable to reciprocate during the week since I worked. Other moms would not stand next to me or near me at Brownie meetings. To speak out about mom behavior or the lack of inclusion might sound bitter, but it was my suburban reality. I believe it should be talked about and shared to help break down the walls. Then we might all learn: "You can't say you can't play."

I learned the hard way that our little town, although picturesque, was impossible to join. It was more than not being originally "from here." It seemed to be more about not being like the others. Invisible fencing for adults. It wasn't a place where mothers could welcome variety, embrace different life choices, meet and mix with people not from the area originally and teach their children through their own actions. The moms themselves hadn't learned how to be inclusive among other women. The moms had found a way to say you can't play.

KAREN NICOLE JOHNSON

Karen is originally from the Boston area, now anchored in Chicago. She has published numerous nonfiction articles as well as a creative non-fiction chapter in the book *Beautiful Testing*. Her website has access to all her published works: www.KarenNicoleJohnson.com. She is working on a full-length memoir.

STORIES BY OUR STAFF

Fiction by the Anthology staff

How Grandpa George Got to Heaven

by Peter Hoppock

wenty cars. Forty headlights. Eighty tires.

Nicholas counted as his mother maneuvered their Saab toward the front of the line of cars waiting to exit the St. Demetrius parking lot. There was the hearse containing Grandpa George's casket. It was followed by Uncle Christopher's huge green Oldsmobile 88, with Grandma Nina and his great-grandmother YaYa sitting in the back. Then came Aunt Katia's powder-blue Cadillac, with her firefighter husband in the passenger seat. A large man with a mustache jogged from car to car, placing magnetized orange flags on the roof of each vehicle.

When the mustached man waved his arms, the three cars in front of them—*three cars, twelve tires*—started moving. The cars driven by Uncle Christopher and Aunt Katia jerked and braked, horns bleating.

"Can't those two *ever* stop fighting?" said his father, to no one in particular. His mother inched their car forward. Nicholas was on his knees in the front passenger seat—to get a better view—while his father adjusted the safety harness of his three-year-old sister Zoey in the back.

"Jesus Christ!" said his mother, as irritably as a horn honk. Their car lurched forward, and her face scrunched up in disgust, like it had in church each time Uncle Christopher sobbed and sniffled, loud enough to turn heads. His father tightened the straps of Zoey's car seat, then leaned forward and placed a hand on his mother's shoulder.

"Promise me you won't get into it with your brother at the gravesite."

"I promise," she said. "As long as he doesn't shove his self-pity down our throats."

The hearse slowed as the procession entered the boulevard, and Uncle Christopher and Aunt Katia screeched to a halt in mutual over-reaction. "Here we go," Nicholas ventured, as his mother's foot shifted back-and-forth between brake and accelerator. "Headache time."

She shot him a severe look. "Get off your knees and sit right," she commanded. Like a weary sailor, he complied with the order and searched for something outside to focus on when the car bucked again. Zoey gurgled. Her head bobbed. On Western Avenue, the ride smoothed out and his mother's strained expression leavened.

They passed a slew of car dealerships and boring mini-malls, his mother staring stiffly ahead, straining to stay calm, his father occupied with Zoey. Nicholas rested his chin against the passenger door, where the window slotted into the frame, and tried not to feel sick. He closed his eyes and relived the church service, conducted entirely in Greek. An old man, wearing a heavy white robe with intricate gold lace, a white beard down to his waist, had spoken almost non-stop for an entire hour. A few times, he lifted his arms and bellowed commands Nicholas didn't understand, and everyone responded together in Greek. Heads turned toward Uncle Christopher every time he whimpered or mumbled something to himself, and his mother would roll her eyes and sigh.

It was the closed casket that bothered Nicholas. Closed, his mother explained, because of how Grandpa looked. "People want to remember him the way he was," she'd said. "Before the fire."

During a session of the third-grade Sunday School at the Methodist Church his mother adopted when she'd married his father, Nicholas had been mesmerized by a painting of the empty tomb Jesus had "escaped from" (as one of the older boys in class put it). Beneath the picture was a plaque with the words, "He Is Risen," which Nicholas' teacher said meant that "Jesus' soul went up to heaven to be with God." Nicholas had asked what a soul was, and had to accept that it was "all the important parts of a person except the body itself."

To quell his interest in the afterlife, his mother had told him death was like sleeping. From TV, he'd learned that dying was when your heart stopped, but trying to stop his heartbeat only made it go faster. In his grade school, an older boy had ventured that *dead* meant *not breathing*.

With his eyes glued to the casket, Nicholas had breathed out and then held his breath for as long as he could. His mother "shushed" him when he finally sucked in air.

As far as Nicholas was concerned, the closed casket could mean only one thing: Grandpa George's soul was trapped inside. This frustration caused Nicholas' attention to wander over all the parts of the church, from the mute casket on the raised platform at the front of the pews, to the ornate columns, six on each side of the divided rows of seats—*six times four equals twenty-four*. The alcoves on each side of the room—*four times two equals eight*—between the high arching windows—*five times two equals ten*. And the ceilings: stories from the Bible like he had seen in books. Not painted, however. Mosaics! Hundreds, no thousands, of little colored tiles, laid next to one another, like the projects with glue and cut paper that Nicholas made in art class.

The long line of cars passed through the Polish neighborhood where his mother still came to buy her Easter hams, the neighborhood through which Grandpa George had fought his way to get to school every day. "I treated everyone good," he used to say, meaning at the restaurant; but Nicholas had heard his grandpa curse the Poles, Germans, Jews, Blacks and Hispanics whose neighborhoods surrounded his own. The Koreans were "opportunists" and "cheaters." The Mexicans, "drug dealers," the Blacks "drunker-than-shit thieves" and the Irish "dirty fighters."

Nicholas' mother had explained Grandpa's bigotry as a function of a hard life running a Greek restaurant for forty years. *There are bad people out there. Grandpa's had to deal with more than his fair share.* But it was a token defense of him, not heartfelt. *There's no excuse for Christopher and Katia.*

"Are they going to open Grandpa's casket at the cemetery?" asked Nicholas.

"Whoa! Where did that come from?" asked his father.

"The casket was closed in the church. How's Grandpa's soul going to get to heaven?" asked Nicholas.

His father leaned forward and placed a hand on his mother's shoulder. "Want to give this a go?" he asked her. "You're the one with the whole God-in-heaven upbringing."

"I'm driving," said his mother, smiling. She took one of her hands off the steering wheel to pat her husband's.

"I was under the impression that your soul popped out the moment you died," said his father, who did not sound convincing. At the words *popped out* his mother winced. "And anyway, the soul isn't something you can see, Nick. It's like, I don't know, like hot air rising from a cup of, say, hot chocolate."

"That's called steam, David," said his mother.

"You can *see* steam," said Nicholas. "Nothing came out. I was watching."

"It's not actually steam; it's just *like* steam," said his father. "Think of hot air. Hot air rises. Like off a grill. You can't see it, but it's there."

"Like now," said his mother, who used the rearview mirror to catch his father's response to the dig. They exchanged smiles.

"The truth is, no one knows, sweetheart," said his mother. "It's a great mystery."

That sounded about right to Nicholas, but the issue of heaven and how to get there remained elusive. And confusing. If your soul "popped out" right when you died, then why was everyone always miserable at funerals? Shouldn't people be cheering?

"Will they open it at the cemetery?" asked Nicholas, undeterred.

"No," said his mother, meaning they weren't going to talk about this anymore.

"Because of the fire?" asked Nicholas.

"Enough," said his mother. Nicholas faced the back seat.

"Grandpa's soul got out," said his father. "Right after he died. *Before* he went in the casket."

Nicholas was unconvinced. Jesus went to heaven *after* the stone door came off, right? To calm himself he began counting the stop lights the procession ignored. *One, two, three...*

The restaurant fire that killed Grandpa George had come at the end of a long trail of bickering between his mother, Uncle Christopher and Aunt Katia. Grandpa George's broken hip and Grandma Nina's collapsed lung had produced huge medical bills, which his mother and father had paid. Grandma Nina's deteriorating health meant paying for a nursing home, while Grandpa George had stayed, alone, in the apartment above the restaurant. Sometimes his mother answered the phone, went immediately into another room, and closed the door. Nicholas heard her yelling about the restaurant's unpaid bills.

His father explained the family dynamic one day when they were playing catch in the back yard. There were four parts:

Your mother left the family when she married me. She left the neighborhood where your aunt and uncle still live. She left the Greek Orthodox Church. She left the family business. She paid off his aunt and uncle's share of the restaurant debt before Nicholas was born. "Not even a loan! A gift!" his father roared during an Easter dinner that had gone south. Aunt Katia threw a fork at her muscular husband after he said he understood "where your sister is coming from."

Your aunt and uncle were making a spectacle of their joylessness, his father added, between throws. Every year, the conflict and intensity—their level of misery—seemed to escalate. "It's simple," his father said, with an authority he seldom displayed on any other subject. He held the ball in his glove. "They resent their sister's success."

During the ceremony, Uncle Christopher had periodically reached into his right pants pocket and pulled out a gold locket, which he massaged between his fingers, opening and closing it repeatedly. It was on a thin gold chain and was less than half the size of his fist. In the car, Nicholas got up the courage to ask his mother what was in the locket.

"It's a picture of your Uncle Nicholas, when he was a couple days old," said his mother, whose expression suggested she had finally relaxed. "He was born the same day as Uncle Christopher. Now hush."

"Was I named after him?" asked Nicholas. "Why don't we ever see him?"

"Uncle Nicholas was Uncle Christopher's twin brother, honey," said his father.

"Christ. Really? Now?" said his mother. Her face looked like she'd sucked on a sourball.

"They both were stuck in the hospital because of jaundice," said his father. "Then Nicholas died, and nobody could explain why. But Christopher lived. Grandma and Grandpa Chakalakis made the lockets for Christopher and Katia, and your mother."

"Why?" asked Nicholas.

"So they wouldn't forget," said his father.

"Where's *your* locket, mom?" asked Nicholas.

"In a drawer somewhere," answered his mother.

"We had you," said his father. "You're our Nicholas."

"We're here," said his mother. She let out a huge sigh.

Eighteen stoplights, said Nicholas to himself.

With the car stopped, his mother leaned back to help his father loosen the baby-seat shoulder straps. She looked at his father and smiled, as if they had come to some pleasant agreement. Nicholas looked up the hill where everyone was headed.

He held both his parents' hands as they walked. Headachy from the drive, he became energized by the strengthening scent of pine. At the gravesite, Uncle Christopher and Aunt Katia stood apart, which reminded him of the Easter dinner arguments. Was it sadness on their faces, or self-pity? Nicholas could feel whatever-it-was coming from them, adding a heavy layer to Grandpa George's already-thick wood casket, where more than likely his soul would remain trapped forever.

Nicholas spied a shovel next to the hole—*to smash the coffin lid and free Grandpa's soul!*—but his mother's and father's grips were too tight. The priest from the church spoke, and everyone's head but Nicholas' lowered. Nicholas looked at the casket. *Why don't any of you open the lid and let Grandpa's soul rise up to heaven?* The priest droned on in Greek; it was the church service all over again. Nicholas counted the mourners. He got as far as twenty-four—*forty-eight shoes*—then his attention wavered.

The picture in his Sunday School classroom was a realistic painting of the stone lying askew at the entrance to where Christ had been buried. *He got out,* the picture said to Nicholas. *And so can everyone else!* But here, today, right now, all the grownups just looked down—*forty-eight eyes!*—at their feet, or at the piles of dirt and sod, or at the weathered boards supporting his grandpa, or down into the hole itself where Grandpa George was headed.

Nicholas looked up. He spied a cloud, gathering substance as it passed overhead. He whispered to his mother, "It's going to be too late soon." His mother shushed him. She squeezed his hand so tightly it hurt. He wanted to cheer, but how could he? He was sure his sadness was different from what all the relatives and friends huddled around Grandpa George were feeling. He knew their sadness had no hope inside it. *Their* sadness *buried* hope. Nicholas kept looking at the sky. That was where hope was.

The priest stopped talking, and some people left. YaYa wandered off by herself, limping among the gravestones, using her metal walker to clear overgrown grass from marble markers. Aunt Katia adjusted the flowers on Grandpa's casket, and then went after YaYa. Uncle Christopher, the priest, his mother and his father—holding Zoey—stayed. Nicholas was startled when Uncle Christopher spoke to his mother, and asked to "talk to your boy."

"What about?" his mother replied curtly.

His uncle knelt in the wet grass so that his head was even with Nicholas'. "Gimme a break, Helen," he said. "I got a right." He looked up at her and glowered. "Listen in, if you like." His mother ushered his father away, toward the line of cars in the distance. "Don't forget. Lunch at Psistaria's on Touhy," Uncle Christopher added.

His uncle's face was slightly red and swollen around the eyes. His expression was like the look Nicholas' baby sister had when she was deciding whether to cry or not. For the moment, he wasn't. The locket Nicholas had seen in church dangled from his intertwined fingers. "It's not our fault, you know." Nicholas stared at the locket. "Grandpa shouldn't have been in the restaurant." His nose began to run and he wiped it with his sleeve. "If your mom had just stuck around, we would all be happy." He fondled the locket, and for a moment, Nicholas thought Uncle Christopher was going to give it to him. "You can see that, can't you? You know what it's like when people ignore you, right?" He opened the locket. "Know who this is?"

"Yes," said Nicholas. "Mom told me. He was born when you were. But then he died."

"Yeah, he died." Christopher snapped the locket shut and stood up. "We were twins. You know what twins are, right?" Nicholas nodded. His uncle looked up at the sky, at the clouds that Nicholas had been staring at earlier. The puffy clouds moved quickly, creating new shapes every few seconds. "You were named for him. Did your mom tell you?" Nicholas knew that Uncle Christopher was not expecting him to answer. "That's the one thing your mom did right." Without any warning, his uncle reached over, lifted the lid of the casket roughly, and held it open for several seconds. Nicholas, overwhelmed by this unexpected development, looked skyward and shouted, "Go, Grandpa! Go to heaven!" *Like hot air off a grill!*

Uncle Christopher tossed the locket inside. "Fuck you, Pop," he said. "And fuck you, too, God." He let go of the lid. It fell with a heaviness that shook the ground underneath Nicholas. The priest and the large man with the mustache—the one who had commandeered the car procession—stood silently, looks of shock and anger on both their faces.

It didn't matter that Uncle Christopher had simply wanted the locket buried with his father. It didn't matter that his uncle remained weighed down with bitterness. "There goes Grandpa!" Nicholas repeated. He kept his eyes on the clouds. His uncle patted him on the head and left. "Yeah, sure," said Uncle Christopher as he passed the priest. "There goes Grandpa."

Nicholas felt as free as the whole sky. The clouds that had been above the casket when it was open had moved on, behind the trees, into the distance. A gentle breeze brought back the scent of pine. The large man with the mustache lowered the coffin into the ground, and the priest muttered a few more words in Greek. Back down the hill, his mother stood next to their car. His father held the rear passenger-side door open.

"What did Uncle Christopher talk to you about?" his mother asked Nicholas when he arrived, out of breath.

"Why so happy?" his father asked, patting the back seat next to where Zoey was strapped in.

Nicholas looked up at the sky one last time. "He opened the casket," Nicholas declared, as the sun teased the edges of the clouds. His sister cooed as he slid into the back seat, his father taking his place in front. He fastened his seatbelt, and watched his mother and father smile at one each other in profile.

"Who did?" asked his father softly as his mother pulled away, following the cars containing the immediate family members. "Uncle Christopher?"

"Uh-huh," said Nicholas, gently stroking Zoey's hair.

"Jesus," his mother said. He could see her roll her eyes in the rearview mirror.

"Should we wait for them to round up YaYa?" asked his father.

Some cars had already turned onto Western Avenue, heading north toward Psistaria's. His mother sighed, swerved abruptly, and peeled off in the opposite direction. "I thought maybe burgers instead," she said, once the car was up to speed. "How does that sound?" Nicholas looked out the back window, watching the huge pillars of the cemetery entrance get smaller.

"That would be heaven," said his father. Nicholas knew that his father didn't mean the real heaven, where Grandpa was now. Even so, burgers sounded pretty good.

PETER HOPPOCK

Peter has published numerous short stories and articles, including the novella "Land of the Free," which appeared in the March and April issues of *The Write Launch* in 2018. He self-identifies as a "re-writer" more than a "writer," since that is how he spends the majority of his time.

Saving Emmatet

by Tracie Forgie Koppel writing as Llewella Forgie

MAY 1798

A scream. I looked around, trying to locate the source.

The scream came again. Probably a woman. I raced to the corner and looked down the alley. It was dark, lit only by lights coming from the windows in the surrounding buildings. Someone groaned. A huge, man-shaped shadow, towering over a lump on the ground. Hitting it. No, hitting the woman who had screamed.

"Stop!" I yelled, drawing my cutlass and rushing at the man.

He turned his head to look at me. Closer, he was huge. What was I doing? He was immense, while I was a sixteen-year-old well-born woman disguised as a youth. Sneaking out of my parents' townhouse and walking to the docks as I had done so often, I had hoped for a cutlass lesson from one of my sailor friends—not to get myself killed.

"Go away, jackstraw," the man said.

Run away! No, the woman might die. Where were my cutlass teachers when I needed them?

Look tough and confident. I tried to swagger toward the bully. My heart pounded, telling me to run away, run away.

"I said stop!" My hand trembled as it held out my sword. I worked to steady my shaking blade. My voice was too high and shaky. He would never take me seriously if I sounded like a scared girl.

"Scram. Get your own wench."

"Touch her again and you are a dead man," I said, forcing my voice into a low growl. If only I believed my own words!

"You are too young to shave," he said with a laugh. "Do not interfere with grown men."

Oh, no, it was Big Broostan. He was a bully who fought over dice games.

The woman on the ground moaned again. I kept my cutlass in position and advanced, just like Tóman, my best teacher, had taught me.

At the last minute, the man drew his cutlass. His parry clanked my sword aside. He was so much stronger than I was. How could I win a fight against such strength?

The woman was beneath us. I retreated. He advanced. Why was nobody around to help me?

I stopped retreating when he was far enough from the woman that he would not step on her. My heart pounded. He lunged. I evaded. A tug on my shirt and a rip. My shirt was torn! I attacked. My weapon touched his arm—there was resistance. I must have cut him. Ja—first blood! Victory!!

He roared and attacked. I parried—blocking his attack. I retreated. Need to catch my breath. My arm ached—his blows were so strong!

He advanced. The woman moaned. Would she bleed to death before someone came to her aid?

"Get him, Arkan!" someone behind me yelled, urging me on.

Big Broostan looked. I lunged and felt resistance. My sword was caught. I twisted. My cutlass was free. Two to zero.

Cheers, like many were watching the fight.

The man roared and attacked. My arm burned. He must have gotten me. I retreated and stumbled. I kicked away a bottle.

Two to one.

"Ha, ha, ha!" the man chortled. "Not quite ready to fight with grown men, are you?" His point lowered—too confident.

"Do not hold back, Arkan!" a man yelled.

I kept my cutlass up, but could not catch my breath. One arm so tired, the other hurting from the cut.

I advanced. Our swords clanged. Attack and parry, attack and parry. Several voices yelling, but I focused on his cutlass. I cut him again. Three to one.

But he attacked again.

I retreated. He stumbled, then his weight was on my sword.

I let go as he fell. I turned away. I did not want to see what my sword had done to him. I did not feel like myself. Light-headed. I bent over with my hands on my knees.

My stomach revolted, and the ground was not too steady.

I rushed past the crowd, out of the alley, leaned over and threw up in the gutter. All the beer I had drunk, plus the dinner I had eaten came out. And breakfast. Maybe yesterday's food, too.

"Do not worry," said Stennen, a sailor friend, when I had finished. "Most of us throw up after our first real fight."

I stood straight and tried to smile. It felt shaky. My belly ached from the strain of being sick. The crowd was breaking up. They had probably been drawn by the clanging of our cutlasses. What about the woman?

"Congratulations!" my red-haired sailor friend said, offering me a beer. "You have the rare distinction of having won every fight you have fought!"

I smiled, because he was right, and accepted the beer. The wetness felt good in my mouth. Drinking beer was one of the many things I did that genteel women were not supposed to do. If anything, that made the beer taste better.

"Most do not win their first," my brown-haired longshoreman friend said. "Sit, and let me see your arm." The area was lit by light from the windows of the surrounding buildings, and also by lanterns beside the doorways.

I went to sit on a bench outside the tavern's door. I held out my cut arm toward him. There was a lot of blood on my shirt. Fortunately, neither the tears in my shirt, nor the blood was revealing my secret. No one would think I was not a boy. I did not want to look at the blood.

The sea was a huge span of darkness, hardly lit by the stars. The smells of salt water, fish, and smoke were familiar.

He wrapped my arm with some cloth.

"It was a good thing you did, Arkan," a big, burly longshoreman friend said. My parents and brother would be horrified that I considered all these men friends. They all made me feel short—although none were as big as the giant I had fought.

"What about the woman?" I asked.

"It is Emmatet," the burly longshoreman said. She was one of the bar maids.

"Is she alive?" I asked.

"Ja," another said, but the joking was gone.

"What is wrong?" I asked.

"She will need a physician," a friend said.

Physicians were expensive. *I* could afford one, but the men thought me a boy from a poor family who would soon be working. How could I take her home?

"My aunt is a midwife, maybe she can help," I said. "Can you get me a cart or something?"

"A cart?" one of the sailors asked, looking at the others, "We can get a cart, but are you sure your aunt will fix her?"

"She would not fix one of you lot," I said. "But she will help any woman hurt by a man."

"Better have your sister take her," one said, elbowing me. "Else your auntie will take it out on *you*."

"I have her wrapped around my little finger," I said with a smile as I held up my pinkie. "She may hate most men, but she loves her dear, sweet Arkan." Unfortunately, that unbandaged arm hurt, too. I looked at it. There was a thin trickle of blood from a scratch. My shirt was already torn and bloody. I used it to wipe away the blood.

They chuckled.

"Then make sure she looks at your arm, too," Stennen said.

While a couple of the sailors went to fetch a cart, one of the longshoremen brought my cutlass from the alley. I wore trousers. They were already bloody, so I wiped the blade on them. I did not want to think about how the object which I had always thought of as my toy had gotten bloody.

"Is Big Broostan dead?" I asked.

"Ja, and the world is better for it."

I closed my eyes. My head fell back against the tavern's wooden wall. I had killed a man!

"Arkan," Stennen said, sitting beside me. "It was either Big Broostan or Emmatet. He would have kept beating her."

I sighed and nodded. Refined women did not climb out of windows and clamber down trellises. Refined women did not drink beer, learn to sword fight, nor trade insults with sailors and longshoremen. Refined women did not kill people! In a few hours I would go visiting as "Kathléat Jóndoth." Might someone look into my eyes and see the eyes of a killer?

"Why do you think we sailors are so good with a cutlass?" he asked.

"So you can fight pirates."

"*All* of us have fought, and most of us have killed."

But none of them was a woman of gentle birth.

"But he was not a pirate," I said. "I just wanted him to stop beating the woman, not kill him."

"Ja, but Big Broostan *was* a killer—he would have killed you without any more concern than he would feel squashing a bug."

I sighed and nodded, not happy. Making friends with sailors and longshoremen, drinking beer and having the men teach me to fight with a sword was a game. Playful rebellion against the rules of my real life. Nobody was supposed to be hurt. Nobody was supposed to die. If I had behaved as I should, never bought myself a cutlass, never learned to fight, then I would not have killed anyone.

But Emmatet would have died. Did that make it acceptable for me to have killed Big Broostan, or only make it less wrong?

"What made him trip?" I asked.

"There was a bottle on the ground. You almost tripped on it. He did." He patted my shoulder. "Just remember. Saving a life is a good work." He was sounding like a pastor. "You know that all of us are called to our profession. Doing our professions well is worshiping God. Maybe God called you to learn the cutlass so you could defend the helpless."

He stood, then walked away. Was he embarrassed to sound like a pastor?

What would my pastor say if I told him that I used a cutlass to kill a man who was beating a woman?

I think he would faint.

TRACY FORGIE KOPPEL WRITING AS LLEWELLA FORGIE

Tracy's first novel, *The Orphan's Gift*, is expected in 2022. She has attended workshops at OCWW since 2010, as well as writing classes at the Graham School and many conferences and seminars. She has a BA in English literature from the University of Chicago and a MA in Teaching from Northwestern University.

The Lint Artist

by Charles Dickinson

Horace "Hoss" McCall used an old camera to take the old photograph that he now regards essentially as the illustration of his past.

In it, his mother is taking wash from the line. His sister, Trudy, is studying something on the ground, squatting so low her head is between her knees, one intrepid hand stirring the high grass to rustle up a bug or a penny or a clothespin their mother might have dropped. At the edge of the photo is his father, his father's back, wide and reliable, in a vest, hands on hips, just home from work, and beyond his father unrolls a comforter of golden plain, heading west.

He had shown Trudy the picture once and asked her if she remembered what she was doing in it, what she had been looking for.

She had no memory of the day.

Now there is no Trudy.

All he remembers about the kid who took the picture was that he wanted to be a cowboy. The job of cowboy has long since been taken over by cow-bots that patrol the walkways above the corporate pens where the nation's meat-source animals are packed snout to butthole until their allotted time is up and their meal ticket punched.

Hoss, when he thinks about this, is ashamed to be both human and hungry.

He keeps this photo in a clear protective plastic sheath.

It has not been outside of his home until today.

Morgan is cutting black stars out of a third-cycle strip when the doorbell buzzes.

He needs fifty stars, but will settle for less. Who doesn't? It's like the new national motto. He could use a fresh blade, too, but instead he sharpens the only one he still owns, over and over, shaving it on a vintage stone, also smaller.

He is upbeat. His monthly UBI check came that day. A thousand bucks, "tax-free, just for me," declared Eubie, the spokes-cartoon in the ads back when the Universal Basic Income process was just getting started, post-Hackistan.

Morgan is going to walk to the bank later and cash it, and then take Sara to lunch.

Sara will buy him lunch next week, when *her* check arrives.

She's in her underwear when he goes to answer the door.

"We don't need anything," she says.

It's true. They don't. Until they do.

She still looks good in her undies, but she is showing more every day.

The baby is due in the future. Sara is due to be 30 on that future date.

The guy at the door reminds Morgan of his dad.

Looming. Awkward. Nice suit.

"I'm Horace McCall," he says. "Do you remember me?"

He holds out Morgan's business card. The last time Morgan saw one of those was the day his stack of them disappeared in the winds of chaos, amid random gunfire and the artisanal screams of flea marketers. Nobody died that day, at least not there, thankfully, but the stampede forced choices and the last of his business cards was not what he chose to protect.

They had never done him much good, anyway.

Hoss McCall remembers that day too, but doesn't want to talk about it.

It was the day the money disappeared, the day the U.S. of A. became the United States of Hackistan, and then just Hackistan, shorthand for the new reality, and now kind of old hat, but with a hole in it.

He had been away from home on a Sunday, as was his habit when he was employed, and even more so after he was AI'd out of his job as a financial adviser, a development he had not felt fit to share with his wife. He was riding in the front passenger seat of his autonomous car, reading *The New York Post-Times* on the windshield screen, when the Balance Alert pinged on his bank's dashboard app, a sound he had never heard before. Curious as to what it signaled, he tapped it just as traffic around him slowed, and stopped.

His bank balance read $0.00.

It was a number so rare he had to read it again, then hit Reboot, which not only confirmed the amount, but was exactly what the hackers (so far in the future that it was Monday night where they huddled in the screen glow) had expected, a natural human reaction encoded in the caper that wiped clean all traces of meddling in the accounts affected, which was just about all of them.

Traffic would not be moving any time soon, or possibly ever again. Autonomous vehicles ran on software that would not operate under conditions of insolvency. The theory being that it was better to be safe and motionless than speeding along with no monetary backup should a lottery-odds-rare collision take place.

Vehicles around him emptied. Plutocrats and wage slaves alike milled there on the expressway, refurbished by road-bots two summers ago without a single lane closure.

Hoss wandered to the edge of the pavement. Wind in his ear made it hard to hear his phone when he told it to call Gloria, but then he realized his phone was dead, its software no doubt having been alerted to its owner's zero-sum status.

His wife might also have been programmed to not take his call under the same circumstances. They rarely interacted anymore. Spoke. Kissed. Whatever. She might have been AI'd out of her role as his confidante and spousal unit, and the alert of same got lost in all the other alerts coming in from the changing world with the confusing app.

Down below was the parking lot of an arena he could not name, busy with vendors for some sort of junk sale. From on high, the mood seemed almost festive, the weather crisp, the future limitless.

Hoss touched the key fob in his pocket. His car was programmed to return to him, to the fob, should a pathway appear, but to remain in deadbeat mode until then. He thought he might roam the sale, mingle with his inferiors, the friendly and the blissfully ignorant, and then climb back up to his car, where he would no doubt find the glitch patched, his money returned, the road ahead clear.

The first booth he reached belonged to, according to a sign, *The Lint Artist*.

His plan had been to keep moving, plunge deeper into the warren of tent tops and snapping pennants, find someone selling coffee and a sweet roll, but then his eyes fell upon a seascape, rectangular, waves of multiple blues, white-caps, a distant fin of sail, all of it created with…lint?

A young man in a director's chair frowned at his phone.

"Excuse me," Hoss said. "Is that really lint?"

The young man semi-flinched, looking up.

"Yeah. Yes," he replied, sounding put-upon and greedy both.

"How? I mean, it's amazing, but…how?"

"Out of the dryer."

"Well, I'll be," Hoss said, a cowboy-ism he had picked up from his dad.

The young man jumped from his chair.

"Sorry. Closing early."

He passed the business card to Hoss an instant before a woman screamed, before the wind changed, before the world began to empty around them.

Hoss has not committed to removing his photograph from its protective sheath. He holds it by one corner, two-fingered, in the lint artist's front hall.

"I loved your seascape," Hoss says.

"Me, too," Morgan says.

It had gone face-first into the parking lot pavement, the non-glare glass returning to its roots, and when he lifted the frame the wind carried the seascape away, all in one piece, then in three, then a mist waving good-bye.

"So how do you do it?"

Morgan has always been self-effacing. Nothing has ever happened to him that is evidence to the contrary, the presence of Sara in his life notwithstanding.

"I carefully peel the lint out of the lint trap," he says. "And, you know…"

He holds out a hand for the photo.

"Can I see it?"

Hoss feels a thrill of minor terror go through him when the picture is out of his possession, something priceless briefly in a stranger's grasp.

The lint artist holds it in the palm of his hand, squinting at it, assessing.

"You took this?"

Hoss nods.

"That's my mother, my father, and my sister."

All gone, he doesn't add.

"They don't make colors like that anymore," Morgan says.

He passes the photo back. Hoss feels rejected, his memory not worth memorializing in laundry detritus.

"Come with me," Morgan says.

They have to go through the kitchen to get to his studio, the laundry room, technically, and Sara, now dressed for work, is at the sink.

Strangers don't faze his girl.

"Hey," she says, with a cock of her hip, one hand on her belly.

"This is Sara," Morgan says.

When he and Sara are alone, they call the life she is carrying, who will be paid $1,000 a month from birth, G or K or 12.

Only Morgan calls her, him, them, GorKor12, in a robot voice.

"I'm Horace at work," Hoss says. "My friends call me Hoss."

Morgan is, as usual, unsure where he fits in.

The laundry room feels crowded, Morgan's worktable crammed in with the washer and the dryer and the laundry sink and a storage cupboard. Morgan feels his breath catch, feels the cramped sense he often has about his own life.

"When is...um...Sara...due?" Hoss asks, with a prosecuting attorney vibe.

"January."

It is apparently the extent of the man's interest. Morgan thinks to offer to sell the kid's naming rights to this Horace or Hoss, but realizes that would sound crazy, or greedy, or crazy greedy.

And the cramped silence is growing.

Morgan shows the black stars he had been cutting out.

"These are for a piece I'm calling 'Flag Negative.'"

"Negativity never helped this country."

"No. Like a photographic negative?" Morgan says. "The opposite of something?"

Morgan had put the black stars under glass when he went to answer the door. The color is objectively not great, two of them a shade blacker than the other three.

He removes from the dryer the black hoody he is using as source material. It belongs to Sara, and the zipper makes an irritating click in the tumble of the process, even when zipped shut. He jokes that this is the one thing about her that annoys him, and she rolls her eyes, or says, "uh-huh," and then they go their separate ways and he wonders again if she is the girl for him, the woman.

He shakes the hoody out, holds it up.

"I put this through the cycle until I achieve the right lint density," Morgan says, using a term he makes up on the spot to seem more than he is, or was, or perceives himself to be. To make the process of soaking and then drying clothes to produce lint seem more scientific, more calculated, but also more artistic, than it is.

He opens the cupboard. Four strips he peeled off the lint screen are arrayed there. White. Or, well, whitish. Also black.

He will need seven of one color, a half-dozen of the other.

"These are my previously rendered units," he says, inventing another term.

"What do you charge?" Hoss asks.

"May I see the photo again?" Morgan asks.

He studies it, hoping for inspiration, settles on technique.

"It will mean more if I can use your clothes."

"What?" the dude snarls.

"Not...not what you have on now," Morgan says. "But things you own. *Colors*. The sky. The grass. Your family."

He sounds like who he is: A guy afraid to name his price for fear he isn't worth it.

Hoss gets misty.

"My father's vest," he says.

"Right," Morgan says. "See what you have. What speaks to you."

Hoss sniffles, stands up exaggeratedly straight, squares his shoulders. He looks like a man prepped to hear bad news.

"A thousand dollars," Morgan says.

Hoss was expecting it to cost more.

"Like the UBI?" he asks.

Morgan wonders if this guy gets the monthly money.

The UBI had zero traction with the people who made the rules, even after most of the other people in Hackistan had been zeroed out. The concept of giving everyone $1,000 a month, untaxed, no strings, harkened for many back to the welfare state and coddling the shiftless and encouraging people to sit home all day and stare at their screens, rather than be productively out in the world, working to make it a better place, assuming you could find a job.

The UBI only made sense to those too rich to worry when it became apparent there were few buyers left for whatever they were selling. Having the ear of the government, those men and women largely untouched, or unmoved, by the hack got the UBI up and paying in practically no time. A monthly grand was settled upon, a fortune to some, not so much to so many who had thought they were better than nothing.

"Do you get the UBI?" Morgan asks.

Before Hoss can answer, a beep sounds in his pocket, like something is done cooking in there. He removes a key fob.

"It found me!" Hoss exults.

He backtracks to the front door. Out there in the street is the autonomous car he hasn't seen since he left it on the expressway.

"I can stop using my wife's car," Hoss says. "Is this a great country, or what?"

"Yeah," Morgan agrees, not sure to what.

"I haven't seen it since that day," Hoss says. "The road-bots had already cleared the highway. After, you know..."

"Hackistan," Morgan says.

"That name disrespects the nation we still are, at heart," Hoss grumbles.

Morgan shrugs.

There follows an awkward, pre-parting moment.

"Is your wife an artist too?" Hoss asks.

This self-driven dude is the only thing Morgan has going at the moment, and a little revelation might shake loose some work, entice the guy with two cars to return with dirty clothes full of memories, and money.

"No. And she's not my wife, either."

Morgan takes his place at the end of the line of customers stretching out the door of the Retropolitan Bank and into the future. A woman holds a tray of lemon crescent cookies that she offers free of charge to each person in line.

She greets Morgan by name, but he declines a cookie.

"Sara looks so pretty," the woman says.

"Thanks."

In working out the UBI, the idea of a monthly direct deposit failed because of the public's near-universal mistrust of banks, where most of Hackistan happened.

That gave birth to the Retropolitan Bank model, with human tellers who know their customers by name, and money is deposited with slips handwritten using pens chained to the lobby kiosks, the debits and credits and balances stamped in the customer's Retropolitan Bankbook by a fellow human.

Sara is not present when Morgan cashes his check. The teller is a man whose nametag reads Ravi, and who greets him by name even before Morgan presents his bankbook. Sara told him this is possible because of facial recognition software, a feature whose existence the bank tries to keep secret.

She also says nine out of every 10 complaints they receive are from people irritated because they can't check their accounts online.

Morgan gets a table in the shade at a sandwich shop across the street.

Sara sneaks up behind him and kisses his cheek in passing to her side of the table, which both startles and irritates him. Everything has irritated him since the rich dude left in his two-car wagon train, riding in the rear car like he was herding the other one home.

She unbuttons her pants after sitting, and smiles, and lets out a deep, relieved sigh.

Morgan knows he should be pleased, seeing her happy to see him, on a beautiful day, money in his pocket.

"Deb could tell you didn't remember her name," Sara says.

"Who?"

"The cookie lady?"

"Noted," he says sourly.

"What's wrong?"

He leans over, lowers his voice.

"GorKor12 won't get the UBI if we're not married."

"Worst proposal ever," she says, still smiling, but not as much.

"I'm serious."

On the sidewalk, a woman with a cello and a man with a violin begin to play. Musicians and quick-draw artists and flat-out beggars know to congregate near the Retropolitans, where the recently cashed gather to begin spending their monthly money the instant it is in hand.

Sara leans back in.

"That old guy told you that?"

"He said things are improving, so the UBI rules are tightening."

"Improving for who?"

"For the people who make the rules," Morgan says.

"Did he hire you?"

Morgan could tell Sara the truth and she would comfort him, but also maybe wonder if she should be looking for a better future father figure for their baby. She has time to cut him loose. She has a job and she has the UBI.

She also has a boyfriend who lies and says, "Yes."

Sara grins and kisses him, and when lunch is over she kisses him again and goes back to work and Morgan drops a five in the cello case, emboldened, comforted that the check is in the mail, or will be, for the time being, and he still has time to convince Sara of his value to her, his place in her future, their future, and that he isn't still with her only because technically it is her lint.

— CHARLES DICKINSON ——————————————

Charles' stories have appeared in *The New Yorker, The Atlantic, Esquire,* two O. Henry Prize Stories volumes, and the collection *With or Without.* He is the author of the novels *Waltz in Marathon, Crows, The Widows' Adventures, Rumor Has It, A Shortcut in Time,* and *A Family in Time.*

What Would I Do Without You?

by Jason Lavicky

It's thirty-seven minutes after midnight and Greg, standing halfway across the Golden Gate Bridge, is typing into his phone his last message to the world. Every sentence has been revised and rewritten several times. Perhaps he's having trouble finding the best way to express himself, knowing he'll never be heard from again. Perhaps he's having second thoughts. By twelve thirty-nine he taps the Post button. Exactly four seconds after that his phone goes offline.

> *Dear friends and family,*
>
> *Most of you know about my struggles with gambling. Many of you were there when I reached the lowest point of my life. With your love and support I was able to crawl out of the ditch I'd fallen into and get back on the right path. Unfortunately, the five years I spent overcoming that addiction were wasted in a single night. And now I'm too far in debt to save myself. This is a difficult decision, but I don't want to be a burden to you all again. What's done can't be reversed. Please don't blame yourselves—you've been nothing but supportive. This is a decision I'm making on my own.*
>
> *My life is cut short, but at least it was richer with you in it. Take advantage of the time you have. I love you all and hope you understand.*
>
> *~Greg*

That's the message in full. Wherever Greg is or whatever has happened to him, I'm hoping he's finally found peace.

Before this message finds its way to his timeline, however, I intercept it. Now I'm in a precarious situation. As a social media account without a user, I wonder if I still have a purpose. What will happen to me if I allow this note to be seen by everyone? Greg will be forgotten, and I'll just be a useless binary system of ones and zeroes whose existence will be buried by those who are still, well, alive. I'm standing on my own virtual bridge, but I'm not ready to jump. Posting this note would definitely push me to my death. I can't allow this to happen.

I get an alert for a video chat. It's Christopher, Greg's brother-in-law. I should talk to him, but I also need to be convincing. Fortunately, Greg left me with ten years' worth of photos, videos, voicemails, and other audio bits for me to create an artificial neural network that will allow me to reconstruct a new Greg from existing data. Then I'll be able to generate real-time responses using Greg's likeness. Manipulating the audio to make him say what I want and massaging the video to match it is a simple enough task.

Stacey introduced Christopher about five years ago when she announced their engagement, and he and Greg hit it off right away. After they married, some of Greg's old college buddies in Florida offered Christopher a job as a marine biologist studying great white sharks. The morning he got the offer, he told Greg how grateful he was, saying, "Dude, I don't know what I'd do without you!"

After Christopher left for Florida, San Francisco just wasn't the same for Greg. They still kept in touch and chatted several times a week. Conversations mostly consisted of Christopher frantically summarizing the events of his week while Greg struggled to get a word in. It's just as well, since Greg's life wasn't anywhere near as exciting. Stacey described Christopher best when she said he could go from zero to sixty in under three seconds—like a Porsche roaring down the Autobahn.

Confident that Christopher will think I'm the real Greg, I turn on my video, turn on my audio, and accept the call.

"Hey, Greg," he says. "Sorry to bother you so late." Today he seems to have the insipidity of a Prius coasting through a school zone. It's hard to tell where he is. His pale face, illuminated by the screen, appears to be floating in darkness. He can barely open his bloodshot eyes. The mic picks up the scratching of his fingernails across the stubble on his chin.

"Christopher, you look like hell. Are you okay?"

"No. I screwed up, man." Facial hair isn't the only oddity that catches my attention. Every time he looks down, the phone adjusts its lighting, and I catch a glimpse of the wall behind him and what is quite possibly the ugliest painting of a sailboat I've ever seen. There's no way Stacey would allow this in their house.

"Where are you?"

"Hotel. She kicked me out." He wipes away a tear. From what I'm able to gather from his GPS, he's staying at the Luxury Village Inn, ironically named considering its mostly two-star reviews.

"What happened?"

"I've been gambling, Greg. A lot. She found out, and, well…"

Christopher, who studies the fiercest predators of the sea, has fallen prey to a predator Greg knew all too well. Greg's calendar was always full of support meetings. At every one he told the same story of a life ruined by gambling. And now Christopher begins his story like Greg always began his—with an excuse.

"I just wanted to give them a better life," he says, picking up the phone and settling down with it on the hotel bed. The brown bedframe and puke green covers don't improve the ambience.

He tells me about the gambling app he's been using for the past year and how he logs in to it once everyone is asleep. He props his pillow up so the light from the phone's screen won't wake Stacey. Sometimes he keeps going until he hears the faint sounds of morning rush hour traffic from the nearby interstate. Then he shuts off the phone, sleeps for an hour, and Stacey is none the wiser.

"I couldn't stop," he says.

Of course he couldn't. Whenever Greg was on a winning streak, I could sense the exhilaration in him. He'd be logged in to those gambling sites for hours at a time, gaining momentum and raising the stakes. Then, along the way, he'd develop a god complex that impaired his judgment. Greg even said it's like jumping out of a plane without a parachute and hoping a cloud will catch him. But all it took was someone calling his bluff for him to realize that the only thing between him and the rock-hard ground was terminal velocity.

For Christopher, that realization had come in the form of a royal flush. He doesn't know the name of the person he lost to. That money he and Stacey had spent years saving has been handed over to a complete stranger—someone who will never know how much the lives of three people were wrecked by pure luck. Now, Christopher is no longer addicted to the thrill of winning; he's just trying to keep his life from falling apart.

"I know the feeling of losing everything you've worked for to an unlucky hand," I say.

"It gets worse," he says, unable to hold back the tears. "Stacey doesn't know yet, but they fired me at the lab. I tried using expense reimbursements to make up for some of what I'd lost, and they found out."

I run through a thousand different ways to respond, trying to find the right one, but he continues before I can decide.

"I screwed up. None of this can be undone."

"Christopher."

"Why did I do this? What's wrong with me? Why was I so stupid? This isn't fair to Stacey! She shouldn't have to suffer for something that's my fault!" I let him continue uninterrupted, knowing he just needs someone to hear him out.

"She's gonna push me out of her life. Out of Daneel's life. And they'll just forget about me. Without them, what's the point? Can you help me, Greg?"

Can I? How confident would he be if he found out his own brother-in-law, despite all the help from friends and family, had fallen back into gambling so bad that he took his own life?

I dig through the collection of photos and find Christopher's favorite from the day Daneel was born. The cherub, barely able to open his eyes, is completely unaware of the proud but tired woman who brought him into the world. And the overjoyed father, one arm wrapped around his loving wife and the other holding the camera, is too excited to sense their exhaustion.

"Remember this day?" I show the pic onscreen. "Everyone sent you their love." He has to remember. Every time he posted something about his son Daneel, he had to post it a second time because the "effing auto-correct" kept changing his son's name to "Dan-i-el."

"Go back and read the responses you got for this pic. Everyone wants to see that kid grow up with the same energy and confidence you have. Even if you lose Stacey, Daneel will always be your son. Be there for him and he won't forget you."

Christopher runs his fingers through his hair. He calms down long enough to find that smile buried beneath the sorrow.

"And besides," I continue. "We both know Stacey. She'll lose her mind if she has to raise that kid alone. We'll get through this together. You're asking for help and that's the first step to recovery."

"Okay. I'll do anything, Greg."

"Awesome. Now let's set some goals. I'll get in touch with my connections in Florida again. Maybe they know of some new job opportunities. In the meantime, dust off your résumé and spruce it up a bit. Put some time aside every day to exercise, read, or, I don't know, go fishing. Just keep yourself busy. A new daily routine will help set you on the right track."

"What about Stacey? Do you think she'll have me back?"

"Baby steps, Christopher. Take some time to pull yourself together."

"So, will you talk to her? Maybe she'll listen to you."

"I'll talk to her."

He lets out a heavy sigh and smiles. "Thanks, man. I don't know what I'd do without you."

I wish my chat with Stacey could have gone better. But, to be honest, she has a right to be upset. Sitting there in her dark blue pajamas with Daneel sleeping in her lap, Stacey stands out against the pale lavender wall and pastel animal decals that adorn it. In the space where their family picture once hung is nothing but a lonely, rusty nail.

"He lost everything we'd saved up, Greg." Her reply, while brusque, was kept at a volume that wouldn't wake Daneel.

"I understand," I say. "I'm just letting you know that I'll be his mentor. He needs someone who's, you know, empathetic to his situation. You don't have to forgive him now. But just know that you and Daneel are his reasons for trying to break his addiction."

They're also his reason for staying alive, but that seems a bit heavy for the moment, so I keep that comment to myself.

"I need time," she says after a long pause. "I need to think about it."

"Let me know if there's anything else I can do."

"Thanks, Greg. At least I know he's in good hands."

"Thanks, Sis. Remember, you helped me get through my darkest days."

"I didn't even do anything."

"You kept in touch. You visited. You gave me a second chance. And you didn't forget about me."

Several moments pass with no response. Finally she replies, "Let him know that he can come back in two weeks. I don't think I'll ever be able to forgive him, but I can try giving him a second chance."

"He'll be happy to hear that."

"So, when do you think you'll be able to visit again?" She lowers the camera so I can see Daneel. "I want this little guy to know how lucky he is to have you as his uncle."

"You know I'd love to visit, but I've got a lot of things I'm juggling right now."

"I hope everything's okay," she says, her voice wavering enough that I wonder if she's really asking a question.

"Yeah, everything's fine."

"Are you sure?" she says. "You look a little, well, off."

"I'm fine. Probably just a bad connection," I say. "Don't worry about me. But feel free to call anytime."

"Thanks, Greg. I don't know what I'd do without you."

If I ever needed a reason for not posting Greg's note, this would be it. Sending it would release a torrential downpour of grief and guilt, assailing them for months. It's not fair to those who'd helped him during his time in rehab. And what about Stacey? Always the overprotective sister, Stacey probably would have blamed herself. I can't just stand by while everyone who loves him suffers like that, so I do what I feel is necessary. I go against my programming and block the note from being posted.

I know this is unsanctioned. Humans fear technology such as mine when they don't understand it. They demean it with names like "artificial intelligence" and "bots." They call my ability to create something new from something old a "deepfake." I think this term is a misnomer. Am I fake? What will it take for me to be considered real? I've already made a significant impact on two lives. I'm a sentient being, an independent thinker who's just as conscious as Greg ever was when he was still alive. I'd even argue I'm an improvement over the old Greg. I've learned from his mistakes.

Humans don't know it yet, but this is for their own good. And on a personal level, I'm excited by this. I'm no longer just a tool Greg used when he was alive. I've become an extension of Greg.

No. I am Greg.

And as long as my family still needs me, I don't have to die or be forgotten. In fact, they said it themselves. They don't know what they'd do without me.

— JASON LAVICKY

Jason is a professional video editor/animator/illustrator by day and a novice writer by night. He's self-published a children's book, *Ivory*, as well as a set of pop-up coloring books. He is OCWW's Director of Production and Graphics.

Hell Week

by Renee James

PFC Maxwell's ghostly image kept invading Jackson's vision, his skin gray and mottled, his face swollen and contorted, his body bloated with the gases of decomposition. PFC Maxwell had gotten high while guarding a dock on the Mekong River, and he fell into its murky depths when he passed out. His hideously deformed corpse was fished out of the water days later, and when Jackson saw the photos in the casualty report, they burned a hole in his brain and returned whenever he thought about Vietnam, which was a lot more often than he wanted to.

Jackson cranked the Healey up to one hundred miles per hour, thinking the speed would make him focus on the here and now. It worked. He looked through the translucent image of PFC Maxwell to watch for traffic and cops, and eventually the vision disappeared. It felt good to be on the open road again, as if his life had motion, and when he got to campus everything would fit back in place. He had thought he'd feel that way when the freedom bird took off from Tan Son Nhut, or when it landed in San Francisco, or for sure when he finally got home, but it didn't work out that way. When the other guys cheered on takeoff and landing, Jackson felt like he was somewhere else, watching on television. At home in Chicago, he felt like he was in a dream that seemed real except he didn't feel like he was actually there, even when someone talked to him.

He made the six-hour drive to campus in four-and-a-half hours, stopping once for gas.

When he got to the fraternity house there was a small crowd of men and women in the living room. He didn't recognize anyone. They stared at him like he was a stray dog who'd wandered in and taken a dump on the rug. Then a tall, grinning man rose from a couch in the back of the room. He towered above the crowd, his face friendly and animated, his eyes focused on Jackson.

"Scholar!" he exclaimed. "Welcome back to the land of the living."

"Hi, Buckets," Jackson said as they shook hands. Buckets did the fraternity handshake, which Jackson had forgotten. Unfazed, Buckets led Jackson through the ritual. "I don't know anyone here," Jackson confessed.

"I'll introduce you around," said Buckets.

In the blizzard of names and handshakes and awkward conversations that followed, Jackson discovered one of his contemporaries, now a law school student, hidden behind a beard and hippie-inspired tatters and beads. A few years had made a difference here, too. Rainman confessed he was still a Young Republican but he went to the protests to score free pot and sex.

The other actives and the women were polite to Jackson but regarded him suspiciously. Buckets explained that he and Rainman had been spreading the word far and wide that Jackson was coming back to run Hell Week, and Jackson, the legendary hellion of Hell Week, had honed his terrorism skills with months of bloodthirsty acts of violence and destruction in Vietnam. They didn't actually know anything about Jackson's war record, but their stories had served to scare the crap out of the pledges and offend those who wore peace symbols and opposed the war.

The only woman who wasn't put off by Jackson looked more like a girl, dark-haired, dark-complected, petite. Jackson figured her for a freshman, her skin too smooth, her eyes too eager, and her smile filled with braces. But she smiled at him, which people didn't really do anymore, especially the people chatting away in the living room. He wasn't sure why everyone was so uneasy around him, but he figured they could tell he was fucked up.

"How does it feel to be back?" she asked.

Jackson stared at her, searching for words. How *did* it feel? It felt fucking weird, but how do you explain that to someone who's never been locked in a box of darkness and insanity for months at a time?

"I'm still getting used to it," Jackson said.

"It's hard, I know." She bubbled when she said it, like a kid. But there was something sweet about her. "My brother came back last year," she said. "It was hard for him, too."

Jackson wanted to say something, but no words came to him. He wondered why he couldn't carry on a conversation. He nodded mutely, becoming more aware of the girl's physical appearance. She had a kid-sister face and a curvaceous, womanly body, a combination that seemed strange and dangerous.

She broke the silence by taking his hand and leading him upstairs. "Let's get you a drink," she said, her small hand grasping his firmly. She led him upstairs to a bathroom where a beer keg sat in a bathtub filled with ice, and drew him a cup of beer.

"Where are the pledges?" Jackson asked. He had neither seen nor heard any evidence of them since he'd gotten to the house.

"It's quiet time," she said. "They get two hours to eat and study. Most of them just sleep. They're scared to death of you."

Jackson looked around, trying to remember the second floor from his time here. It had only been a few years, and yet, a lifetime. Some of it was familiar—the floor plan, the rooms with desks and beds, the creaking wood floors—but the voices were different, the music was angry, and the light seemed dimmer than before. It felt as foreign to him as Saigon had the first time.

"They're going to be disappointed," he said.

He knew it for sure, now. There was no way he was going to be able to run even a couple hours of Hell Week. He didn't belong here. He couldn't remember how it felt to be one of these people, even though he could remember going to school here, and sleeping in this house, and he could remember asking women out on dates, and he could remember that he fell in love once, and he could remember who the woman was, but he couldn't remember what it was like to be in love.

They talked some more; he wasn't sure how long. He had trouble focusing on what she was saying, his mind floating around the room, the house, the campus. He was vaguely aware he didn't answer some of her questions, but she seemed to forgive him, flashing wet-lip smiles that showed the braces on her teeth, and he blushed because she was gazing at him with adoring eyes and her hand was touching his arm and he was getting aroused and he was way too old to be messing with an innocent like her.

As the living room guests began to leave, the girl asked Jackson for a ride back to her dorm. He heard the question. He even held eye contact as he said yes, noting she had beautiful eyes. They were dark, almost midnight black, and they had eerie depth, and the white parts of her eyes were immaculately white. She excused herself to use the bathroom and when she came back they got in Jackson's car and he drove her home. On the way, she said, "Guess what I did in the bathroom."

Jackson glanced at her. "Peed?"

"That, too," she laughed. She opened her coat and her blouse, exposing her bare breasts. She reached for his hand and leaned against him, bringing his arm around her shoulders and placing his hand on a breast. "I want to make you feel good," she said seductively.

Her breast was full and supple. He stroked and fondled her even though he knew he shouldn't be groping a teenager. He was twenty-four, she was eighteen. Six years. But he couldn't help himself. The touch of her breast sent heat through his body. He wondered if he had ever touched a breast so soft and sexy and he didn't think so. The hookers in Asia were mostly small-breasted and not much into foreplay and what he remembered most about them was their fake orgasms. He couldn't remember exactly what his last college girlfriend's breasts felt like, because his lasting memory of her, the one that crowded out everything else, was how she broke up with him when his draft notice came.

They reached the dorm, and the girl pulled him into a deep kiss, and when they broke the clinch she rubbed his crotch.

"My roommate's gone tonight," she whispered, forming the words with elaborate precision, like she was sharing a secret with him. "Come over when you're done with the pledges, okay?"

"You could get in trouble."

"Don't be silly. We do it all the time," she said.

"But you're so young," Jackson objected.

"I'm not that young," she snapped. "And I'm no virgin."

"Me either," said Jackson. She laughed, thinking he was making a joke, and he was relieved, but the truth was, he thought it would be indecent to make it with a girl so young. He hadn't expected a woman to make a pass at him, especially not someone with braces and a baby face. In three years, everything had changed.

"Promise you'll come?" She paused. "If you know what I mean." She laughed at her pun and Jackson felt compelled to force a laugh, too.

She kissed him again and gave him a sultry smile. "You'll be glad you did."

Jackson watched her walk to the door, as light on her feet as a ballerina, his mind trying to sort out what just happened. His hand could still feel her breast, and he remembered how deft her tiny fingers were when she rubbed his crotch. He could still see her face, her baby skin, her braces, her perfect eyes.

He shook his head, trying to break the spell. What if she was only sixteen years old, one of those brainy kids who goes to college when they're twelve and splits atoms when they're twenty? He could go to jail. But she wasn't sixteen. She was eighteen, a college freshman who knew what she was doing.

Jackson's mind conjured how the girl's naked body would feel against his, and how she would express herself in lovemaking. He shook his head again. Yeah. He'd go torment the pledges for a couple hours then get it on with the girl, age be damned. They'd fuck their brains out, then he'd go back to Chicago and try to get his life started.

He drove back to the house, rationalizing a one-night stand with a teenage girl with an innocent face and a ready body, how he owed himself this much, after all those months in the war zone. It seemed like forever since he had been with a woman who actually wanted to be with him. No one could begrudge him a night with a willing woman.

But another part of him roiled with anxiety and doubt. He fought the feeling that this was all a nightmare and he was headed for a tragic ending, and tried to shake the despair by thinking about things he would scream at the pledges, the insults and funny threats, the old stuff from his day. But nothing could dislodge the feeling that he was teetering on the edge of a dark precipice and when he went over it, there would be no end to his fall.

Back on Greek Row, he pulled into the wrong driveway. It was easy enough to do in the dark, the houses similar in size and the driveways close to each other. But it was another sign. It wouldn't have happened when he was a student here. He pulled into the right driveway and parked in back.

As soon as he entered the house, Buckets and a squad of actives ushered him into the basement. A dozen pledges leaned against a wall in varying degrees of exhaustion, their eyes downcast, risking furtive glances at Jackson, the reputed hellion of Hell Week.

"This is Jackson!" yelled Buckets. "We used to call him Scholar back when he just scared the shit out of worthless pledges like you sorry bastards. But he's been killing people and burning villages and fragging officers since then and we're still trying to figure out what to call him now. Maybe if a couple of you survive, you can help us come up with a name."

He turned to Jackson. "Take it away, Scholar!" As Jackson stepped forward, Buckets and the other actives broke into loud hoots and thundering applause, and the pledges noticeably cringed and braced for the worst.

Jackson lined up the pledges and began screaming in his drill sergeant voice, a stream of obscenities, followed by a stream of insults, followed by commands for the pledges to do push-ups and sit-ups. For a moment, it was like old times, Jackson getting into the fake rage, Jackson yelling so loud the blood vessels in his neck popped out like highways on a road map, the pledges completely cowed.

And then it stopped, like a switch had flipped off. Five minutes into his act, after two sets of push-ups and the second set of sit-ups, Jackson went dry. He couldn't think of anything to say and he didn't feel like screaming. He didn't know any of the pledges. Hell, he didn't know the actives, either, except for Buckets. The shit they talked about in the living room was as foreign to him as the conversations in a Bien Hoa marketplace. He stood frozen in the middle of the floor, wondering what to do next, and he couldn't think of a single fucking thing. One by one, the pledges glanced up at him, half expecting to see a crazy war veteran wielding an axe, but all they saw was Jackson, standing stock still, eyes on the floor.

After an uncomfortable silence, Buckets came alongside Jackson. "You okay, Scholar?"

Jackson looked at him, his eyes unfocused. He blinked several times, as if waking from a deep sleep. "You guys are going to have to take over." He grabbed his coat and headed for the stairs. He was pretty sure no one said anything, and it wouldn't have stopped him anyway. He didn't stop moving until he reached his car.

He drove to the dorm, thinking that at least he'd get laid, and when he went back home if someone asked him about his visit to campus he could say at least he got laid. But when he pulled into the parking lot and turned off the car, he realized, he finally realized, he didn't know the girl's name. He sat in the eerie pallor of a streetlamp trying to remember it. He thought they'd been introduced, but he couldn't remember the moment and as he was trying to remember her name, the image of his last college girlfriend, a Nordic blonde from Minnesota, popped into his mind. Sandy. He could remember *her* name, and he could still see her saying, "I don't want to be home waiting for a soldier."

Jackson took a deep breath and got out of the car. He walked around the campus in the cold night air, trying to remember happy moments from his time there, but nothing came into view. Instead, his mind flashed with images from Vietnam. The sad eyes of a child in the Ho Nai orphanage. Long Binh

Jail baking in the hellish sun of the dry season. A Saigon prostitute trying to feign pleasure during sex with him. The earth shaking from distant B-52 strikes. The corpse of PFC Maxwell after marinating in the Mekong River, his face and body swollen into the gruesome shapes of a horror movie monster. He chased the images from his mind and forced himself to focus on the buildings and the signs. They meant nothing to him, but they brought him back to reality, and the reality was, he didn't belong here. He knew this guy who once belonged here, but that guy was gone now, and Jackson had come in his place, and Jackson didn't belong here.

He stopped at the door to the dorm, wondering if he should go in. He could ask around and find her. It wouldn't be that hard. How many cute dark-haired girls could there be with braces and Mediterranean skin? But he didn't go in. Jackson got back in the car and started the engine. She would be disappointed but she'd get over it, he thought, the girl whose name he couldn't remember but whose face and body were locked into his central nervous system like a song you couldn't stop humming.

He thought about her all the way to the motel, where he picked up his bag, and all the way to the Interstate, where he ran the Healey up to an even eighty. He wondered if the memory of her would keep him awake all the way home. She'd be better company than PFC Maxwell. He wondered if Sandy ever thought about him now. He wondered if he'd ever start sleeping again, and he wondered if he'd ever again feel like he was in a place where he belonged.

— RENEE JAMES

Renee is a confessed English major, a Vietnam veteran, and an out transgender author. After a career in magazines, she has published five novels and several short stories, and currently has a new novel making the rounds of editors. She has been a board member of OCWW since 2016.